praise for mending the soul

This is a very thorough and biblical analysis of abuse and how to overcome it. Every pastor and biblical counselor should have a copy of *Mending the Soul*.

Dr. Neil T. Anderson, founder and president emeritus of Freedom in Christ Ministries

Mending the Soul integrates very well the biblical-theological-psychological understanding of abuse. It is a pragmatic, insightful, candid evaluation of the problem and contains specific recommendations for healing psychologically, emotionally, and spiritually.

Ralph Earle, Ph. D., family therapist and psychologist, author of *Lonely All the Time*

Steve Tracy has made an enormous contribution to our understanding of the biblical, social, and psychological dimensions of abuse and its impact on our society and the church. As a p⸺ who deals often with the effects of abuse, I am deeply indebt⸺ ⸻viding this useful instrument to help heal and m⸺

⸻yne R. Lehsten, pastor of counseling and ⸺age ministries, Scottsdale Bible Church, Scottsdale, Arizona

As a family physician for thirty years, I saw the faces of many of my patients as I read the pages of Dr. Tracy's book—patients who presented with difficult sets of cryptic symptoms—and realized what their real diagnosis was. I will have multiple copies of this book on hand to help patients suffering from these issues, and I'll be recommending it for all my colleagues, including residents and medical students, for whom this should be required reading to sensitize them to this devastating problem.

Jacqueline A. Chadwick, M.D., vice dean of academic affairs, University of Arizona College of Medicine, Phoenix Campus

Mending the Soul is by far the best book I've seen for integrating biblical foundations and scientific research as it describes abuse and its effects, reaching its height in the comprehensive model for healing abuse emotionally, relationally, and spiritually. Pastors, counselors, and teachers alike will relish this excellent resource.

Gerry Breshears, Ph.D., professor of theology,
Western Seminary Portland, Oregon

Steven Tracy deals honestly and profoundly with the troubling and long-neglected issue of abuse in this much-needed work. It demonstrates biblical fidelity and pastoral concern while raising awareness of the problem—especially for the church—and showing the path to healing.

Dr. Kenneth Magnuson, associate professor
of Christian ethics, The Southern Baptist
Theological Seminary, Louisville, Kentucky

With the biblical wisdom of a theologian and the counseling insights of a therapist, Steve Tracy has crafted an invaluable resource for those concerned with abuse in all its forms. Tracy offers a scripturally anchored model of abuse recovery that includes practical suggestions and copious real-life examples. Chapter 9 by itself (on rebuilding intimacy with God) is worth the price of the book. This volume deserves to be read and reread by every pastor, counselor, and serious people helper.

Sandra D. Wilson, Ph.D., seminary professor,
spiritual director, and author of *Released from Shame*
and *Into Abba's Arms*

Steven Tracy's book on abuse skillfully weaves together sound theology, insightful biblical exegesis, and the best of psychological findings about the horrors of abuse and the road to recovery. Featuring many case examples from his extensive work with survivors, the book stands as a substantial challenge to the church: Stop revictimizing survivors and begin facilitating their healing.

James R. Beck, Ph.D., professor of counseling,
Denver Seminary

understanding and healing abuse

mending *the* soul

STEVEN R. TRACY

ZONDERVAN®

ZONDERVAN.com/
AUTHORTRACKER
follow your favorite authors

Mending the Soul
Copyright © 2005 by Steven R. Tracy

Requests for information should be addressed to:

Zondervan, *Grand Rapids, Michigan 49530*

ISBN 978-0-310-28529-8

Library of Congress Cataloging-in-Publication Data

Tracy, Steven R.
     Mending the Soul : understanding and healing abuse / Steven R. Tracy.—1st ed.
       p. cm.
     Includes bibliographical references and indexes.
      1. Sexually abused children—Pastoral counseling of.   2. Adult child sexual abuse
victims—Pastoral counseling of.   3. Child sexual abuse—Religious aspects—Christianity.
4. Abused children—Pastoral counseling of.   5. Adult abuse victims—Pastoral counseling of.   6.
Child abuse—Religious aspects—Christianity.   I. Title.
     BV4464.3.T73 2005
     259'.1—dc22   2004025695

Interior design by Tracey Walker

Printed in the United States of America

14 15 16 17 • 23 22 21 20 19 18 17 16 15 14 13 12 11

contents

acknowledgments

Many individuals have graciously made this book possible, including our supporters who several years ago helped to make my doctoral research in England a reality. While I was on the pastoral staff at First Baptist Church in Tempe, Arizona, Dr. Roger Ball and other church leaders believed in me and graciously allowed me to apply many of the principles and policies in this book to my pastoral ministry there. I'm grateful to the leadership teams of Mending the Soul Ministries and Phoenix Seminary for their encouragement and excitement regarding this project. I'm exceedingly thankful for those who have entrusted to me their own stories of abuse and healing. I have countless reasons to be thankful for my own family, which has been incredibly supportive and patient while I have labored over this project. I am particularly thankful for Celestia, my life partner and soul mate, whose love and God-given expertise at healing wounded souls have transformed this book and me. Finally, I am most grateful for Mary. Her courage to face the pain and truth of her abuse and to wrestle with God until she experienced his healing touch has inspired me more than she will ever know. By God's grace, her story will inspire countless others. I dedicate this book to her. To God alone be the glory!

part 1

the nature of abuse

✳

chapter 1

a wake-up call regarding
the extent and power
of abuse

Mary sobbed uncontrollably on the bathroom floor. Her mother stroked her hair and held her until she could finally speak. Mary's first day of high school had been a parent's worst nightmare. She had gotten into a fight with a classmate, had threatened the principal, and was on the verge of being expelled from school. Mary's parents, missionaries with a Christian organization in the inner city of San Francisco, were beside themselves. Ever since she entered adolescence, Mary had grown increasingly rebellious and withdrawn. The precocious little girl who wore fairy dresses and drew pictures of puppies now wore black and drew pictures of corpses. Mary attempted suicide twice in junior high. In fits of rage she would curse her parents for not aborting her before she was born. Her parents sought help from counselors, their youth pastor, and even the family doctor, but nothing seemed to help. It felt as though they were in a losing battle with an invisible demon that was consuming their daughter's very soul.

Finally Mary began to speak to her mother in barely audible whispers. She told about a boy at school who had threatened her friend. As her mother began to question the depth of her rage at the boy, the long-invisible dragon began to take shape. Her cruel classmate had triggered dark memories she had spent years trying to escape. Finally she could no longer hold back the terrible images. She shamefully recounted that five years earlier, her cousin had sexually molested her over a period of two years while he was babysitting her. The molesting stopped once her family moved to San Francisco, but her cousin continued to make sexually suggestive comments whenever she came to visit.

Priest would lay sins upon it then send into the wilderness

Mary's parents immediately contacted the authorities and the rest of the family. The authorities chose not to prosecute the case, since there was no physical evidence. The extended family turned on Mary and her parents with a vengeance. They accused Mary of trying to destroy the family by making up lies. They accused Mary's parents of using the cousin as a scapegoat for their poor parenting. They threatened to report Mary's parents to the mission board to get them removed from their ministry. Even when three other children came forward and reported that the cousin had fondled them, the entire extended family refused to believe or support Mary. They argued that if the cousin had done something inappropriate to Mary, it was in the past, and she was obligated to forgive and forget. To add insult to injury, they rebuked Mary for her anger toward her cousin and said it showed how sinful and unchristian she really was. Two years after disclosing the abuse, Mary still wasn't sure she could believe in a God who watched her cousin molest her but did nothing to stop it.

I wish Mary's story were merely a hypothetical example. It is not. My ministry to Mary and her family has permanently transformed my understanding of abuse. It also raises troubling questions for all Christians:

- How widespread is abuse?
- How can abuse that happened years earlier continue to have an impact?
- How can parents, youth workers, and single adults looking for life partners identify potential abusers?
- How can abuse victims heal?
- What does genuine healing look like?
- Where does forgiveness fit in?

These are some of the questions this book seeks to answer. For all too long the church has ignored or even covered up abuse. By God's grace this must change.

Mending the Soul is divided into three parts. Part 1 addresses the nature of abuse. Here I will seek to give a biblical explanation for abuse, define exactly what constitutes abuse, and look at the characteristics of abusers and abusive families. I'll examine five different kinds of abuse, all of which distort the image of God and hence are very damaging.

Part 2 explains the effects of abuse. Abuse victims and those who seek to minister to them must understand the way abuse impacts the soul before a plan for healing can be mapped out. All too often, well-meaning Christians spout Bible verses to cure very complex problems such as abuse. Scripture does give us a path to healing, but we cannot use Scripture properly until we have a keen grasp of the nature of abuse and the damage that needs to be healed.[1] More specifically, I'll look at shame, deadness, powerlessness, and isolation as four of the most persistent and destructive effects of abuse. I will also relate these effects of abuse to our being made in the image of God, for it is only when we see abuse from the vantage point of our unique creation as divine image bearers that we can understand the soul damage created by abuse.

Part 3 will provide a path to healing. I'll specifically discuss facing the brokenness caused by the abuse, coming alive from deadness and numbness, learning to love and trust God, and understanding the role and practice of forgiveness. This section will conclude with an epilogue written by a sexual abuse survivor, who shares how God helped her heal, and will also include her thoughts on how churches and Christian leaders can minister to the abused.

I've also included five appendixes I developed in pastoral ministry: a sample child protection policy, a written application to work with minors, an oral screening form, a summary of warning signs of potential abusers, and a listing of Bible passages that address abuse. I've written this book to be an accessible handbook for the wounded and for the shepherds (both lay and professional) who seek to care for them. Therefore, I have tried to keep technical discussion to a minimum. For those who desire a more nuanced discussion of the issues and documentation of sources, I have provided ample endnotes.

Before we begin our formal look at the nature of abuse, I'd like you to be aware of three of the premises that shape my model of abuse and healing.

ABUSE IS RAMPANT

I, like many who were blessed to have grown up in a loving home, have had a very difficult time accepting the reality of abuse, particularly in Christian homes. Years ago, when I was a young pastor in a vibrant church, I was deeply offended when the women's ministry invited a special speaker to address the topic of domestic violence. Little did I (or anyone else) realize that one of our elders had been beating his wife for years, having put her in the hospital several times, and that at that very time one of our ministers was about to be arrested for felony child abuse. I've come to realize that abuse is not the odd exception but is rampant both in the church and in secular society. The evidence for this tragic assertion is overwhelming.

Domestic violence perpetrated against adult women is one form of abuse rampant in most cultures around the world. The World Health Organization notes that research from every country where reliable, large-scale studies have

Car accidents/muggings/cancer < Abuse > where does it differ?

been conducted reveals that 16 to 52 percent of women have been assaulted by an intimate partner, and violence against women (which often takes place in the home) is as significant a cause of death and incapacity among women of reproductive age as cancer.[2] Domestic violence is also an enormous problem in the United States. A 1992 report prepared for the U.S. Senate Judiciary Committee cited two U.S. surgeons general, declaring that domestic violence is the number one public health risk to adult women in the United States.[3] Furthermore, domestic violence was named as the leading cause of injury to women ages fifteen to forty-four, more common than traffic accidents, muggings, and cancer deaths combined.[4] The United States Department of Justice reports that approximately one-third of women who are murdered are killed by an intimate (husband, ex-husband, or boyfriend), and most victims of intimate partner homicide are killed by their husbands.[5] In 1998, women experienced about 900,000 violent offenses at the hands of an intimate partner—a rate five times higher than the violence men experience from women.[6] It is estimated that in America, in their lifetimes, one in three adult women will experience a physical assault by an intimate partner.[7]

Tragically, domestic violence in Christian homes appears to mirror the high rates of the general society. For example, Lee Bowker's survey of one thousand battered women from all sections of the United States revealed that most of the battered women and their husbands "were part of mainstream American religious bodies," and denominational preference did not significantly differ between the violent and the nonviolent families.[8]

Sexual assaults, particularly date rape, on adolescent and adult women are also shockingly common.[9] One of the largest (over 6,000 students) and most widely cited surveys of sexual assault among female college students was conducted in 1987 by Mary Koss.[10] She and her fellow researchers found that over one-fourth of the women had experienced a rape or attempted rape since age fourteen, and another 14 percent of the women had experienced unwanted sexual contact. Another researcher put these sexual assault rates in perspective: "[These findings] made acquaintance rape and date rape more common than left-handedness or heart attack or alcoholism. These rapes are no recent campus fad or the fantasy of a few jilted females. They are real. They are happening all around us."[11]

betrayed by lover

Large-scale research on child abuse reveals that physical and sexual abuse of minors is also rampant. It is impossible to know for certain how prevalent child abuse is, because the vast majority of abuse is not reported to the authorities. The most reliable survey methods (retrospective surveys of adult nonclinical

looking back on past events

no observable symptoms

populations) show that in North America at least 20 to 25 percent of girls and 5 to 15 percent of boys experience contact sexual abuse.[12] The U.S. Department of Health and Human Services collates data annually from Child Protective Services in all fifty states. Their most recently published study observes that reports of suspected child abuse were made on over 2.8 million children in 1998. One of the most respected and thorough studies of child abuse is the congressionally mandated National Incidence Study of Child Abuse and Neglect. Its most recent report, using very strict criteria, found that over 1.5 million children were abused or neglected in the United States in 1993.[13] What is most alarming is that in the seven years between the second and third National Incidence studies, there were sharp increases in all categories of abuse and neglect, except educational neglect. Overall, the estimated number of seriously injured abused children essentially quadrupled between 1986 and 1993.[14]

[margin note: What continues to feed abuse?]

To put some of these statistics in perspective, physician and abuse expert Charles Whitfield notes that there are approximately 50,000 names on the Vietnam War Memorial in Washington, D.C. If we were to make a memorial to children in our society who have been sexually abused, it would need to be more than 1,300 times the size of the Vietnam Memorial. If we broadened it to include other forms of child maltreatment (physical abuse and neglect), the monument would need to be over 7,500 times the size of the Vietnam War Memorial.[15]

It is exceedingly difficult for us to accept the fact that abuse is rampant.[16] I have vivid memories of a pastor who was highly offended when I gave him a Christian book about sexual abuse. He dogmatically asserted that the book's author (a noted evangelical authority on sexual abuse) didn't know what he was talking about when he wrote that abuse is prevalent in the church. This pastor reasoned that he had been a shepherd in a large church for several years, and of the several thousand individuals in his congregation, he only knew of a couple individuals who had been sexually abused. Furthermore, he contended that the book's discussion of sexual abuse put impure thoughts into people's minds. It apparently hadn't occurred to him that, given his mind-set, it was unlikely anyone would disclose sexual abuse to him. Ironically, my wife and I knew of several dozen individuals in his church who *had* been sexually abused.

[margin note: so don't speak of it]

[margin note: Not him]

ABUSE IS PREDICTABLE

[margin note: Shock vs Surprise]

While the prevalence of abuse should shock us, it should not surprise us. Orthodox Christianity has always declared that we live in a fallen world. Humans are born not morally neutral but sinfully depraved. While evangelical theologians

debate the effects of human depravity (especially the nature of (free will),) none
question its universal presence. The biblical record makes this indictment
inescapable, for no sooner had the forbidden fruit cleared Adam's and Eve's lips
than a host of destructive and even abusive behaviors ensued. On the heels of the
first human sin (Genesis 3:1–6) came hiding from God (Genesis 3:8–10), blame
shifting (Genesis 3:12–13), murder (Genesis 4:8), and universal evil so great that
God destroyed almost the entire human race (Genesis 6:5–8).

The Bible is patently clear that all humans from the moment of conception
are corrupted by sin (Psalm 51:5) and thus have the potential for evil cruelty.
The Bible repeatedly warns of evil people whose greatest delight is to violate and
overpower the weak and vulnerable, shed their blood, and consume them (Psalm
17:8–12; Proverbs 1:16–19; Micah 2:1–2; 3:1–3). Even if we do not murder with
our hands, we are all quite capable of abusively murdering with our tongues
(Proverbs 18:21; James 3:2–12). In the apostle Paul's overwhelming exposé of
universal human depravity and resultant guilt, he notes that in their natural
condition all humans are depraved and inclined to abuse others (Romans 3:9–
18). He cites various Old Testament passages to show that the entire human
race and every aspect of every human is depraved and often abusively destructive. Specifically, humans possess throats that are an open grave (they want to
destructively consume); they have the poison of asps under their lips, curse with
their mouths, have feet swift to shed blood, and leave nothing but misery and
destruction in their wake (Romans 3:13–16). This graphic language (drawn from
Psalm 5:9; 10:7; 140:3; and Isaiah 59:7–8) describes the way universal human
depravity is displayed in widespread abusive behavior.

Paul's assertions about how depravity results in widespread abuse are validated from Genesis to Revelation by hundreds of accounts of verbal, physical,
and sexual abuse. We read of abusive behavior that penetrates all sociodemo-
graphic sectors of biblical society. Various forms of abuse are committed by Jews
as well as Gentiles, worshipers of Yahweh as well as worshipers of Baal, kings as
well as peasants, men as well as women.[17] Joseph's brothers abusively sought to
kill him and eventually sold him into slavery in Egypt (Genesis 37:20–28), but
Joseph also experienced abuse from the Egyptians (Genesis 39:11–20). The
pagan prince Shechem raped Dinah (Genesis 34:1–2), but the Jewish prince
Amnon raped his own sister, Tamar (2 Samuel 13:1–19). Pharaoh, king of Egypt,
ordered the slaughter of baby Jewish boys (Exodus 1:15–22), but so did Herod,
the king of Judea (Matthew 2:16–18). Idol-worshiping King Ahab used his power
to murder the innocent (1 Kings 21), but so did King David, the writer of many
psalms (2 Samuel 11:6–27).

The pagan inhabitants of Sodom sought to rape two men visiting their town (Genesis 19:1–6), but in similar circumstances Israelite men fatally gang-raped a traveling woman (Judges 19:16–28). The Egyptians physically abused their Israelite slaves (Exodus 1:11–14; 2:11), but Israelites physically abused their inspired prophets (Jeremiah 20:1–2). The agents of the antichrist will behead saints for refusing to worship the beast (Revelation 20:4), while Herodias had John the Baptist beheaded for refusing to overlook her adulterous affair (Matthew 14:1–12). Jesus was tortured and executed by the barbaric Romans, but the sophisticated Jewish religious leaders had already tried to stone him to death (John 8:59) and peasants from Nazareth tried to throw him off a cliff (Luke 4:29). Arameans ripped open the wombs of pregnant women and killed their unborn children (2 Kings 8:12), but Israelite parents burned their own infants alive as an act of worship (2 Kings 17:17; Jeremiah 32:35).

Lest we attempt to limit abuse to the ranks of evil degenerates and religious hypocrites, we should tease out the biblical data a bit more. In the biblical record, orthodox religious leaders and even mature believers are repeatedly indicted for abuse and collaborating with abuse:

- Abraham, the greatest Jewish patriarch and hero of faith (Genesis 22; Hebrews 11:8–9, 17–19), twice deceitfully tried to protect himself by exposing his wife to sexual exploitation by a foreign monarch (Genesis 12:10–15; 20:2, 11).
- Sarah, the heroine of faith, almost fatally abused her own handmaid and child (Hebrews 11:11; Genesis 21:9–21).
- David, the man whose heart was wholly devoted to God and the greatest human monarch in Jewish history (1 Kings 11:4, 36–38), was guilty of murder and adultery (2 Samuel 11). He also failed to protect his own daughter from incestuous rape and engaged in a conspiracy of silence with her rapist (2 Samuel 13:7, 20–39).
- Lot, who in some respects was "righteous" (2 Peter 2:7–8), offered his own daughters to be gang-raped by the men of Sodom (Genesis 19:8).
- Judah, the father of one of the greatest tribes of Israel, tried to have his own daughter-in-law burned to death after he impregnated her (Genesis 38).
- Monotheistic Israelite priests used their religious power to sexually prey on women serving in the tabernacle (1 Samuel 2:22).
- Priests and other religious leaders used their power to physically exploit the vulnerable, especially widows and orphans (Micah 2:8–9; Malachi 3:5).

- Christians in the Corinthian church engaged in a form of incest that was more perverted than that practiced by their pagan neighbors (1 Corinthians 5:1).

We must not sanitize the biblical record to avoid the implications for our own families, churches, and communities. Humans are no less sinfully depraved now than they were in the past. Abuse is rampant today, as it has been throughout human history—a point we must emphasize because few Christians, even Christian leaders, truly believe abuse is rampant through all segments of society and is even committed by Christian leaders. Over and over, parents, congregations, and religious leaders deny abuse reports, regardless of the weight of the evidence. We must *never* assume the child who reports that dear uncle Bob has been touching the child's private parts must be lying. Unspeakable damage can occur when we deny the possibility that a pastor who powerfully communicates God's word on Sunday could beat his wife or molest his daughter on Monday.

A few years ago I asked a team of child abuse professionals to lecture in my seminary class. One of the presenters was a judge and former government prosecutor with years of experience in the criminal court system, particularly with child abusers. She soberly warned my students that twenty years in the courtroom had shown her that Christians were extremely gullible when it came to child abusers and persistently unwilling to accept the potential for abuse in their own religious community. She said she shuddered when church members testified in her courtroom as "character witnesses" for those accused of child abuse. Again and again she hears Christians defend the moral integrity of individuals who end up being convicted of child abuse. These Christians simply can't believe a person they've experienced as "nice" could commit abuse.

After this guest lecture, John, one of my students, came up to me with a sheepish look on his face. He told me he knew this judge, and in fact he had been guilty of doing just what she had warned us about—serving as a character witness in her courtroom for a youth leader in his home church accused of sexually molesting a junior high girl in the youth group. John recounted how he gave eloquent testimony about how wonderful this man was and how there was no way he could have abused a child; he just wasn't capable of that kind of behavior. John then told me that, after his glowing character witness testimony, the prosecuting attorney cross-examined him and asked him if he knew that this "wonderful man" had previously been convicted in another state of raping a teenager at knifepoint. John had been flabbergasted. He hadn't known about this criminal abuse history, and yet he still couldn't believe that a leader in his church could molest a teenager. The jury disregarded John's naive judgment, and the youth leader was convicted of child molestation and sentenced to several years in prison. John deeply regretted his destructive assumption that a Christian leader could not molest a child. Christians must take the implications of universal depravity seriously and accept the fact that *all* humans are capable of abuse.

In addition to human depravity, another factor in human history makes abuse predictable, namely, the role of Satan and his demonic legions.[18] Contemporary culture often makes Satan the butt of jokes, as evidenced in Adam Sandler's portrayal of Satan in the movie *Little Nicky* and in Gary Larson's comic images in the "Far Side" cartoons. Liberal theologians often assert that Satan and demons reflect the prescientific mythology of the biblical writers, and that evil is best understood as the result not of dark angelic forces but of unjust social-political structures.[19] The writers of Scripture, however, treat Satan as real and unimaginably destructive.

- Nineteen of the twenty-seven books of the New Testament refer to Satan, and seven Old Testament books refer to him.
- Of the eight New Testament books that do not refer to Satan, four refer to demons.
- Of the twenty-nine references to Satan in the gospels, twenty-five are made by Jesus himself.
- Satan's power and influence is vast. He is declared the ruler and god of this world (John 12:31; 2 Corinthians 4:4).
- Unbelievers are held captive to do his will (2 Timothy 2:26).
- He is the one who deceives nations and the whole world (Revelation 12:9; 20:3). Thus—temporarily—Satan is carrying out his will throughout world history.

One of the biblical titles given to Satan helps make the link between Satan's character and human abuse. Satan is repeatedly called "the evil one" (Matthew 6:13 NIV; John 17:15; 1 John 2:13–14; 5:18–19). This phrase in Greek indicates that Satan is "the one intrinsically wicked who is not content to be corrupt in himself but must seek to corrupt others."[20] As we'll see in the following chapters, abuse is one of Satan's most powerful tools for corrupting and destroying individuals in every aspect of their being (physically, emotionally, relationally, and spiritually). Repeatedly, the Bible describes Satan's work and influence in the world as one of abusive evil. Cain, the man who committed the first act of physical abuse recorded in Scripture, drew his inspiration from Satan, the "evil one" who was a butcher (physically abusing murderer) from the very beginning (John 8:44; 1 John 3:12).[21] Satan is said to promote the persecution, abuse, and even murder of God's people (Revelation 2:10; 12:13). In this context, the most significant satanic title is found in Revelation 9:11, where Satan is called Apollyon (that is, the Destroyer), the king of the demons. In this passage Satan the destroyer sends out demons with scorpionlike tails to abuse and physically torment humans all over the earth.

As evil personified; the ruler and god of this world; and the one who promotes evil, death, and destruction from the Garden of Eden to the end of the age, Satan clearly is promoting abuse in our own generation and culture. The Bible's teaching about the person and work of Satan makes abuse sadly predictable.

ABUSE IS REDEEMABLE

Thus far we've seen a very grim portrait. If abuse is widely distributed throughout all sectors of society—and it has been so throughout human history—due to human depravity and satanic influence, what hope is there? It is precisely at the juncture of intractable evil, abuse, and human misery that the Christian gospel offers the only possible hope. The God declared in the Bible is not like the Greek gods on Mount Olympus who drank ambrosia and consorted with nymphs while humans squirmed on earth. Rather, God is deeply moved by human suffering (Hosea 11:8; Matthew 9:36; John 11:35) and is committed to heal and redeem the broken at the greatest possible cost (Exodus 2:23–25; 12:1–42; Romans 5:8). Jesus Christ did not come for the healthy, but to redeem the sick and broken (Matthew 9:12–13). The writer of Hebrews beautifully declares that Christ took on human flesh so that he could die and, in so doing, render Satan and death impotent and break the chains of human bondage (Hebrews 2:14–15).

The incredible irony of the gospel for abuse victims is that Jesus suffered the most extreme form of physical abuse so that the broken could be healed ("by His scourging we are healed" [Isaiah 53:5]). In fact, this irony is so great that the dominant symbol of Christianity is an instrument of sadistic abuse—a cross. When one understands the grotesque nature of crucifixion, by which the founder of Christianity and many early Christian leaders were tortured to death, it's amazing that Christians image their faith with a cross (1 Corinthians 2:2). It would be comparable to Jews making the symbol of Judaism a miniature crematorium they wear around their necks and place on their synagogues. The cross is the most powerful symbol imaginable of God's ability to heal and redeem abuse.

This side of heaven, no one can offer a fully satisfactory answer for why God continues to allow evil and suffering. We do know, however, that God delights in taking suffering and evil and creating great good out of them (Romans 8:28; 2 Corinthians 4:8–18; Philippians 1:12–14). One of the most beautiful statements of such divine redemption of damaging evil is found in Genesis 50:20, when Joseph declared to his abusive brothers, "You meant evil against me, but God meant it for good." This statement highlights the fact that God is sovereign, even over evil. What the brothers intended for Joseph's destruction, God providentially redeemed in the most dramatic fashion. He brought individual healing and restoration to Joseph but also used the very circumstances created by their abuse to bring about the deliverance of their entire family—and ultimately the Israelite nation. The apostle Paul, a collaborator in the fatal abuse of Stephen and the former physical abuser of Christians (Acts 8:1–3),[22] became the Christian church's greatest missionary and teacher. He, in turn, experienced much abuse—slander, beatings, whippings, stonings, imprisonments, and even murder attempts (2 Corinthians 11:23–33). After enduring incredible suffering, Paul declared that through all of the abuse, Christ was sweeter and stronger in his life (2 Corinthians 4:8–18; 12:10). God always desires to heal our brokenness and to use it as the very nutrient to draw us into a deeper experience of joyful intimacy with him and to give us an opportunity for more fruitful ministry to others who are also broken (Romans 8:17; 2 Corinthians 1:4–6).

Mary, the missionary daughter abused by her cousin, is now a young woman. She is an eloquent testimony to God's power to heal a shattered soul from the ravages of evil. Mary still bears scars on her body from the many times she cut herself with a razor. For years after the abuse, the cutting was the only thing that made her feel better. Now the most noticeable features on Mary's body are not the scars on her arms and legs but the light in her eyes and the impish smile on her lips. Mary has slowly learned to trust God. She is slowly learning to trust men. Mary has devoted her professional career to working with abused children. She is still growing and healing, but she recently told me that, for the first time in her life, she truly believes God has redeemed her abuse. This book is dedicated to all the Marys in this world who have suffered the evil of abuse and who need to experience the healing redemption that only the crucified Christ can bring.

chapter 2

✳

abuse as a perversion of
the image of God

U ntil God brought Mary into my life, I simply didn't comprehend the staggering impact of abuse. I was particularly shocked at the images of this beautiful little girl who had haunting memories of abuse that would repeatedly engulf her in such toxic clouds of self-annihilating shame that she would viciously slice her own body with a razor. How could sexual fondling that had occurred years before cause a bright and gifted young girl who had grown up in a loving Christian family to have such self-loathing and shame that cutting herself with a razor actually brought a twisted sense of release?

After Mary had disclosed her abuse, her parents sought counsel from Dr. Susan Jones, a godly Christian pediatrician who specialized in working with high-risk adolescents in the California juvenile justice system. Dr. Jones explained to Mary's confused parents that in ten years of treating adolescents, she had worked with hundreds of teens who cut themselves. Nearly all of her young adolescent patients who self-mutilated had been sexually abused. In some strange way, the uninvited pain in their souls was temporarily assuaged by deliberately creating pain in their bodies.[1] How is it that sexual abuse generates such powerful self-destructive urges?

Abuse opens a Pandora's box of long-term, destructive fallout that raises a host of troubling questions: Why is it that women who have been abused during childhood are significantly more likely to be revictimized in adulthood? Why are adult female prostitutes three to four times more likely than nonprostitutes to have been physically or sexually abused in childhood?[2] Why is it that 70 to 80 percent of sex addicts are survivors of physical or sexual abuse?[3] Why is it that 50 to 70 percent of psychiatric inpatients and 70 percent of all psychiatric emergency room patients report a history of childhood physical or sexual

22

Image of God = Need for intimacy/relationship.
Try to fit God in a box — make visible the invisible
Care for creation

chapter 2: abuse as a perversion of the image of God   23

abuse?[4] Why is it that the majority of men who beat their wives and/or children experienced childhood physical abuse?[5] One might logically expect that men who experienced the horror of abuse in childhood would be the *least* likely to be abusers themselves, not wanting to inflict the kind of pain on their loved ones that was inflicted on them. *Yes!*

The unpleasant truth is that abuse has profound, wildly irrational consequences. It tears the soul. The only way we can truly understand the effects of abuse is to clarify what it means to be a human being made in the image of God. To understand the devastating impact of abuse, we need to understand the manner in which abuse perverts the image of God in humans.

their perception of who God is.

MADE IN THE IMAGE OF GOD — GENESIS 1 AND 2

"Define image"

Christian theology asserts that humans are not just the most highly evolved mammals at the top of the food chain; we are not simply the most complex machines that accidentally arose out of "primordial soup" millions of years ago. Rather, humans are dazzlingly unique among the entire created realm, for only humans are made in the very image of God. As one theologian wisely notes, being made in God's image "confers on the human subject the highest possible distinction, leaving the world of the animals far behind. Here is language used of no other creature, language that teaches us to understand ourselves in terms of God rather than in terms of the animals."[6] The Bible is very clear that all humans are uniquely made in the image of God (Genesis 1:26–28; 9:6; James 3:9). In fact, being made in God's image lies at the core of what it means to be human, for when God chose to create humans, he made them "in His own image" (Genesis 1:27).

Our challenge is to understand more precisely what "image of God" means, since the Bible nowhere defines this monumentally important phrase. The best way to make sense of the image of God is to look at the creation account in Genesis 1:26–28, where this phrase first appears. We should note first that the biblical account of human creation is distinctly different from other ancient Mesopotamian creation accounts in which humans are created as an afterthought to provide the gods with food and relieve them of work. Moses, on the other hand, tells us that humans are the apex of all creation, for only after Adam and Eve are created does God pronounce his finished work as "very good" (Genesis 1:31). The first chapter of the Bible tells us that God did a magnificent, unique work when he created humans, for they alone are created in such a way that they mirror the sovereign Lord of the universe.

While there are many theories about the nature of being made in God's image, I believe it's best to understand it as referring to *all that we are* as humans. Thus, there are various aspects to the image of God that can be seen in the creation account.[7] The first aspect of the image of God seen in Genesis 1:26 is the *relational* aspect. By virtue of being made in God's image, humans have the capacity, longing, and need for intimate relationship based on the truth that God himself is a relational God who is in intimate relationship within his own divine being. Jesus himself spoke of the loving intimacy he had with the Father and prays that his children would reflect God through intimate human relationships (John 17:21–23). Apparently when God chose to create creatures who would mirror who he is, the best (and maybe the only) way to do so was to create not just an individual but a pair whose very sexuality as male and female complements and draws each to the other.[8]

The relational aspect of being made in God's image has profound implications. The New Testament teaches that intimate relationships in the Christian community are essential for spiritual growth (Acts 4:32–34; Hebrews 10:24–25; James 5:16). Furthermore, social scientists have discovered that healthy relationships are essential for social, intellectual, and emotional growth. Children who are completely cut off from human contact develop permanent social and intellectual impairment. Research on attachment has shown the tremendous long-term social and emotional significance for children to have a secure attachment with their parents.[9] The human need for relationship is so profound that infants who are fed, clothed, and given medical care but are deprived of physical touch will often fail to thrive and, left untouched, may actually die.[10] Yet we must remember that our very capacity for intimate relationships based on being made in God's image creates great vulnerability in a sinful, abusive world.

A second aspect of the image of God is seen in the language of Genesis 1:26: "in Our image, according to Our likeness." We might call this the *visible* aspect of the image of God. It is the aspect of the image of God in which humans visibly demonstrate God's attributes. We see this in the very terminology of this verse ("image" and "likeness").[11] The point here is that humans are to visibly manifest who God is, that is, they are to make visible the invisible God (cf. Colossians 1:15). As with the first aspect of the image of God, we can anticipate great damage when humans (especially children who are idealistic and vulnerable) look to key adults, expecting to get a glimpse of what God is like but in reality getting a picture of what Satan is like.

This can be compared to a lost child who is dehydrated and in desperate need of water. If the thirsty child finds a bottle of clear fluid labeled "mineral water," it would be particularly perverse if the child, after drinking the liquid in good faith, became gravely ill because the fluid was actually poison. The child would come to fear the very thing needed to sustain life—water. Children need and deserve to glean a sense of the character of God from watching their adult caregivers. Adults who distort the image of God cause great harm to spiritually thirsty children.

A third and final aspect of the image of God is often called the *functional* aspect—the aspect in which humans function as God's representatives on earth.[12] In terms of creation, we are his vice-regents, or representatives, in caring for the creation. The Bible's account of creation suggests this aspect of the image of God, for in Genesis 1:26, "Let Us make man in Our image" is immediately followed by "and let them rule." We also see this in Genesis 2, for God waited to create some of the plants until Adam had been created to care for them (Genesis 2:5). God put Adam in the garden to "cultivate it and keep it" (Genesis 2:15). While the Bible ultimately assigns the providential care over the created world to God himself (Psalm 104:14–30; 135:7; Acts 14:17), God made humans in his image as his functional representatives to care for creation. This involves both control (Genesis 1:26; Psalm 8:5–6) and cultivation (Genesis 2:15). We can easily see how this aspect of the image of God can be distorted. Instead of functioning properly as God's representatives to care for creation, we can rule harshly over creation and grossly misrepresent who God is. When humans do not function as God's representatives but use their power to dominate rather than nurture, much long-term damage is done.

THE EFFECTS OF SIN — GENESIS 3

While Genesis 2 ends on an incredibly beautiful note of relational intimacy ("the man and his wife were both naked and were not ashamed"), this intimacy is immediately shattered by sin in Genesis 3. As soon as Adam and Eve eat the forbidden fruit, all three aspects of the image of God are disrupted and distorted. Instead of mirroring and enjoying relational intimacy, immediately after eating the fruit they try to hide from each other and from God (Genesis 3:7–8); soul-satisfying intimacy is perverted into shameful hiding. Instead of visibly manifesting the character of God, they manifest ungodliness and unholiness. Instead of functioning as God's representatives in caring for creation, their sin caused creation to be harmed and cursed (Genesis 3:14–16). At every level, sin corrupted the image of God, though it did not eliminate it.

At this juncture we should note the relevance of the curse recorded in Genesis 3:16 to the issue of abuse:

[Handwritten margin notes at top:] Was Birth before a plan SIN?

[Handwritten notes at top:] men = 80-90% Child sexual abuse
men abuse women 5X more
65% of abuse child cases are by women
abuse among parents = 75% of time is the mother
Children a 2X more likely abused by female then male.

part 1: the nature of abuse

[Handwritten margin note on left, vertical:] WOMEN

- Instead of joyfully living out the image of God through physical reproduction (a very Godlike activity), the woman would now experience pain in childbirth.
- Instead of acting as a spiritual equal who complements the man, the woman would have an unhealthy, slavish dependence on the man ("your desire will be for your husband").[13]
- Instead of the man treating the woman as a divine gift who could complement him as an intimate equal, the fallen man would seek to harshly rule over the woman as an inferior.[14]

Scripture and human history repeatedly bear out the accuracy of this horrible prediction. Throughout history men have repeatedly abused their power, and women have repeatedly been inappropriately and dangerously dependent on men. The Bible describes numerous instances (Isaiah 10:1–2; Ezekiel 22:6–12; Micah 2:9; 3:1–3, for example) where those with power (typically males) used this power to exploit and abuse those with less power (typically females and children). In a clarification of who is great in the kingdom, Jesus reminds his disciples that the Gentile political rulers (who were virtually all male) used their authority to dominate harshly those under their care, whereas in the kingdom of God, greatness is expressed through humble servitude (Luke 22:25–26).[15]

In short, in a fallen world, our Godlike privilege of creating and nurturing life is perverted through the abuse of power. Because men typically have greater physical and social power, they are often the perpetrators of abuse.[16] For instance, research shows that men are responsible for about 80 to 90 percent of child sexual abuse.[17] The United States Department of Justice reports that in 1998, women experienced physical violence by an intimate partner (in most instances a man) at a rate five times higher than the violence men experience from their predominantly female partners.[18] At the same time, when women are in positions of power (especially over their children), they as fallen sinners will also abuse that power. The most recent National Incidence Study shows that 65 percent of all maltreated (abused) children are maltreated by a female, and when children are maltreated by a birth parent, 75 percent of the time they are maltreated by their mother.[19] The National Incidence Study also found that children are twice as likely to be neglected by a female as a male. The dynamic of the abuse of power helps us understand why over three-fourths of abused or neglected children are abused by their own birth parents, for birth parents typically have the greatest power over a child.[20]

ABUSE AS A PERVERSION OF THE IMAGE OF GOD

Abuse is invariably about the abuse of power over another individual—an abuse that perverts the divinely ordained image of God. In the next few pages we'll define five different kinds of abuse and describe how they are a perversion of the image of God.[21]

Five Kinds of Abuse

Sexual abuse	A perversion of "one flesh"	Genesis 2:24
Physical abuse	A perversion of "let them rule"	Genesis 1:26
Neglect abuse	A perversion of "cultivate the ground"	Genesis 2:5
Spiritual abuse	A perversion of "image"	Genesis 1:26
Verbal abuse	A perversion of "be fruitful"	Genesis 1:28

Sexual Abuse — A Perversion of "One Flesh"

A teacher recently told me about a call she had received from a woman in her Sunday school class seeking advice on a moral dilemma. She and her husband frequently traveled with their three adolescent children. As do most families on a limited budget, they shared a hotel room when they traveled. Her dilemma? Her husband, an active member of a vibrant evangelical church known for solid Bible exposition, was pressuring her to have sex with him in the motel room with their three children in other beds a few feet away from theirs. He reasoned that the Bible nowhere prohibited this, so she was obligated to comply with his demand. Apparently this man did not realize (or care) that by deliberately exposing his children to his sex acts with his wife, he could be prosecuted by the state for child sexual abuse, and he could cause damage to his children. *pressure/shame*

Sexual abuse is the exploitation of a minor for the sexual gratification of another person through sexual contact or sexual interaction.[22] Abusive sexual contact can be described on a descending continuum and includes intercourse, attempted intercourse, oral sex, genital contact, breast contact, intentional sexual touching of buttocks or thighs, simulated intercourse, touching of clothed breasts, and sexual kissing.[23] Abusive sexual interaction includes deliberate exposure of a minor to pornography or sexual activity and exhibitionism. This graphic description is necessary because many people mistakenly believe sexual abuse must involve sexual intercourse, or at least genital contact, with a minor.

Furthermore, even when people accept that sexual abuse encompasses a broad range of behaviors, they often assume that only abuse involving intercourse creates severe damage. On the contrary, all sexual abuse is extremely damaging. Diana Russell, one of America's foremost authorities on sexual abuse, found that in the cases of the "least severe" forms of sexual abuse (sexual kissing, sexual touching of buttocks or thighs, etc.), almost 20 percent of the abuse victims experienced extreme trauma, and in the next to least severe forms of sexual abuse (touching of clothed breasts, etc.) 35 percent of victims experienced extreme trauma.[24] I've repeatedly witnessed the devastating effects of sexual abuse that did not involve sexual intercourse.

Sexual abuse is incredibly damaging because, as creatures made in God's image, sex is the most powerful bonding activity in which we can engage. God's intention is that in marriage a man shall leave his father and mother and cleave to his wife and become one flesh (Genesis 2:24). Loving marital sex can powerfully bond, but through abuse it can just as powerfully wound. I often hear church leaders express great impatience with sexual abuse survivors who continue to experience the damaging effects of their abuse. They make remarks such as, "For crying out loud, that happened years ago." "Lots of girls get touched like that. Get over it!" "How long is this woman going to nurse this abuse?" These kinds of ignorant and destructive comments completely ignore the biblical data. In 1 Corinthians 6:15–18, drawing on the bonding imagery of Genesis 1 and 2, Paul declares that the sex act is unlike any other act we commit. When we sin sexually (or, by implication, are sinned against sexually), it forms a unique bonding, which creates damage that goes beyond anything else we can do with our body.[25] As Paul concludes in 1 Corinthians 6:18: "Flee immorality. Every other sin that a man commits is outside the body, but the immoral man sins against his own body."

Sexual relations are to be a beautiful divine gift that expresses unconditional love and should be a source of emotional and even physical life. Sexual abuse grotesquely distorts the relational aspect of the image of God and the divine plan for sexuality. With sexual abuse, sex no longer gives life but destroys life. With sexual abuse, sex does not express selfless love but destructive selfishness. As a result, sexual abuse survivors struggle to accept their own sexuality and their own bodies. They also struggle in marriage to enjoy sanctified sex. Women who have been abused often can't admit to being enjoyed and desired by a godly man. Sexual abuse is a sad perversion of the "one flesh" relationship.

Physical Abuse — A Perversion of "Let Them Rule"

With respect to child abuse, physical abuse is legally defined as any nonaccidental injury to a minor by an adult or caregiver. This could include blows, shakings, burnings, or other physical assaults that cause injury to the child. Domestic abuse can be broadly described as the use or threat of physical violence to control an adult family member, particularly a spouse.[26] This can include threats, shovings, slaps, hair pulling, punches, kicks, injuring or killing of pets, destruction of personal possessions, assaults with inanimate objects, and assaults with lethal weapons.

Physical abuse of children and spouses is a great perversion of the functional aspect of the image of God. We are to care for creation as God's representatives by cultivating and exercising responsible dominion. Through physical abuse we injure and demolish what we should nurture, sustain, and enhance. Instead of functioning as God's gracious representatives to care for creation, physical abuse distorts the image and character of God. Since God has put it in the human heart for children and spouses to crave love and affection from family members, physical abuse at the hands of parents and spouses, the very ones whose hands should caress us, is most destructive.

Various people in our church had told me that Jessica was a very angry young woman who was a difficult person for her family to live with. One day Jessica's husband, Don, a successful restaurant owner, called me and reported that he and Jessica were on the verge of divorce. He was distraught over the prospect of losing his wife. When I probed for the root of the problem, he said they just couldn't communicate and kept getting very angry at each other. He trolled for sympathy by telling me that Jessica had left him for several weeks to live with her parents. I grew increasingly concerned when Don admitted he got so angry that he couldn't think rationally and often couldn't remember what he had said or done after their fights. He didn't tell me what I later learned—he grew up watching his own father beat his mother. That was his posttraumatic training for family life. What he also failed to tell me was that he had been threatening, slapping, and shoving Jessica on a regular basis. She lived in stark terror of his violent rages, which had been intensifying. Don had recently slapped Jessica so hard that he split her lip and knocked her to the ground. Up until this point other church leaders had unanimously concluded that Jessica was simply an immature Christian who needed to be more cooperative in her marriage. The truth was, Jessica was experiencing physical and emotional trauma from Don's physical abuse. Don and Jessica's three young children were also experiencing significant damage from their violent home environment.[27]

Can't hide abuse from family

Neglect — A Perversion of "Cultivate the Ground"

Neglect is closely connected with physical abuse. Overtly it is the opposite of physical abuse but produces similar results. Instead of a failure of actions (physical abuse), it is failure to act. Neglect is the failure of a parent or guardian to provide a minor with adequate food, clothing, medical care, protection, supervision, and emotional support. It is a perversion of the functional aspect of the image of God, in which humans are to cultivate the ground (Genesis 2:5) — to function as God's representatives by tenderly caring for his creation. If we are called to responsibly care for the plants and animals God created, how much more should parents tenderly care for their own children, who are utterly dependent on them. Neglect can be chronic or occasional and is very damaging in either instance. God has harsh words for professing Christian parents who refuse to provide adequately for their own children (see 1 Timothy 5:8).

Spiritual Abuse — A Perversion of "Image"

Christy had grown up at First Presbyterian Church. Many of her relatives attended there. When Christy was in junior high, Mark, her twenty-one-year-old lay youth pastor, formed a special relationship with her over an extended period of time. Mark took advantage of his spiritual authority in Christy's life to develop a sexualized relationship with her. He told Christy that their relationship was pure and that it was ordained by God. He also implied she would experience physical harm if she reported their relationship. Christy loved the attention but was in emotional turmoil over her "special" relationship with Mark. His caresses and sexual touch felt very wrong. In time Christy developed a severe eating disorder. She eventually gathered the courage to go to the senior pastor and disclose Mark's behavior toward her. She documented her story and shared it with her pastor in his office. He read her letter and then asked her to sit down. As she watched, he tore the letter into tiny pieces and informed her that the Bible tells us we must forgive others. He furthermore declared that she had a sinful heart in being angry toward Mark, and that she needed to confess to God her sin of anger. The pastor prayed with Christy over her "sin" and admonished her to never repeat the accusations.

Shortly after this, Christy's bulimia spun out of control. Sadly, Mark's abuse continued for several more years. Eventually through the help of a counselor, Christy gained the strength to oppose her church authorities and report Mark to the police. He was eventually convicted of felony sexual abuse for acts he perpetrated on other girls in the youth group. He was given a ten-year prison sentence. Even after his conviction, Mark's church continued to run a weekly notice in the bulletin, publicizing the opportunity to donate toward Pastor Mark's legal defense fund. To this day, this church has never apologized to Christy or her family and still pretends the abuse never happened.

While Mark's sexual abuse of Christy was in the least severe category (it didn't involve sexual intercourse or even fondling of the genitals or breasts), it was still extremely damaging, especially in combination with spiritual abuse. When Christy began getting counseling in junior high, her Christian therapist asked her to draw a self-portrait—a helpful way for counselors to assess the impact of abuse on the child's sense of self. To the counselor's astonishment, Christy drew a picture of her back (see figure 1).[28] She had such overwhelming shame she couldn't even draw a picture of her own face. The sexual and spiritual abuse had had a powerful synergistic effect.

Figure 1

Christy's experience illustrates graphic spiritual abuse by two different pastors who should have been her protectors. Spiritual abuse is the inappropriate use of spiritual authority (the Bible, ecclesiastical tradition, or church authority) to force a person to do that which is unhealthy.[29] Often it will involve a forceful or manipulative denial of that person's feelings and convictions. Ultimately, spiritual abuse is based on a denial of one of the most precious pillar doctrines of Protestant Christianity, namely, the priesthood of the believer. This doctrine teaches that, while church leaders and spiritual teachers are appropriate and helpful (Ephesians 4:11–12), every individual believer has the Holy Spirit and has direct access to God (Romans 14:4–5; 1 John 2:27). Thus, every believer has a right to discern the will of God through the Scriptures and the leading of the Spirit without needing a human "priest" to intercede to God for him or her.

The clearest biblical example of spiritual abusers is seen in the Pharisees, who had honed spiritual manipulation into an art form. They habitually twisted the Scriptures to selfishly manipulate others under the guise of spirituality (Matthew 15:1–9; 23:16–36; Mark 7:11–13). It's worth noting that the harshest words attributed to Jesus in all four gospels are found in Matthew 23, and they are directed at the Pharisees for their spiritual abuse.[30] Jesus excoriated them for using Scripture and their own legalistic rules of spirituality to place unbearable, crushing spiritual demands on those under their authority, all for their own self-advancement (Matthew 23:1–8). Jesus notes that if the Pharisees had used their spiritual authority properly, they would have de-emphasized their authority, rejected authoritative titles, and humbly served those under them (Matthew 23:8–12). Jesus places their spiritual abuse in the same category as the most severe physical abuse, for he says these hypocritical Pharisees are "sons of those who murdered the prophets" (Matthew 23:31).

David Johnson and Jeff VanVonderen give four characteristics of a spiritually abusive system:[31]

- *Power posturing.* The leaders are preoccupied with their authority and continually remind people of it. This runs contrary to the Bible's teaching that church leaders are not to excessively leverage their authority but are to lead by example, not decree (Luke 22:25–26; 1 Peter 5:3).
- *Performance preoccupation.* Spirituality becomes a matter of external performance, not internal character (Matthew 15:1–12).
- *Unspoken rules.* Spiritually abusive churches have unspoken rules such as, "Don't ever disagree with the pastor or you are disloyal and

unspiritual"; these rules are not discussed openly but are enforced rigidly.

- *Lack of balance.* Spiritually abusive churches have little or no spiritual balance, and the leaders exhibit either extreme objectivity ("you must have graduate degrees to have any spiritual knowledge") or extreme subjectivity ("the Lord gave me this message, and you must accept it").

The Bible is very clear that spiritual abuse by religious leaders is extremely destructive. Religious leaders can, in the name of God and Scripture, manipulate and destroy others for their own selfish purposes (Ezekiel 22:25–28; cf. Galatians 6:12–13). Spiritual abuse often creates tremendous damage, for it can generate great confusion and perversion regarding the character of God, the people of God, and the Word of God. Often victims of spiritual abuse find church attendance, Bible teaching, and even the Scriptures themselves to be emotionally disturbing because these were the very things employed to manipulate and harm them. Spiritual abuse is also damaging because it programs people to continually distrust their own emotions and convictions and give in to the demands of someone who claims to be more spiritual. Because spiritual abuse leaves no physical marks, it is often minimized by Christians.

Some of the most destructive spiritual abuse is that which is subtle and not obviously heretical. Several years ago my wife, Celestia, had a counseling session with a client named Cathy, who potently demonstrated the destructive power of subtle spiritual abuse. Cathy, immaculately dressed, sat on the edge of the sofa. Her beautiful auburn hair and brown eyes were a stark contrast to her stiff demeanor. In her hour-long session she never relaxed or even leaned back on the sofa. From the outset she cried and repeatedly apologized for being sad.

Cathy didn't know what she was feeling. She had no vocabulary for her sorrow. She had come to see Celestia because of a debilitating anxiety that was making it difficult for her to leave her own home. Cathy was married to a well-known elder in a large evangelical community church. She homeschooled her four children. She had few friends and had "no time" for personal friendships or for discretionary reading and activities. When Celestia asked her about this, she dispassionately explained that five years earlier she had made a $50 purchase without her husband's permission. When he found out, he became enraged, and in front of the children he lectured her on how God in his love punished the children of Israel when they disobeyed. He declared that he was to "love" her in the same way. She was to be punished from that point on. He would no longer give her money for groceries and other household expenses. She would need to babysit to "earn" that money in her spare hours. That evening he confiscated her checkbook and credit cards. In the days that followed, he continued to make reference to "God's loving punishment" and threatened her with even greater punishment if she didn't exhibit total obedience.

As Celestia heard her story and began to describe the true nature of God's love reflected in the way Jesus respectfully and gently responded to Mary Magdalene and to other women, Cathy sobbed uncontrollably. Her heart resonated with this truth. She was created for that kind of love. She was starving for godly love, having been manipulated and bullied by a self-righteous husband who twisted Scripture to humiliate her as an inferior. Cathy left the session in tears, continuing to apologize for her well-earned sorrow. Sadly, she never came back. It's unlikely that anyone in Cathy's church will ever realize how profoundly and destructively her husband had spiritually abused her.

Verbal Abuse — A Perversion of "Be Fruitful"

Verbal abuse is a form of emotional maltreatment in which words are systematically used to belittle, undermine, scapegoat, or maliciously manipulate another person. Verbal abuse can be every bit as damaging as physical or sexual abuse, and in some cases it's even more damaging. Those who haven't experienced abuse often can't understand this. The somewhat subjective nature of verbal abuse can make it more insidious and difficult to confront (which can also make it more damaging).

Verbal abuse perverts the beautiful truth of divine creation. Nine times in Genesis 1 Moses tells us, "Then God said," and six times follows it up with, "and it was so." Thus God's very words are efficacious; they have the power to create the universe and all life that exists in it. Humans as "image of God" creatures are also called to create life ("be fruitful and multiply" [Genesis 1:28]). While humans obviously do this through sexual relations, we also metaphorically give life through our words. The Bible tells us "death and life are in the power of the tongue" (Proverbs 18:21). Pleasant words are "sweet to the soul and healing to the bones" (16:24). Good words have the power to awaken and heal a troubled heart (12:25). Given the power of words to encourage and to give life, Satan will surely prompt people to use their God-given verbal power not to bless but to curse, not to give life but to take life. The perversion of life-giving words helps explain why almost half of the seven sins identified as the ones God particularly hates are expressly verbal (a lying tongue; a false witness; one who spreads strife among brothers—Proverbs 6:16–19).

While the psychological community readily accepts the axiom that verbal abuse can cause tremendous long-term emotional damage, any Christian familiar with the Bible should easily accept this postulate as well. Rash words ravage the soul the way a sword can ravage the body (Proverbs 12:18). A godly tongue gives life, but a perverted tongue crushes the spirit (Proverbs 15:4). The tongue's power for emotional and spiritual destruction is so great that James describes it as a fire that burns up life and is set on fire by hell itself (James 3:6).

Betty, an extremely pleasant woman with a soft Northern accent, has a gentle demeanor that belies her troubled soul. In the course of discussing her troubled marriage and family life, Betty disclosed one of the most tragic stories of abuse I've ever heard. Betty's father was a musician who frequently moved his family from town to town as he sought work. Sadly, he was also an alcoholic, who became very destructive when he had been drinking. Betty would lie awake at night listening to her drunken father curse and sometimes beat her mother. On several occasions he beat Betty and her brothers.

On one occasion, when Betty was six, her father came home drunk in the middle of the night. Betty heard his footsteps coming up the stairs, but instead of hearing him stumble into his own bedroom to curse at her mother, he suddenly appeared in the doorway of her bedroom. A few moments later he came to Betty's bed and raped her. The rapes continued for ten years until Betty was sixteen. Betty went to bed every night not knowing if her father would appear in the middle of the night to assault her. Betty dreaded hearing music when she came home from school. It usually meant her father was celebrating—which invariably meant that he would soon come to her in the middle of the night. Now a middle-aged woman, Betty summarized her abusive childhood to me. I was shocked when she said that twenty years of physical abuse and ten years of rape by her father weren't as painful as the verbal abuse she endured from her mother.

One of her most vivid and life-imprinting incidents occurred, again, at the tender age of six. She was practicing her spelling words with her mother. When Betty misspelled the word *butter*, her mother scowled, and with piercing eyes she declared, "You are such a stupid little bastard." Now, almost fifty years later, Betty choked back the tears as she recounted her mother's venomous words. Though she had been a Christian for many years, Betty still struggled with the deep-seated conviction that she really is nothing more than a stupid little bastard. In fact, acting on this message had all but destroyed her marriage, as well as her relationship with her son (who at the time of our session had just been sentenced to life in prison).

Undoubtedly, one of the things that greatly reinforced the horrible message of this verbal abuse incident was additional verbal abuse she experienced several years later from her mother. When Betty was twelve, she had finally gathered the courage to tell her mother that her father had been molesting her. When she did so, her mother flew into a rage and accused her of trying to destroy their family by slandering her father. Betty did not bring up the topic again.[32] The sexual abuse continued, and an adolescent girl concluded that she must not be able to trust her feelings and that she deserved to be abused.[33]

BORN TO SHIMMER

All forms of abuse—sexual, physical, neglect, spiritual, and verbal—can be highly damaging because of the manner in which they pervert the image of God in humans. Apart from the redeeming grace of God, abuse often leaves lifelong scars on the soul.

Shawn Mullins has captured the battle humans face in living out their divinely ordained destiny in a fallen world. He declares that we are born to shimmer, born to shine, born to radiate. This is God's beautiful plan, which abuse perverts.

Shimmer

Sharing with us what he knows
shining eyes are big and blue
and all around him water flows
this world to him is new, this world to him is new
to touch a face
to kiss a smile
and new eyes see no race
the essence of a child, the essence
he's born to shimmer, he's born to shine
he's born to radiate
he's born to live, he's born to love
but we'll teach him how to hate
and true love it is a rock
smoothed over by a stream
and no ticking of a clock
truly measures what that means, truly measures
what that means

and this thing they call our time
heard a brilliant woman say
she said you know it's crazy how I want to capture mine
I think I love this woman's way
I think I love this woman's
way she shimmers, the way she shines
the way she radiates
the way she lives, the way she loves
the way she never hates
sometimes I think of all of this that can surround me
I know it all as being mine
but she kisses me and wraps herself around me
she gives me love, she gives me time
yeah . . . and I feel fine
but time I cannot change
so here's to looking back
you know I drink a whole bottle of my pride
and I toast to change
to keep these demons off my back
get these demons off my back
cause I want to shimmer, I want to shine
I want to radiate
I want to live, I want to love
I want to try to learn not to hate
try not to hate
we're born to shimmer
we're born to shine
we're born to radiate
we're born to live, we're born to love
we're born to never hate[34]

✳

Now that I've defined abuse and explained the ways in which it perverts the image of God, I'll take a look at some general and specific characteristics of abusers. In other words, since abuse is so damaging, just what kind of person would abuse another? What are the profiles of various types of abusers? Chapter 3 addresses these kinds of questions.

chapter 3

✳

profiles of abusers

John was a well-known member of the community. As a successful businessman, his baritone voice was widely recognized from his radio commercials. He was heavily involved in civic events and charitable organizations and had even dabbled in local politics. So his arrest for the sexual exploitation of a minor made headlines in the midsize city where he lived. The community quickly polarized, with dozens of friends, neighbors, and employees coming to his defense. After a lengthy trial, John was convicted of sex crimes against two adolescent girls. Reporters immediately sought interviews with John's friends and neighbors, most of whom declared that John was innocent and had been railroaded by the district attorney. What I found most amazing was the logic used by his defenders. Several told reporters he couldn't possibly be guilty of sex crimes because he was such a nice guy who had helped many people in the community. One elderly neighbor recounted how he had shoveled her sidewalks one winter—something she was quite sure a child molester would never do. After much questioning by the reporter regarding John's guilt or innocence, one exasperated defender declared, "Just look at this man. Look at his face. Anybody with half a brain can see he's not a child molester."

This instinctual response is one of the most common myths regarding abusers, namely, that you'll know one when you see one. It's very disturbing to discover that this comforting bromide has no factual basis. In 1960, the Israelis captured Nazi war criminal Adolf Eichmann and put him on trial in Jerusalem for war crimes and crimes against humanity—for his extensive role in orchestrating the murders of up to six million Jews in Nazi death camps. When Eichmann's trial began in 1961, *The New Yorker* magazine sent philosopher and writer Hannah Arendt to Jerusalem to cover the trial. Her reaction upon seeing Eichmann for the first time was one of shock, because, as she looked into the face of this indescribably evil man, she did not recognize evil. She mused that his deeds were monstrous, but the doer appeared quite ordinary and commonplace. As she continued to reflect on Eichmann, she coined a phrase to describe him: "the banality of evil."[1]

It is highly disturbing to realize that evil abusers often have a banal quality to their existence. And what stands out about banality, by definition, is that it does not stand out.

Thus, what is exceptional about abusers is their commonness. Abusers come from all strata of society. For instance, several years ago the U.S. Customs Office undertook a large child pornography sting operation. They arrested dozens of men and in the process documented approximately sixty different professions represented among the defendants. The list read like a vocational cross section of American society: attorney (2), actuary, butcher, college music teacher, janitor, owner of a funeral home, salesman (3), police officer (3), farmer, graphic artist (2), defense contractor, school bus driver, house painter, and structural engineer.[2] Abusers cannot be predicted by race, occupation, demeanor, education level, or facial features. Thus, one of the most chilling aspects of physical and sexual abusers is their invisibility. This presents a disturbing situation for all of us who want to protect ourselves and our children from abuse. If the family dentist, our child's Sunday school teacher, the retired engineer next door, or our auto mechanic could be a dangerous abuser, then what do we look for? If abusers cannot be visually identified, then what common characteristics do they possess? Let's look first at four general characteristics of abusers, and then I'll briefly profile six kinds of abusers.

GENERAL CHARACTERISTICS OF ABUSERS

Pervasive Denial of Responsibility

In the twelve years my wife, Celestia, and I have worked with abusers and abuse victims, the single most consistent characteristic we've seen in abusers is their utter unwillingness to accept full responsibility for their behavior. I have rarely seen abusers confess to abuse unless there was crystal-clear, overwhelming evidence of their behavior—and even then they'd typically minimize what they had done and shift the blame. Over and over Adolf Eichmann declared he was not criminally responsible for the murder of millions of Jews in Nazi death camps, for he was simply "following orders."[3] Rapists sometimes blame victims for dressing seductively. Date rapists invariably say the sex was consensual. Physical abusers blame family members for making them mad. Several times I've heard child molesters say the child seduced them into having sex.[4] One time I heard a molester, who was later convicted for raping two children, tell the jury that the children held him down and forced him to have sex with them. What made this denial even more outrageous was the fact that the children he molested were five and seven years old, and the man was a full-grown adult who weighed over three hundred pounds. Needless to say, the jury didn't buy his repulsive blame shifting, but it does demonstrate how extravagantly abusers deny responsibility. Similarly, spiritual abusers customarily offer biblical justification for their abuse. When caught red-handed, they will (if pressed to the wall) admit to some inappropriate behavior but will fixate on the sins (real or imagined) of the other person. In short, most abusers have an utter inability to fully own their sin.

Two studies illustrate the incredibly pervasive denial of responsibility on the part of abusers. When two researchers interviewed eighty-six convicted child molesters about their sexual offenses against children, they were given 250 different verbal justifications by these molesters for their actions. The most frequent excuse for child molesting was that the child had consented to having sex (29 percent of the molesters said this). Other justifications given were that they did it because they had been deprived of conventional sex by their wives or girlfriends (24 percent), because they had been intoxicated (23 percent), or because the child had initiated the sexual activity (22 percent).[5]

Similar gross denial of responsibility can be seen in wife batterers. James Ptacek conducted interviews with men who had been in a Boston-area counseling service for physically abusive men. He discovered incredible patterns of denial of responsibility with these men. Most frequently they said they beat their wives because they had lost control due to alcohol or built-up frustration. They made such statements as,

> I think I reach a point where I can't tolerate anything anymore, and it's at that time whatever it is that shouldn't be tolerated in the first place now is a major issue in my life. . . . I couldn't hold it back anymore.

*

> It was all the booze. I didn't think. . . . It was temporary insanity. I really, all's I really wanted to do was crush her.[6]

The second primary way these men denied responsibility was by blaming their wives for causing them to beat them.[7] The following statements reflect ways they blamed the victims:

Women can verbally abuse you. They can rip your clothes off, without even touching you, the way women know how to talk, converse. But men don't . . . so it was a resort to violence if I couldn't get through to her by words.

✳

On some occasions she was the provoker. . . . You know, you're married for that long, if somebody gets antagonistic, you want to defend yourself.

✳

It [the beating] was over sex, and it happened I guess because I was trying to motivate her [to want sex more often] and she didn't seem too motivated.[8]

The final way in which these wife-battering men rationalized their behavior was by denying that beating their wives was abusive or physically injurious. Here are some examples:

I never beat my wife. I responded physically to her.

✳

[Did you injure your wife?] Not really. Pinching does leave bruises and I guess, slapping. I guess women bruise easily, too. They bump into a door and they bruise.

✳

These people told her that she had to get all of these orders of protection and stuff like that because I was going to kill her. . . . I mean, I'd yell at her and scream, and stuff like that, and maybe I'd whack her once or twice, you know, but I wasn't going to kill her. That's for sure.[9]

These quotes demonstrate the extreme break with reality abusers reach in their pervasive denial of responsibility. Christian leaders must recognize this dynamic, lest they buy into the abusers' lies and contribute to victim blaming. Furthermore, abusers must be held to the highest levels of accountability. Nothing less than total ownership for their abusive behavior should be accepted by their churches; anything less contributes to their denial and in essence justifies their sin.

Justifying the wicked is considered an abomination to God (Proverbs 17:15). When Nathan the prophet confronted King David for his evil abuse, he held him fully accountable for his actions. He did not entertain a discussion of how Bathsheba was partially responsible for bathing on the roof, or how the servants were somewhat to blame for bringing Bathsheba to David when they knew he was having a midlife crisis. Nathan boldly declared, "You are the man!" David responded without qualification: "I have sinned against the LORD" (2 Samuel 12:7, 13).

Conversely, David's predecessor, King Saul, gives one of the clearest examples in all of Scripture of the extremes to which abusers will go to avoid taking responsibility for their sins. Saul attempted to kill his own son Jonathan to cover up his own foolishness, but the people prevented Saul from doing so (1 Samuel 14:44–45). Saul later assaulted David with a deadly weapon and repeatedly attempted to kill him (1 Samuel 18:11). The turning point in Saul's life occurred when God commanded him to destroy the evil Amalekites and to save nothing, not even livestock (1 Samuel 15). Saul partially obeyed by attacking and defeating the Amalekites, but he kept the choicest spoil and did not kill their king as he was commanded. The amazing part of the story is that, when Samuel came to Saul after the battle, Saul greeted him by declaring that he had carried out the Lord's command—a bald-faced distortion he actually seemed to believe. Abusers can get so caught up in their denial that they lose touch with reality.

When Samuel confronted him with the facts, Saul cleverly explained that they had destroyed everything as God commanded, except for the best livestock, which they planned to offer to the Lord as a sacrifice (1 Samuel 15:15). Notice the way abusers can use religion to justify their sins. Samuel confronted Saul with his disobedience, telling him he had done an evil thing. Samuel asked, "Why then did you not obey the voice of the LORD, but rushed upon the spoil and did what was evil in the sight of the LORD?" (verse 19). Saul insisted that *he* had obeyed, but that the people had disobeyed: "I did obey the voice of the LORD.... But the people took some of the spoil" (verses 20–21). At this point Saul resorted to blame shifting, one of abusers' favorite tactics.

Only after being persistently confronted with the facts of his disobedience did Saul acknowledge his sin. Even then he was more concerned about saving face than about the way he had dishonored God. Saul pleaded, "I have sinned; but please honor me now before the elders of my people and before Israel" (verse 30). After this incident, Samuel didn't go to see Saul again, but he grieved over Saul's tragic moral condition (verse 35). Saul's pervasive denial of responsibility is characteristic of virtually all abusers. Vulnerable adults and those who are responsible for protecting minors must recognize this powerful denial dynamic and courageously battle it.

Bold Deceitfulness

Closely connected with the abuser's unwillingness to own his or her destructive behavior is bold deceitfulness—a "skill" abusers need in order to maintain their innocence, avoid the discomfort of changing long-established patterns of behavior, escape the painful consequences of their actions, and assuage their own nagging consciences. Families, congregations, and secular leaders often find the audacity and persuasiveness of abusers' deceitfulness to be overwhelming. Abusers can be masterful at manipulating words and actions to confuse, confound, and put others on the defensive.[10]

There are biblical examples of such bold deceit, particularly in 2 Samuel 11. After David took sexual advantage of Bathsheba, the unmistakable physical evidence (her pregnancy) signaled his sinful behavior. Instead of repenting of his sin and taking the appropriate steps of correction and restitution, David sought to cover his tracks by bringing Bathsheba's husband home from battle so he could have sexual relations with his wife (verses 5–6). David deceitfully pretended to have called Uriah home so David could get news of the battle and honor Uriah. We read, "David asked concerning the welfare of Joab and the people and the state of the war" (verse 7). This was a sham, of course. David was fixated on his own welfare, not the people's. When David sent Uriah home and encouraged him to have sexual relations with his wife, he sent him a gift (verse 8).[11] The irony is that David had already stolen a most precious gift from Uriah. What breathtakingly bold deception—showering gifts and kindness on the very man whose wife you have impregnated!

When Uriah's loyalty to his soldiers prevented him from going to his wife, David plied him with wine to get him drunk, thinking it would serve as the necessary disinhibiting aphrodisiac. When that failed, David took advantage of Uriah's godly character. Knowing that Uriah was fiercely loyal to God and to the king, David had Uriah carry the very sealed message containing instructions for his own murder.[12] The message read, "Place Uriah in the front line of the fiercest battle and withdraw from him, so that he may be struck down and die" (verse 15). Abusers are often very cunning, and they deceitfully prey on the very virtues of those they abuse, counting on the fact that their victims will not act treacherously, as they do. The message David sent to his general, Joab, was equally deceitful, orchestrating Uriah's death in battle in such a way that it would appear to be an accident.

Finally, David's feigned response to the news of Uriah's death reflects hardened, calculated deceit, as he said, in effect, "Don't let this thing discourage you [literally, 'do not let it be evil in your sight']. People on both sides get killed in war. Redouble your efforts, and you will succeed" (see verse 25). The wickedness of this response is as obvious as it is deceptive. People on both sides *do* get killed in battle, but solders are killed by the enemy, not by their king. Joab did need to resign himself to the vagaries of war—but not to the venalities of his king. Redoubling their efforts was irrelevant. Defeat in the previous battle was not the result of military failure by the general but moral failure by the monarch. All reality had been veiled by David's fog of deception, but the fog lifted in the very last statement of the chapter: "But the thing that David had done was evil in the sight of the LORD." Those who deal with abusers must have the courage and wisdom to see through the fog and cling to truth.

Those who work with abusers must anticipate bold deceitfulness. One of Celestia's earliest clients was a three-year-old who had been referred by a local pastor. This girl came home from Sunday school one day and told her parents about a man at church who had touched her private parts. It turned out that a longtime elderly member of the church, a grandfather figure to most of the children, had fondled her in the church office while others were coming in and out of the office. He was so deceitfully clever that he was able to abuse this girl while appearing to be reading to her as she sat on his lap. The boldness of this abuser's deceit was seen in the fact that one week after this church confronted him, contacted the police, and forbade this man from having any contact with the children of the church, he visited another church less than a five-minute drive from this one and offered to serve in their children's ministry.

Harsh Judgmentalism

In spite of (and even because of) their own destructive behavior, abusers are often very judgmental and harsh toward others. This allows them to maintain the "high moral ground" and deflect attention from themselves onto others. To do so is often an effective way of maintaining their moral facade; thus, it perpetuates their denial of responsibility. This harsh judgmentalism is also a godless method for unrepentant abusers to deal with their own shame. Instead of facing their shame, much of which is a gracious, God-given, internal witness to their sin, they displace it onto others. Abusers often become quite sophisticated at this technique, for it is generally developed over long periods of time. Eric Leberg notes this tendency in child molesters:

> Because the offender is still minimizing his guilt, he will desperately try to maintain secrecy through verbal taunts and accusations that will sidetrack all meaningful discussion. . . . Thus, he will remember the number of times the wife refused his demands for sex, the times she got intoxicated, or the times she didn't clean the house to his satisfaction or forgot his birthday wishes or left her dirty socks on the floor. He'll remember the times the children fought, disturbed his sleep, came home late, did poorly in school, wasted their allowance, spilled milk during dinner. . . . To each of these events he will attach some value judgment that, although it may be absurd, again deflects the discussion away from his sexual abuse of his child or children.[13]

The tendency of abusers to harshly judge others is well attested in Scripture. While King David was sleeping with the very woman he stole from his faithful servant, whose faithfulness he rewarded by murdering him, David expressed great outrage that a rich man would steal a lamb from his poor neighbor. In fact, David's moral outrage was so great that he said the rich man deserved to die (2 Samuel 12:5), even though stealing was never deemed a capital offense in the Torah. Rather, the Torah prescribed restitution for theft (Exodus 22:12).[14] On the other hand, murder, rape, and adultery with a married woman were all capital offenses.[15] Thus, David's response to the rich man who stole a sheep evidences an ironically harsh judgment from one who had committed and continued to cover up not one but multiple capital offenses.

The intensity with which abusers maintain their hypocritical judgmentalism is often ferocious. The more counselors and family members try to confront an abuser's sin, the more aggressive he or she becomes in identifying and scrutinizing the sins, mistakes, or weaknesses of others.

Shaun grew up in an affluent, religious home in the Deep South. As an adolescent, he took advantage of his prestige and wealth. He developed a callous disregard for women once he got what he wanted from them. In college he started going to church again, as it afforded him ample opportunity to meet attractive and often naive young women. Shaun began to date a shy woman named Beth, who had little social experience. Shaun pressured Beth into having sex early in their relationship. Once this happened, his disrespect for Beth became palpable. He ridiculed her for not being able to meet his needs. He demanded she clean his house and do his laundry. He constantly joked about the anatomies of other women and accused Beth of sinful jealousy when she asked him to stop. She felt trapped and guilty about their sexual relationship and, against her better judgment, agreed to marry Shaun.

Once they got married, Shaun's abusive behaviors intensified. He repeatedly threatened Beth physically and put his fist through a wall in an effort to strike her. His escalating use of pornography and his repeated online affairs caused him to make twisted, abusive sexual demands of Beth. He raged at her for not being a godly wife, for not responding to his leadership by meeting his sexual needs. Shaun's verbal, physical, and spiritual abuse intensified.

Eventually, after their third child was born, Beth decided she could no longer endure her abusive marriage. With the help of a Christian psychologist and a godly neighbor who was a retired medical missionary, Beth began to gain the strength to set appropriate boundaries around her husband's destructive behavior. She separated from Shaun and insisted he get counseling. Shaun wrote the following letter to Beth after she, her pastor, and the psychologist insisted Shaun not contact her directly:

> I believe the reason you are so angry and bitter toward me is not because I was such a horrible person but because you got into a relationship you didn't want to be in in the first place. You felt pressured to get married, and you got married. This isn't my fault. . . .
>
> If you actually loved me, a lot of the bitterness and resentment you have inside you would not be there. Love covers a multitude of sins. Beth, you did some pretty horrible things to me as well. Please don't forget that you called me every name in the book. You swore at me. You've hit me dozens of times. You've withheld sex from me. You refused to get close to me, and you leave every time life gets tough. . . . I have done nothing a little forgiveness won't take care of. . . . You refuse to help me overcome my sin. That is why I have fallen.

Clearly, Shaun placed the blame for his marital problems squarely on Beth's shoulders—she was to blame for their problems, including his sexual sin; she was to blame for being bitter. In fact, his letter ends with a demand that she start being gracious and Christlike. Shaun offers a sad example of the harsh judgmentalism of abusers.

Abusers' judgmentalism can greatly compound the damaging effects of abuse. Abuse creates a shame that makes victims feel they are bad, worthless, defective, and responsible for the abuse. In some cases, even the anticipation of abuse can launch this self-blaming dynamic. For instance, in 1 Kings 18:9, godly Obadiah thought he was about to be murdered by King Ahab, so he asked Elijah what sin he had committed that he was about to be abused. In reality, God had spoken through the prophet Elijah to declare he would send a severe drought on the land as judgment for Ahab's wickedness in leading the people into idolatry (1 Kings 16:29–17:1). After several years of severe drought, when Ahab saw Elijah, the first words out of his mouth were, "Is this you, you troubler of Israel?" (18:17). In fact, Ahab's harshness had no basis in reality. Ahab himself was the troubler of Israel. In this case, Elijah was mature enough not to accept Ahab's judgmental message. Most abuse victims are not as spiritually mature as this seasoned prophet, and their abusers' judgmentalism compounds the damage to their souls.

Calculated Intimidation

Because abusers' lives are built around twisting reality, avoiding consequences, and engaging in behavior that brings temporary relief to their inner torment, they typically cannot face the reality of their destructive actions. Most abusers are desperate to keep their victims from revealing the truth. Thus, they often strategize to intimidate their victims into silence and submission, which allows them to continue to abuse with impunity. This also creates further damage to the victims, for it adds to their emotional trauma and can intensify feelings of powerlessness and vulnerability.

Biblical Examples of Intimidation

There are examples in the Bible that illustrate the various kinds of intimidation used by abusers. The most extreme is the direct promise of severe bodily harm, as seen in wicked Queen Jezebel's threat to have Elijah killed within twenty-four hours after he carried out divine judgment on the priests of Baal (1 Kings 19:1–2). Sadistic sex offenders are known to tell their victims ahead of time what horrible things they plan to do to them, as this kind of intimidation brings them pleasure.[16]

Sometimes opaque threats are just as traumatizing as direct threats, because they create a general sense of dread. This is what King Ahab did with the prophet Micaiah when he put him in prison after the prophet gave a prophecy Ahab didn't want to hear. Before he left for battle, Ahab told Micaiah and the prison guards that Micaiah was only to be given a sparse diet of bread and water "until I return" (1 Kings 22:27), implying that a much worse fate would befall the prophet when the king came back victorious from battle.

One of the most common types of intimidation used by abusers is the verbal threat of harm unless they are given what they want. Rabshakeh, general of an Assyrian army infamous for its sadistic cruelty, threatened extreme harm to the Judeans unless they gave in to him (2 Kings 18:27–35). This was no idle threat, for the Assyrians were well-known for extreme cruelty to their enemies. Archaeologists have discovered various ancient texts in which the Assyrians, with great braggadocio, recount the utter destruction of cities they conquered. They graphically recorded how, after defeating enemy armies, they would pile up the severed heads of enemy soldiers, slaughter the defeated citizens, torture the defeated royal family, flay political leaders, and place conquered women in the royal harem.[17] Thus, Rabshakeh's threats must have been extremely intimidating.

The Diabolical Creativity of Intimidation

The creativity of abusers to intimidate is quite diabolical, for it is often based on a serious calculation of the victim's weaknesses, points of vulnerability, and greatest fears. I've often heard sexual abuse victims say they passively endured their fathers' abuse as long as they did because the fathers threatened to molest the younger siblings if they resisted. One sixteen-year-old serial physical and sexual abuser of adolescents told his young victims he would come back and kill their family members if they told anyone what he had done to them. Furthermore, he told these naive young children that he could see and hear through walls, so he would always know if they told anyone. Sadly, they believed him.

A few years ago in Arizona, a Christian school principal was convicted of child abuse for forcing a fifteen-year-old girl who was considering enrolling at the school to completely disrobe, bend over, and receive swats on her buttocks. At first she refused to comply, but he threatened to give her twelve swats unless she immediately stripped. He said he wanted her to understand corporal punishment *before* she attended the school. The girl, who had gotten in trouble in a previous school, was told she deserved the punishment. The girl's mother, who witnessed the incident, told police she was too frightened to stop the headmaster. In fact, the mother was so intimidated that in the middle of this incident she told her daughter to "just do whatever he tells you to do, so we can get this over with." The principal was given a one-year prison sentence for abusing this teenage girl and another young boy. In the process of prosecution, it was discovered that this man had been kicked out of another school district in another state for what appeared to be physically abusive behavior. Shortly after the principal was released from prison, he moved to Europe, where he quickly opened another private religious school. No doubt he continued to intimidate parents and children, just as he had done for many years. Parents and others who care for minors must be just as strategic and determined to protect children as abusers are to intimidate them.

TYPES OF ABUSERS

In addition to these general characteristics, it's helpful to note specific characteristics of several types of abusers. Entire books are written on single types, or even subtypes, of abusers, so the best I can do here is to give a brief overview both of sexual molesters of minors and of physical abusers (of adults and children).

General Adult Child Molesters

Child molesters come from all walks of life and are very difficult to identify, even for professionals. The only observable distinctive of adult child molesters is that they are overwhelmingly male (80 to 90 percent).[18] The influences that lead a person to sexually violate a child or adolescent are complex and not entirely understood.[19] For example, it may be a misconception that the majority of child molesters were abused as children. Some current research indicates that 20 to 35 percent of child molesters were themselves sexually abused as children or adolescents.[20] While this figure is certainly much higher than the rate of abuse experienced in the general male population, it shows there must be other factors besides personal sexual victimization that influence adults to sexually violate children. We do know that a high percentage of child molesters report they came from dysfunctional families of origin.[21] The majority of sex offenders describe their fathers as cold, distant, hostile, and aggressive; often report conflicted relationships with their mothers; experienced high rates of physical abuse; and indicate that they communicated less with their parents than did their peers.[22] Recent research suggests that witnessing serious intrafamilial violence and experiencing neglect may be more influential than sexual abuse on sexual abuse victims' becoming sexual abusers themselves.[23]

Thus, the families many adult molesters come from are emotionally and physically hurtful. They do not provide healthy emotional nurturing, respect for the individual, and modeling of healthy conflict resolution and communication skills. These negative relational experiences lead some men to distrust adult relationships and to look to children and adolescents to meet their emotional and sexual needs.

Here are several other characteristics of adult child molesters. These observations can aid churches and organizations as they screen adults who want to work with children and youth.

- They most often molest females.
- They are rarely family members of the victim (only 10 percent) and are most often friends or acquaintances.[24]
- When the molester is a family member, he is much more likely to molest the child repeatedly and more severely.[25]
- Stepparents are up to ten times more likely to molest than natural parents.[26]
- Child molesters often have large numbers of victims. In one study, the molesters of girls had an average of twenty victims, while the molesters of boys had an average of 150 victims.[27]
- Child molesters are rarely caught and thus may not have a criminal record for molesting. They are, however, often guilty of committing nonsexual crimes and may have a criminal record for some of these offenses, which may indicate they are a potential sexual risk to minors. These telltale offenses include drunken driving, drug offenses, trespassing (often connected with voyeurism), shoplifting, and assault.[28]

- Research reveals that as many as half of all molesters had been drinking when they molested.[29]
- Molesters, including incest offenders, often commit various kinds of sex crimes, including rape, exhibitionism, and voyeurism.[30]

Fixated Child Molesters (Pedophiles)

Some child molesters are so consistently sexually aroused by minors that they are placed in a separate category of molesters we call pedophiles (literally, "lovers of children"). These people are often called "fixated molesters" for their sexual fixation with children or adolescents. Most often this sexual attraction is to boys. Pedophiles will typically have a fairly narrow age range of sexual interest. According to some experts, pedophiles attracted to girls usually prefer girls eight to ten years old; pedophiles attracted to boys are often drawn to boys who are slightly older.[31] Some pedophiles are attracted to children of both genders.

Most pedophiles first began molesting children when they themselves were adolescents. Of all the types of child molesters, pedophiles are in many respects the most troublesome, for they have the greatest number of victims, and their sexual proclivity toward children is often the most resistant to treatment. Many experts believe pedophiles cannot be cured—if cure means eliminating sexual desire for children.

Through self-assessment surveys and personality tests, pedophiles are often shown to be introverted, emotionally immature, and fearful of adult heterosexual relationships.[32] Thus, they turn to children for intimate relationships, for they relate much better to children than to adults. This helps us understand why pedophiles often believe they are expressing love to the children they are molesting. Pedophiles tend to use physical force on their victims less frequently than other molesters, though they often utilize threats and psychological manipulation to keep their victims silent about the abuse. Pedophiles are often extremely deliberate, patiently "grooming" potential victims in order to gain their trust and lower their inhibitions so they can have a sexual relationship with the child or adolescent without having to use physical force.[33]

Female Molesters

While female molesters are far less common than male, many experts believe that the number of female perpetrators is significantly underestimated and that females may be responsible for as much as 20 percent of the sexual molestations of minors.[34] There is limited literature on female offenders, but Anna Salter notes that, given what we do know, we can place female molesters in three categories:[35]

- *Women who molest children under the age of six, usually their own children.* This is one of the largest groups of female offenders. These are women whose identities are so amalgamated with their children's that they cannot function as mothers. Rather than nurture children, as healthy mothers do, they use children to meet their own emotional and sexual needs. Tragically, these women often have sadistic tendencies and take twisted pleasure in hurting children.
- *The teacher/lover group of women who primarily molest adolescents.* They are generally emotionally needy women in their thirties who take advantage of their position of authority to build romantic relationships with vulnerable teens.
- *Women who were at least initially coerced into having sexual relations with children by an adult male partner.* Some of these women will then go on to initiate sexual relations on their own with children.

Adolescent Molesters

Adolescent sex offenders provide a very serious challenge. It is estimated that adolescents commit up to half of all child sexual abuse, and their victims tend to be younger children. Adolescent molesters are a diverse population that can be put in several different categories:[36]

- *Experimenters.* These youths are typically sexually naive eleven- to fourteen-years-olds who have little history of acting-out behavior and who have a limited number of exploratory acts with children.
- *Group offenders.* These adolescents with little or no previous delinquency history are influenced by peers to engage in sexual offenses against children.
- *Undersocialized offenders.* These adolescents exhibit chronic social isolation and lack of social skills, and they are motivated to molest children by a need for greater self-importance and intimacy.
- *Pseudosocialized offenders.* These adolescents appear to have good social skills and confidence but are likely to have been extensively sexually abused themselves. They molest for sexual pleasure.
- *Sexually aggressive offenders.* These adolescents typically come from an abusive and out-of-control home and have a personal history of antisocial behavior, substance abuse, and poor impulse control. They often use force to molest, typically so as to experience the power of domination and to humiliate their victims.

While there is a broad range of adolescent offenders, research reveals some common traits of adolescents who molest children:

- They tend to come from families that are rigid and emotionally disengaged.[37]
- They most often molest girls.
- Compared to nonoffending peers, they tend to possess weak social skills, to have learning disabilities, to be more socially isolated, and to have a sense of powerlessness.[38]
- The vast majority of adolescents who molest children are males (up to 90 percent), but the females who do molest children have most often experienced severe maltreatment during childhood, including sexual victimization; typically they will molest boys.[39]

Children Who Violate Other Children

Tragically, children are at risk of sexual victimization not only from adults and adolescents; it is not uncommon for children to sexually violate other children.[40] Children who sexually violate other children have often been sexually abused or have been sexualized through exposure to sexual activity.

While many, if not most, children at one time or another engage in innocent sexual exploration ("playing doctor"), sexual behavior becomes exploitive if it:

- occurs with intimidation or force,
- continues in secrecy after caregivers have advised the child that it's inappropriate,
- involves children of widely varying ages or developmental stages, and
- involves explicit sexual acts (attempted or simulated sexual intercourse, oral sex, and so forth).

Unlike adult and juvenile sex offenders, gender is not a distinctive characteristic of children who sexually violate other children. In fact, 65 percent of preschool children who sexually violate other children are girls, though the most sexually aggressive children are almost always males (91 percent).[41]

Physically Abusive Men

While physically abusive men are found in all ethnic and socioeconomic groups, the lowest income households experience dramatically higher rates of male physical abuse.[42] According to the Centers for Disease Control and Prevention (CDC), men who physically abuse their wives have a 50 percent probability of abusing their children as well, and the most violent wife batterers have almost a 100 percent probability of physically abusing their male children.[43]

One of the most predictable features of physically abusive men is that they experienced family violence during childhood.[44] They were taught that physical violence is an acceptable way to deal with stress and frustration; they weren't taught the practical skills of healthy communication and conflict resolution.

Behaviorally, the most characteristic pattern of physically abusive men is *control*. Abusive men have a pathological need to control much or all of their spouses' and children's lives, and they do so not just through physical force but also through psychological and verbal manipulation and abuse.[45] They often have an underlying sense of insecurity, inadequacy, and powerlessness that results in their need to control family members. They resort to violence when family members do things that threaten their fragile self-concepts.[46]

While there are widely varying types of physically abusive men, the following attitudes and beliefs are characteristic of physically abusive men:[47]

- *Overarching sense of entitlement.* Physically abusive men use this sense of entitlement to justify physical violence toward family members who do not give them what they think they deserve. Family members exist to meet their needs.
- *Selfishness, self-centeredness.* Their needs are of primary importance.
- *Air of superiority.* They believe they are superior to their wives and children. Often this is connected with a global belief in male superiority.
- *Extreme possessiveness.* Family members are viewed as owned objects, which helps explain why physical assault and homicide rates go up dramatically when women separate from their abusive husbands or boyfriends.

＊

Now that we've had an overview of the characteristics of abusers, I'm ready to put this information into a relational context in the next chapter. Abusers rarely act in isolation from other family members. In fact, there are notable characteristics of abusive families that can help us better understand the nature and impact of abuse, and I'll now explore these characteristics.

chapter 4

✳

portrait of an
abusive family

Abusive families (families in which abuse takes place) are identical to and yet radically different from other families. While abusive families typically blend in with all the nonabusive families in their neighborhood, they have certain distinct traits that contribute to and result from the abuse. It is imperative for us to understand these traits; if we don't, we cannot minister effectively to abuse victims—in fact, we can ultimately create additional hurt and damage.

Several years ago, I was ministering in a church in the Pacific Northwest. I had decided to do a series of sermons on family life. I was rather young and naive and did not understand the unique dynamics of abusive families. Thus, even as I tried to minister to our families, I and the other pastors said things that were very hurtful to Tina, a young woman in our congregation who had grown up in an abusive family. In the middle of my preaching series, Tina mustered up the courage to send me the following letter:

Dear Pastoral Staff,

For the past two years I have sat through many Sunday school lessons and sermons, only to go away defeated and hurt by the assumptions you make about families. You do not understand the kind of families some of us grew up in. When you preach about family harmony, communication, resolving family conflict, and honoring your father and mother, do you have any idea how complicated and confusing these topics are for us who grew up in abusive families? Let me tell you a little bit about my family.

By the age of three, I was already well acquainted with family violence. My biological father abused my mother in front of me on many occasions. My mother divorced my father twice before I was three. We were a typical welfare family when my mother met and married a man twice her age. My stepfather was and is an EVIL man in every sense of the word. He beat my brothers and me until we were blobs crying on the floor. In addition, punishment for trying to defend ourselves involved sitting on his lap while he told us why he had to molest us. The abuse continued until I was sixteen. During this time neighbors, teachers, and friends knew what was happening. We often stayed out of the house until well after dark to avoid a confrontation. Anything and everything from not folding the towels correctly to walking in front of the television would result in the cycle of beatings we went through. My mother during this whole time just watched. How could anyone just watch? Only once did she beg him to stop, which resulted in him throwing his keys and breaking her glasses. She never spoke up again. Finally, when I was sixteen, I ran away with my brothers. Only then did my mother wake up. We moved out of Idaho with only the clothes on our backs, and I have not seen him since. Even after twelve years, I still fear him, still look over my shoulder, still believe he can get to me because he is EVIL.

I realize it is hard to understand something unless you have gone through it—but please feel my pain when you speak on abuse, honoring your father and mother, forgiving those who hurt you. I'm not asking you to heal my pain, but you don't have to alienate me either.

Sincerely,
One of the abused in your congregation

My heart broke for Tina and for the way I had inadvertently hurt her. I simply did not understand the unique profile of abusive families. Since this time I've witnessed these dynamics in countless families. I've also seen them lived out in the pages of Scripture. In fact, an incident in King David's family gives a remarkable picture of the dynamics of families in which abuse takes place. It also sheds light on the nature of abuse itself, particularly the dynamics of rape. If I would have paid attention to this Bible story earlier, I'd have understood Tina's family much better. While this biblical text doesn't give a systematic assessment of abuse, it corresponds well with modern research on abuse and has much to teach us about abusive families.

THE STORY OF TAMAR AND AMNON

Before you read on, I encourage you to pick up a Bible and read 2 Samuel 13:1–21, which describes the rape of Tamar by her half brother Amnon. For the rest of this chapter, I'll outline some of the major characteristics of abusive families revealed in this Bible passage.

The Needs of Family Members Are Expendable

The story begins in verse 1 with an introduction of the key players: "Absalom the son of David had a beautiful sister whose name was Tamar, and Amnon the son of David loved her." Like a well-crafted Shakespearean tragedy, this story begins by deftly introducing pregnant phrases that will soon turn sinister. The careful reader will quickly feel something is amiss in this family. First of all, Absalom and Amnon are identified as sons of David, but Tamar is simply Absalom's sister. This is odd, since Tamar is the daughter of King David and Queen Maacah (2 Samuel 3:3). In fact, nowhere in the entire account is Tamar ever referred to as the daughter of David.

In abusive families, family members are not equally valued by the parents. In highly patriarchal families, female children are often given less protection and honor than their male siblings. It's also strange that the story begins by mentioning Absalom first, since Amnon was the royal prince who would succeed David on the throne and thus would normally be honored by being mentioned first. Absalom is probably mentioned first because, in the broad context of 2 Samuel, this particular story is about the quest for an heir to the throne.[1] Unfortunately for Tamar, she ends up a pawn in a family power play. This will become particularly clear in 2 Samuel 13:21 when we see David's failure to respond to Tamar's rape. It also tells us something important about abusive families: *The needs of individual family members are highly expendable.* The weak members of a family can be used up and exploited to feed the appetites of the more powerful family members.

Reality Is Difficult to Discern

We learn two other things about Tamar in this opening verse: she was beautiful, and her brother Amnon loved her. In a healthy family, these would be prescient statements of blessing and happiness. Not so for Tamar. *In abusive families, reality is very difficult to discern.* Nothing is as it appears. Beauty metastasizes into pain and shame. Brotherly love turns out to be bestial lust. What you thought was the safest place on earth—your own family home—turns out to be the most dangerous. No wonder those who grow up in abusive families find it nearly impossible to trust their own perceptions and emotions. No wonder so many abuse victims are so confused they feel they are going insane. Most are quite sane, but they live in insane families.

The Victim Is Made Responsible

While Tamar hadn't seen it yet, verse 2 tips the reader off to Amnon's true character. He was so frustrated because of his "love" for his beautiful sister Tamar that he made himself sick. While Scripture does speak of a healthy, romantic "lovesickness" (Song of Solomon 5:8), that's hardly what we have here. Amnon was specifically said to be frustrated because Tamar was a virgin and it was "hard ... to do anything to her." This probably refers to the fact that royal virgins were kept under close guard, so Amnon was not able to have sexual relations with her. Amnon's "love" was nothing more than an incestuous lust he had fanned into a raging fire. The irony here is that Amnon made himself sick with his own lust for his sister, but Amnon, Jonadab, and David (with varying degrees of knowledge) all placed the responsibility on Tamar to heal Amnon's self-induced sickness. *In abusive families, the victim is made responsible for solving needs—even evil needs—they didn't create and could never legitimately satisfy.*

There are many modern-day Tamars. Sheila was the oldest of six children. Her frail mother was often sick in bed and seemed utterly overwhelmed by life. Sheila learned from a very early age that she was Mommy's little helper. In fact, she was much more of a mother to her siblings than was her mother. She dressed the children for school, prepared the meals, and made the grocery lists. As she looked back on her childhood, she described herself as the model child. She remembered receiving a few beatings when her father had been drinking, but she had experienced emotional neglect virtually every day of her childhood. She was the caregiver for the entire family. While it had given her a sense of responsibility at the time, it had drained her soul and was more damaging than the frequent beatings some of her younger siblings had received. When Sheila turned nine, her father began to molest her once or twice a week. He explained that her mother was not available to meet his needs, and a man's needs must be met. Sheila put up little resistance, though she hated what her father was doing to her. She had been programmed from birth to ignore her own needs and take care of everyone else. That was her job in the family.[2]

The Family Appearance Is Deceptive

Amnon's lust might have eventually died out were it not for his interaction with his shrewd adviser, Jonadab, who had asked about his downcast countenance. Amnon told Jonadab he had been depressed because he was in love with the sister of his brother. The fact that Amnon did not identify Tamar as his own sister might well suggest he had already begun to impersonalize Tamar and his familial relationship with her to justify his lust.[3] In a healthy family, Jonadab would have corrected Amnon and coached him in the proper way to meet his relational and sexual needs.[4] Instead, Jonadab concocted a devious scheme for Amnon to gain physical access to his sister by pretending to be ill and calling for his sister to feed him (verses 3–5). Jonadab was Amnon's cousin, and as a member of the family he should have been concerned for Tamar's welfare and his cousin's moral well-being.

Jonadab reveals another characteristic of abusive families: *Appearances are deceptive. The family's shiny exterior belies a dark inner reality.* "Jonadab" means "the LORD is generous." Sadly, giving your cousin a clever scheme to help him rape his sister hardly shows the generosity of God. The scheme itself also epitomizes the deceptive appearance of abusive families. On the face, it appeared that Tamar was simply being asked to provide physical sustenance (food) and comfort for her sick brother. In reality, her kindness and trust would be skillfully manipulated to shatter her physical safety and to strip her of emotional comfort for the rest of her life.

Jonadab and Amnon weren't the only family members with a deceptive appearance. The entire royal family had a very impressive appearance. David had sinned with Bathsheba, but he had repented and been forgiven. God blessed David and Bathsheba with another son (Solomon), whom Nathan the prophet named Jedidiah, which means "loved by the LORD" (2 Samuel 12:25). Tamar and Absalom were good-looking royal family members who obeyed their father.

Very significantly, immediately before the account of Tamar's rape, the writer tells us that the Israelites had secured a great victory over the Ammonites (2 Samuel 12:26–31). The Jewish general Joab was so concerned about David's appearance and reputation that he asked David to lead the final assault, so that the city would be renamed after David and not Joab. As the chapter concludes, David's positive public persona reaches a crescendo as David is crowned with a massive gold crown taken from the enemy king. But as we've already seen, the royal family was not what it appeared to be.[5]

Judith Lewis Herman notes the deceptive appearance of abusive families in her insightful study of forty abusive families:

> The families in which the informants grew up were conventional to a fault. Most were churchgoing and financially stable; they maintained a facade of respectability. They were for the most part unknown to mental health services, social agencies, or the police. Because they conformed to traditional family norms, their private disturbances were easily overlooked.[6]

The Truth Is Ignored

Amnon followed his cousin's advice perfectly. He feigned illness to get David to send Tamar to feed him bread cakes. David fully cooperated with Amnon's fiendish plan, ordering Tamar to go to Amnon's house and prepare him food. If this was all the information we had regarding David's response to Tamar, we might conclude he had been so thoroughly deceived that he bore little responsibility for the violation of Tamar. David's pattern of behavior toward his children shows otherwise. In fact, David demonstrates another trait of abusive families: *Vulnerable family members are not protected because no one really wants to know the truth.*

The truth is ignored. In other words, maintaining one's own emotional well-being is more important than admitting that dangerous family problems exist. As the God-ordained spiritual leader charged with the well-being of his household (Deuteronomy 6:1–9; Proverbs 1:8–9; 4:1), David should have known, at the very least, that something was wrong with Amnon, whose depression was quite evident to other family members. The fact that Amnon was next in line to the throne made it even more inexcusable that David failed to observe such wholesale moral turmoil in his own son. Amnon's moral character most likely had been eroding over an extended period of time. No spiritually healthy man wakes up one morning and decides he's going to rape his sister. David apparently chose to see nothing and do nothing, and Tamar was eventually raped as a result.

David's actions after Tamar's rape confirm the assessment that he didn't protect her because he didn't want to know the truth. After the rape, when Amnon's predatory deviancy was public knowledge, David did absolutely nothing. His silence shouts in the biblical account. There is no indication that David consoled Tamar, cautioned Absalom, or punished Amnon; he is lamely silent. He does not ask because he apparently does not want to know. Later on, when unavenged Absalom asks for Amnon to go with him to the sheepshearing, David allowed Amnon to go, precipitating his murder (2 Samuel 13:24–29). Later on, when Absalom began to steal away the hearts of the people, which ultimately resulted in civil war, David was oblivious to his son's growing rebellion (15:1–14). David's failure to embrace the truth of Absalom's bitterness cost the lives of at least twenty thousand soldiers (18:7), as well as Absalom's life (18:14–15). It also led directly to ten royal concubines being publicly raped (15:16; 16:22). David did not protect because he did not want to be disturbed with the truth.

Celestia and I have heard hundreds of stories in which palpable evidence of abuse was chronically ignored, with no questions asked. The evidence included a wife's unmistakable facial bruises; children who cower and scream the moment a parent or older sibling comes into the room; the inexplicable discovery of a young child's bloody underwear; a ten-year-old boy who suddenly begins wetting the bed and having nightmares shortly after visiting his aunt and uncle; and a husband who gets up repeatedly in the middle of the night to go to a child's room, shuts the door, and each time afterward washes the child's sheets, leaving them folded on the dryer the next morning. In each of these instances family members asked no questions, and the abuse continued.[7] In abusive families truth is not a friend but the enemy.

Family Abusers Use Force

Amnon's ruse worked, and after sending away the servants, he gained private access to Tamar. At this point he wasted no more time pretending to be a bedridden invalid. He grabbed Tamar and lewdly demanded sex. The language of the text highlights Amnon's abusive use of physical force to hold Tamar against her will. The Hebrew verb translated as "took hold of" (2 Samuel 13:11) is the same one used in 2 Samuel 2:16, where Judean soldiers "seized" enemy soldiers by the head so they could stab them to death.[8]

Amnon's behavior with Tamar highlights the fact that rape victims and other abuse victims should not be blamed for what happened to them. *Family abusers use force to get their sordid way*—be it physical force, emotional blackmail, verbal threats, intimidation, or calculated emotional manipulation to hold victims against their will so they can abuse them.[9]

It's important to recognize that abusers employ a wide range of behaviors other than mere physical force to seize and hold their victims. At the same time, those who are chronically abused develop a sense of powerlessness so that their abuser doesn't have to use force in order to continue to abuse them. This explains many situations in which the abuse victim inexplicably fails to walk away from the abuser. For instance, twelve-year-old Elizabeth Smart was reportedly abducted at knifepoint from her Salt Lake City home by a homeless religious drifter, was held against her will, and was sexually abused; and yet, months after her abduction, when she was discovered by local police, she didn't attempt to flee but rather lied about her identity and remained with her abuser, who had forced her to become his next wife.[10]

There Is No Straightforward, Healthy Communication

Amnon's sexual demand was both crass and confusing; for this was the first and only time he called Tamar "my sister" (2 Samuel 13:11).[11] As we've seen in the previous chapter, abusers manipulate with their words and actions and have little regard for the impact of their manipulation on the victim. For Tamar, "sister" should have been a term denoting a tender familial relationship that elicited steadfast loyalty, care, and protection (Genesis 34:1–31; Leviticus 18:11; cf. 1 Timothy 5:2).[12] Instead, this sister received violent defilement, contempt, and abandonment.

We see here another characteristic of abusive families: *There is no straightforward, healthy communication, and many of the verbal messages are contradictory and confusing.* In abusive families, messages are, at best, ambiguous and confusing. At worst, they are demeaning and destructive. The net effect is tremendous confusion. For instance, Tamar was told by her father that her brother was sick and needed her to feed him bread cakes. Then she found out that he was morally sick and needed her to feed his lust. He called her his sister but asked her to be his lover. Before the rape he called her his sister, but afterward he calls her "this woman" (2 Samuel 13:17). He initially offered her entrance into the most personal place in the household—his bed—but when he was done with her, he threw her out on the street and locked the door. The ambiguity, distortion, and dishonesty of verbal messages in abusive families produce profound confusion and damage.[13]

The Victim's Response Is Often Futile

After Amnon's brash proposition, Tamar had the inner strength to offer a courageous response. The clarity and logic of her response make her rape all the more tragic. While being held against her will, she immediately spoke up and gave Amnon three "don'ts" in 2 Samuel 13:12 (don't violate me; don't do what isn't done in Israel; don't do such a disgraceful thing) and three "ands" in verse 13 (and it would disgrace me so that I'd have to get rid of my reproach somehow; and you will become a public fool; and the king won't deny your request if you ask him for my hand in marriage).

The three "don'ts" emphasize the moral impropriety of forced sexual intercourse—it violates the sacred law of God.[14] The first two "ands" emphasize the terrible results of such a sin (shame for Tamar, social ostracism for Amnon), and the final one suggests an alternative nonsinful course of action (marriage with the king's consent).[15] All of Tamar's statements were accurate, with one exception. She warned that if Amnon proceeded to rape her, he would experience social ostracism. In a just society, Amnon *would* have faced severe social consequences for his sex crime, but nothing in the text suggests this happened. The terrible irony is that Amnon's sinful actions resulted in *Tamar's* social ostracism. As is so often the case in our fallen, unjust world, abuse victims can suffer far worse consequences than do their perpetrators.

Tamar's response was logical, wise, and in harmony with God's standards. But her story teaches us this sad reality when it comes to abuse situations: *The victim's response is often futile.* The tragedy here is that when abuse victims rise above the swirling waves of distorted and hurtful verbal messages and gather the courage to speak the truth, their words often fall on deaf ears. Abusers rarely respond to reason, which is why it's vital for families and churches to focus on listening to, empowering, and protecting abuse victims. It often does little or no good to spend time reasoning with unrepentant abusers.

Several years ago a pastor phoned to ask for my advice. He and other church leaders had been working with a couple who were having severe marital problems. The husband had been asked to leave two previous churches for being contentious and verbally abusive to church members and to his own family members. The husband was extremely domineering toward his entire family. When he didn't get his way, he would scream, threaten, and humiliate his wife and children. This pastor had recently discovered evidence suggesting the man had been hitting his wife and children. Two different Christian counselors who had worked with the couple advised the wife to separate from her husband, believing he posed an immediate threat to his family. The wife had asked the husband to move out until he got counseling and learned to control his abusive anger. The husband refused to leave.

The pastor was convinced this was a dangerous, abusive man and wanted my help in writing a detailed position paper responding to the husband's biblical arguments. He and the other church leaders hoped that by confronting the abusive husband with thorough, sound biblical teaching, he would see the light. Unfortunately, chronic abusers have hard hearts only the Lord can penetrate. They don't respond to logical persuasion.

The apostle Paul understood the fact that hard-hearted sinners cannot be reasoned with. He instructed his colleague Titus that after someone has rejected a clear presentation of the truth, he or she must simply be removed to protect the rest of the spiritual family: "Reject a factious man after a first and second warning, knowing that such a man is perverted and is sinning, being self-condemned" (Titus 3:10–11). I advised this pastor to go ahead and gather the biblical data for the good of this wife and for the church's education but to put 90 percent of his energy into protecting the abused woman and her family. He did write an excellent biblical summary on marriage, anger, and the servant leadership of husbands, but this abusive husband simply responded that he did not have to listen to the church leaders and that he wasn't going to get counseling or change his behavior. Abusers rarely listen to logical biblical arguments.

Power Is Used to Exploit

In contrast to Tamar's courageous, well-reasoned objections, Amnon used his brute strength to ravage his sister: "He violated her and lay with her" (2 Samuel

13:14; the Hebrew text makes crystal clear the brutality of his act, for it literally says, "he forced her and laid her." *In abusive families, power is used to exploit.*

While this may seem like an obvious point, it bears noting that in abusive families, power is used in various ways to exploit. For instance, one major study of incest victims revealed that half of the women who had experienced sexual abuse by their fathers had also been physically battered by their fathers and in some cases by both parents. Another 25 percent of these women had been severely disciplined (which in many cases might have been abusive as well).[16] Similarly, Judith Lewis Herman concludes from her study of abusive families that "one of the most significant distinguishing characteristics of the incestuous fathers was their tendency to dominate their families by the use of force. Half of the informants reported that their fathers were habitually violent"[17]— that is, they physically abused family members.

In abusive families, nonphysical power is used to exploit as well. This can include psychological/emotional manipulation (shaming, threatening to reveal ugly secrets if they don't get what they want, threatening a family member with divine punishment, etc.); social coercion (threatening to tell other family members how horrible the victim is, threatening to cut the victim off from the rest of the family, etc.); and financial coercion (threatening to force the victim—or anyone who protects him or her—out on his or her own, cutting off finances, etc.).

Stated or perceived financial intimidation is a particularly significant force in many abusive families. Research shows that girls with mothers who are sick or poorly educated are at much higher risk of incest by their fathers or stepfathers—largely because these mothers, who are especially vulnerable and financially dependent on their husbands, find it extremely difficult to protect their daughters from abuse.[18] Abusive husbands are typically very good at exploiting their wives' vulnerability.[19]

Both emotional and financial intimidation help explain the findings of a recent research study. This study showed that two of the most significant factors in predicting whether a mother will believe and protect a child who discloses intrafamilial sexual abuse are (1) the age of the mother when she had her first child and (2) the mother's relationship with the perpetrator.[20] Mothers who had their first child at a young age tend to be more emotionally and financially vulnerable than mothers who had their first child when they were older. And mothers of abuse victims are far more likely to experience emotional and financial pressure and deprivation if the perpetrators are the husbands than if the perpetrators are nonspouses.[21]

Abusive Families Are Emotionally Unstable

Immediately after Amnon raped his sister, his lovesickness was suddenly transformed into great hatred. The text says that Amnon "hated her with a very great hatred; for the hatred with which he hated her was greater than the love with which he had loved her" (2 Samuel 13:15). This dynamic of love that turns into hate can seem strange to those who don't understand abuse.[22] It is, however, a common occurrence in abusive families, and it illustrates this characteristic: *Abusive families are emotionally unstable.*

In Amnon's case, his actions clearly show he didn't really love Tamar in the first place, though the extent of his newfound hatred was no doubt exacerbated by his own shame and guilt. Thus, emotional instability can both contribute to and result from abuse.[23] In abusive families, love and hate often dwell side by side. Abuse victims, especially incest victims, are often given special treatment, attention, and "love" by the abuser.[24] As with so many other dynamics in an abusive family, this creates great confusion for abuse victims and makes them distrust their own emotions.

Barbara is a twenty-nine-year-old nurse with three small children.[25] She lives in a New England mill town. She volunteered to share her personal account of growing up in an abusive family because she wanted to encourage others who had also experienced abuse. Barbara grew up in North Carolina in a working-class family. She was the oldest of six children. Her father had gone to Princeton but was drafted before he could graduate. He was a proud man who disdained the South and anyone with a Southern accent, including his own wife.

Barbara's father physically, sexually, and verbally abused his family for twenty years. He began fondling Barbara when she was three years old. The sexual abuse continued until she was well into adolescence. Barbara articulately spoke of the confusing emotional climate of her abusive home, where she and her other family members experienced love and kindness, abuse and rage—all from the same man. Even at the age of twenty-nine, Barbara still feared her father, acknowledging that she had been deeply disturbed by his abuse. She began by describing her father on a positive note:

> He always appeared the family man. He was affectionate. He used to take us fishing. When he was being a father, I suppose he did as well as anyone. He was giving and fun, and we enjoyed his company. But when he was drinking, he was certainly very different.
>
> We knew that there were certain things that had to be done or else. The "or else" was usually physical. He would beat us. But I was exempt from much of it. It's like there were two families because I was different. I was different in many

ways, but I was definitely my father's pet.... I had a bond with my father, which may have been a source of strength even though he was the [sexual] pursuer most of the time. But still I think that bond is important: *to have someone looking out for you even if they are beating you at the same time.*

My father showed my mother a lot of affection around us. When the family was together, he would love her, he would kiss her, and they would appear to be a happy couple. He would express good feelings about her.... But when he was drinking, they would fight. I've seen him hit her and throw her against the wall.

At the time I definitely felt that if I didn't comply [sexually], I would be hurt. He had hit me and knocked me around. I wasn't totally free of what was going on with the other kids. I got less than the others, probably because I was a good kid. I guess I always did what he told me, *and I was always the favorite child.*[26]

The emotional confusion created by Barbara's abusive father was quite obvious. She reflected on her childhood and remembered her father as loving and affectionate and also as abusive. She felt he looked out for her, even though he beat her. She felt she was his favorite, even though she was his victim. Clearly, Barbara continued to be confused about her father and his treatment of her.

The Victim Is Shamed, Blamed, and Demeaned

Tragically, Amnon's abusive behavior did not stop with the rape. After his lust was satiated, hatred welled up in his heart, and he ordered Tamar to "get up, go away!" (2 Samuel 13:15). Tamar refused to leave, arguing that to send her away was more evil than the rape itself. Amnon's response was to order the servants to "throw this woman out" and bolt the door.

While it seems very strange to modern readers that a woman would want to stay with her rapist, we must put Tamar's actions in their historical context. In an ancient patriarchal culture that placed great emphasis on sexual purity and honor, a young woman who had lost her virginity, even through rape, would have few chances of marriage. Without marriage, a woman would have little chance of supporting herself and thus leave her with no social and financial future. She would also be unable to have children, which was the single most important role of women in Jewish culture. For this reason, Old Testament law mandated that when a man raped an unmarried woman, he had to pay a dowry and marry her and could never divorce her.[27] Thus, Tamar cried out that Amnon's second act was a greater wrong than the first, for in kicking her out and not marrying her, he was killing her future.[28]

Amnon thus showed great disdain for Tamar by declaring, in essence, that she wasn't worthy to be married to *anyone*, not even to her rapist. The manner in which Amnon threw Tamar out was also demeaning and abusive—ordering a servant to remove Tamar, a princess. Furthermore, she was no longer viewed as his sister but as "this woman."[29] All this adds up to another sad characteristic of abusive families: *Abuse victims are shamed, blamed, and demeaned.*[30]

The characteristics of abusive families are seen not only in nuclear families but in spiritual families (churches and religious organizations) and in social families (schools, close-knit communities, and the like). Churches and communities often shame, blame, and demean abuse victims. Several years ago, Celestia began working with a troubled teenage client. After a few sessions the girl shared that she had gone to a shopping mall and met some local teen boys, who offered her a ride home. She was flattered and accepted their offer. Instead of taking her home, however, they took her into the desert and gang-raped her. Eventually they let her go and threatened her with great harm if she told anyone what had happened. She had the courage to tell the authorities and to press charges against the boys. When the principal of the conservative Christian high school she attended heard about the incident, he expelled her from school. He stated that only a slut would allow such a thing to happen to her—and they didn't want sluts in their Christian school. Abusive families shame and blame the victim.

Family Members Are Isolated and Lack Intimacy

The unmitigated tragedy of Tamar's story was revealed in her response to being thrown out of Amnon's house. She tore her long robe—the kind worn by virgins—and put ashes on her head, put her hand on her head, and wept bitterly. All of these actions were cultural signs of grief, for from this time on, Tamar would have no social future and would be isolated from society (see 2 Samuel 20:3). While Tamar, like all abuse victims, experienced many destructive consequences from the abuse, this text highlights one in particular: long-term social isolation. Tamar was part of an abusive family in which family members experienced little or no real intimacy.

King David didn't really know his children. He didn't realize Amnon's moral struggles or the danger he had brought on Tamar by sending her to his house. Once he found out his son was a rapist, he was angry, but he never seemed to have confronted Amnon or consoled Tamar (2 Samuel 13:21). Later when Absalom avenged Tamar's rape by having Amnon murdered, David was comforted and longed to go to Absalom, but he refused to speak to Absalom or to see him (2 Samuel 13:37–39; 14:24). Even though David loved Absalom, the only way Absalom could get his father's attention was to manipulate a response by setting the commanding general's field on fire (2 Samuel 14:28–33). In short, the family members in this ancient abusive family knew little or nothing of healthy intimacy; they were isolated from the very family members to whom they should have been closest. Sadly, this dynamic is very common, for *abusive families are characterized by social isolation and a lack of intimate relationships.*[31]

Those who grow up in abusive families may have many people around them, but they are perpetually lonely. Tamar was socially isolated for the rest of her life, for after her rape and expulsion from Amnon's house, "[she] remained and was desolate in her brother Absalom's house" (2 Samuel 13:20). One abuse survivor put it this way: "I had a fantasy of myself screaming inside a block of ice. People were walking right by, but no one saw or heard me. I wanted so much for someone to melt the ice."[32] Because those who grow up in abusive families often experience chronic isolation and loneliness, and because as divine image bearers they long for intimate relationships, they often end up in promiscuous or otherwise unhealthy relationships.[33]

A Strict Code of Silence Is Enacted

The biblical story now shifts to Absalom, who, upon seeing Tamar's visible grief, makes several incredible statements (2 Samuel 13:20). He first asks her if she has been with Amnon. Some interpreters take this as evidence that Absalom and Jonadab were working in concert, and that Absalom had been in on the rape plan all along—which would have given him an excuse to kill Amnon so he could become heir to the throne. I believe Absalom's treatment of Tamar suggests, rather, that he loved her and had not actively conspired with her rape but had passively conspired by ignoring warning signs of Amnon's devious intentions.[34] After all, abusive families aren't intimate, don't know each other well, and don't protect vulnerable family members because they don't really want to know the truth.

Absalom next issues a well-meaning but dreadful injunction: "But now keep silent, my sister, he is your brother." The basis for keeping quiet about the abuse is that the abuser was the victim's brother. This points to another characteristic: *Abusive families enact a strict code of silence, especially if the abuser is a family member.*

For millennia, families have closed ranks and maintained the strictest code of silence when they find out a family member is abusing another family member, particularly if the abuse is sexual. This silence may be due to the fact that, in most cultures, incestuous sexual abuse brings more severe legal and social consequences than do other forms of abuse. Family members often find it difficult to believe a fellow family member could commit such a terrible act. In other instances the abuser has so much power that other family members fear the consequences if he or she is held liable for family abuse. Thus, for a variety of reasons, families place tremendous explicit and implicit pressure on victims of intrafamilial sexual abuse to shut up and to stay quiet.[35]

This conspiracy of silence is one of the most characteristic dynamics of abusive families, and is documented in much of the literature on abuse. For instance, in Diana Russell's landmark study of sexual abuse, her probability sample included 930 women, with 648 cases of sexual abuse before the age of eighteen. Of these, only thirty cases (just 5 percent) were reported to the authorities. Of the women who were sexually abused by a family member, only 2 percent of the cases had been reported to the authorities.[36] While Tamar's family might not have listened to her report, the truth should have been told, for covering up such horrible sin has grave consequences for the victim and for the entire family. The Bible repeatedly condemns covering up, overlooking, or relabeling evil (see Psalm 74:8–9; Isaiah 5:20; Micah 2:6–11).

Abusive Families Deny and Distort Healthy Emotions

Absalom's final command to Tamar is probably also well meaning but equally dreadful. He said, "Do not take this matter to heart"—that is, do not worry about or pay undue attention to the rape. Absalom may well have been trying to comfort Tamar, knowing he intended to get revenge on her rapist. But how could a rape victim not take to heart one of the most violating, damaging events that could ever occur to her? How could she not pay attention to an event that had dramatically changed her life forever? In fact, Tamar's dramatic actions (weeping, tearing her dress, putting ashes on her head) were most appropriate expressions of grief over a tremendous loss.

Absalom's request is in keeping with the characteristics of abusive families, for *abusive families deny and distort proper healthy emotions*. Abusive families pressure victims to go numb and to not express appropriate grief and anger, and the abusers don't express proper emotions either. Other than lust disguised as love, the only emotions Amnon expressed were anger and disgust, and they were directed at the gracious sister he had raped. There is no biblical hint that Amnon had any appropriate emotions (compassion, sorrow, remorse, and the like) toward Tamar.[37] This dynamic helps us understand why abuse victims have such a hard time experiencing healthy, appropriate emotions.

The Wrong Ones Are Protected

King David's response offers a final insight into abusive families. After hearing of Tamar's rape, David was "very angry" (2 Samuel 13:21). What is confusing is that this sovereign monarch was very angry, and yet he did absolutely nothing. David's ambiguous response is explained in some of the Hebrew manuscripts, which add the following to this verse: "but [David] did not curb the excesses of his son Amnon; he favored him because he was his firstborn."[38] In other words, David was angry that Tamar was raped, but because Amnon was the firstborn golden boy, David protected him and not Tamar. Even though God's law dictated that Amnon should either be cut off from the people for committing incest (Leviticus 20:17) or be forced to marry Tamar for raping her (Deuteronomy 22:28–29), David insisted on protecting the abuser—which unveils another characteristic: *In abusive families, the wrong ones are protected.*[39]

We could give countless examples of how families, churches, and denominations protect abusers instead of victims and potential victims. Perhaps the most egregious recent example of such misdirected protection is the sexual abuse scandal in the Roman Catholic Church in America, particularly in Boston, Massachusetts. An investigative team of journalists with the *Boston Globe* won a Pulitzer Prize for the book *Betrayal*, which documents how scores of Catholic priests, particularly in Boston, molested thousands of children for decades, while the church's top leadership (including cardinals) knew of the abuse, systematically covered it up, and tenaciously protected the abusive priests.[40]

In this book the authors give overwhelming evidence that the leadership of the Catholic Church misused their spiritual authority to silence abused children and their parents through direct injunctions, veiled threats, secret settlements, sealed records, and patent lies and deception. Sadly, this pattern seems to have occurred in other parts of the country as well. Some of the worst offenses were reported in New Mexico, where abusive priests were sent to a treatment program at the Paraclete Center. After that they were sent to area churches, where reportedly many continued to molest. One attorney intimately familiar with the situation described the incongruity of the royal treatment the abusive priests received at the treatment center in contrast to the church's disregard for the victims:

> I can tell you what the atmosphere was [at the Paraclete Center]. They flew in fresh fish and special food items and they went on hikes in the mountains and they were released over the weekend into the local parishes, where they continued to abuse children.... There is not a single shred of evidence that anyone gave one whit about the victims.[41]

Tragically, in abusive families and churches, abusers are protected, while innocent, vulnerable victims are not.

CONCLUSION

We can now summarize what Tamar's rape by her brother teaches us about the primary characteristics of abusive families:

- The needs of individual family members are highly expendable.
- Reality is very difficult to discern.
- The victim is made responsible for solving needs they didn't create and could never legitimately satisfy.
- The family's shiny exterior belies a dark inner reality.
- Vulnerable family members are not protected because no one really wants to know the truth.
- Family abusers use force to get their sordid way.
- There is no straightforward healthy communication, and many of the verbal messages are contradictory and confusing.
- The victim's response is futile.
- Power is abused to exploit.
- Abusive families are emotionally unstable.
- The victims are shamed, blamed, and demeaned.
- Members are isolated and lack intimacy.
- A strict code of silence is enacted.
- Abusive families deny and distort proper healthy emotions.
- The wrong ones are protected.

＊

Now that we've examined the nature of abuse, the profiles of abusers, and the characteristics of abusive families, we're ready to move on in part 2 to look at the specific effects of abuse. What is the result of being abused and growing up in an abusive family?

part 2
the effects of abuse

✳

chapter 5

shame

once served as the college pastor in a church near a state university. I met hundreds of college students during my tenure there, but Mary Beth was one of the most memorable. Bill, one of our graduate students, had invited Mary Beth to our church several times during the school year, and she finally agreed to visit.

After I met Mary Beth I understood why Bill had worked so hard to reach out to her. She was neatly dressed and attractive but was so painfully shy and withdrawn it almost hurt to look at her. Her hollow eyes were focused on the floor during her entire visit. I called her later that week to invite her to have lunch with Bill and me at the Memorial Union. She very reluctantly agreed. As soon as we sat down, she informed me she wouldn't be back to our church, as it had been a big mistake for her to visit. I assumed she had some objections to Christianity or to the lesson. I began to gear up for a defense of the faith, but in stammering words she slammed a verbal line drive into the outfield that I could not catch. She began to apologize profusely for visiting our church. She blurted out that she was so sorry she had contaminated our sanctuary, and that if we had only known what kind of evil person she was, we never would have allowed her into the church. I did my best to assure her that everyone in our church was a needy sinner, and that God loved her more than she could imagine, but I sensed my words had penetrated no farther than a fist-sized rock would penetrate the armor of an M1 tank.

I was baffled by Mary Beth's utter inability to accept God's love until later that week when Bill connected the dots. Mary Beth had been molested for years by her stepbrother and was immersed in shame and self-loathing. She was severely anorexic and had been hospitalized several times during the previous year. Compulsive exercise had permanently damaged her knees, but she continued to jog many miles a day. When Mary Beth looked in the mirror, she saw a fat, wicked young woman who deserved to suffer for the sexual acts that had been done to her. Her brother's abuse had filled every cell in her body with destructive shame. I desperately longed to help Mary Beth experience God's healing, but, in spite of our calls and invitations, I never saw her again.

THE NATURE AND CHARACTERISTICS OF SHAME

I'm convinced that shame is the most powerful human emotion. It often overwhelms, directs, and transforms all other emotions, thoughts, and experiences.[1] For instance, no matter what Mary Beth was told by friends, pastors, or her doctor, and no matter what she felt or experienced, the conclusion would always be the same: she was a dirty, wicked, fat girl who deserved to suffer. Her shame hijacked all other internal and external voices.

Once a destructive shame virus has infected our mental hard drive, it's extremely difficult to remove because it filters all thoughts and feelings that could be used to remove it. For example, when abuse victims like Mary Beth experience sensory pleasure (touch, pleasant music, and the like), they often instinctively feel guilty. These guilt feelings then reinforce the internal shame grid and strengthen the core belief that they are disgusting and dirty.

This is true for positive accomplishments as well. For example, when Mary Beth received an A in one of her courses, instead of accepting that the good grade gave evidence of her academic skills and hard work, her shame acted as an emotional parasite. It sucked all the healthy nutrients out of the experience by letting the A in this course make her feel bad for all the times in her life she didn't get an A. It might also have convinced her that she didn't really deserve the A; maybe the teacher just felt sorry for her.[2] Thus, all experiences, including very positive accomplishments, indict and assault the self.

While shame is universally and profoundly experienced, it is seldom understood. For instance, there's no scholarly consensus on what constitutes shame.[3] But I'll risk giving my own definition: *Shame is a deep, painful sense of inadequacy and personal failure based on the inability to live up to a standard of conduct—one's own or one imposed by others.* Regardless of the subjectivity, fickleness, or rationality of the standard that was violated, if it's a standard that we or others who are important to us value, it will produce shame. Because shame is connected with one's failure to live up to an important standard of conduct, shame creates a sense of disgust toward self. Thus, shame makes us want to hide from others and even from ourselves.[4] Longtime Fuller Theological Seminary professor Lewis Smedes paints a clear picture of the feeling of shame:

Shame is a very heavy feeling. It is a feeling that we do not measure up and maybe never will measure up to the sorts of persons we are meant to be. The feeling, when we are conscious of it, gives us a vague disgust with ourselves, which in turn feels like a hunk of lead on our hearts. . . .

[Shame is] like an invisible load that weighs our spirits down and crushes out our joy. It is a lingering sorrow.[5]

While shame is a painful emotion, it is not necessarily an unhealthy one. In fact, shame is a divine gift, but a gift Satan often distorts so that it becomes very destructive. The critical difference between healthy and unhealthy (toxic) shame is the relationship between shame and guilt. Guilt is a moral/legal state that results from having violated the law, thus rendering one liable to a penalty. Shame is the painful emotional response to the perception of being guilty.[6] Thus, healthy shame is an appropriate response to an actual violation of the law of God. It is a divine gift because it signals that something is dreadfully wrong, that we are not living up to our created design, and that we are alienated from our loving, holy Creator (Romans 2:14–15). As Anthony Hoekema notes, "The very greatness of man's sin consists in the fact that he is still an image-bearer of God. What makes sin so heinous is that man is prostituting such splendid gifts. . . . The corruption of the best is the worst."[7]

The point is that healthy shame is based on our unique dignity as bearers of God's image. No matter how much we've sinned, healthy shame is a gracious call to correction and cleansing so we can be what the Lord of the universe meant us to be. In other words, healthy shame sounds an internal foghorn that we are headed toward the jagged rocks. It is a gracious call to repentance.[8] It's the basis for calling believers to lovingly practice church discipline on fellow believers who are engaged in ongoing sinful behavior, so that they will be shamed and prompted to repent (2 Thessalonians 3:14; cf. 1 Corinthians 5:1–13; 2 Corinthians 2:6–8).

Unhealthy or toxic shame, on the other hand, can never redeem; it can only corrode and destroy. For the recipient, toxic shame often feels similar to healthy shame, but it is based on lies and distortions about God, our sin, our worth, and our redeemability. The distortions may be subtle or outrageous, but the result is the same: toxic shame distorts our sense of dignity as divine image bearers and drives us away from God. Toxic shame distorts reality by going beyond convicting us that we've done bad things that need to be forgiven. It whispers to us that we are bad and unforgivable. Instead of pointing out real sin we can address, toxic shame distorts our sin, our worth, and God's grace so that we can do nothing but hide in the shadows. Even when we really *have* sinned against God, toxic shame gives a false interpretation of our sin that strips us of all hope. Lewis Smedes describes well the way toxic shame distorts reality:

> [Unhealthy] shame can be like a signal from a drunken signalman who warns of a train that is not coming. The pain of this shame is not a signal of something wrong in us that needs to be made right. Our shame is what is wrong with us. It is a false shame because the feeling has no basis in reality. It is unhealthy shame because it saps our creative powers and kills our joy. It is a shame we do not deserve because we are not as bad as our feelings tell us we are. Undeserved shame is a good gift gone bad.[9]

The worst aspect of toxic shame is that it isolates us from God, from others, and even from ourselves. Since we are made for relationship with our Creator and with those made in his image, isolation is a debilitating result of shame. Since toxic shame tells us we are defective, irredeemable, and unlovable, all we can do is hide and hope that others won't figure out our ruse. In their song "Creep," the group Radiohead articulates the toxic-shame message that one is permanently defective and hopelessly different from other normal people. The singer compares himself to a friend and bemoans the fact that the friend is beautiful and special, while he is defective in body and soul. He repeats his futile desire to be special, to belong, and to be noticed by others and declares, "But I'm a creep, I'm a weirdo, what the hell am I doing here?" This is the message of shame: *I'm permanently defective. I'm just a creep and a weirdo who will never belong and doesn't deserve to belong.*

SHAME AND ABUSE

Nothing can generate clouds of toxic shame like abuse. Most abuse victims carry massive amounts of toxic shame, and apart from God's healing, they will carry it all the way to the grave. Abuse generates great amounts of shame for several reasons.

Transfer of Shame from Abusers

First of all, the dynamics of abusers and abusive families set the stage for considerable shame for abuse victims. Abusive families deliberately use shame to manipulate and control.[10] As I noted in our examination of the characteristics of abusers, abusers constantly shift blame to their victims, are deceitful, and exhibit harsh judgmentalism. These behaviors largely result from the abusers' own shame that they are unwilling to deal with. Hence, abusers ferociously transfer their own shame to the victim.

When the victim is a child, this transfer of shame can be particularly damaging, since children are most vulnerable, particularly to abusive parents. Children don't have the cognitive or emotional resources to ferret out the truth and to reject the undeserved shame abusive parents heap on them. Pastoral counselor Richard T. Frazier explains the way abusive parents' shame is absorbed by their vulnerable children: "A child is emotionally unable to refuse, modify, or detoxify a parent's abusive projections. The power differential is too great and the projections too toxic and overwhelming. Furthermore, the child actually lives in the emotional world and fantasy life of the parent. This is the child's reality."[11]

Given these characteristics of abusers, along with the debasing nature of abuse itself, it is understandable that abuse victims come to believe they are so disgusting that they deserve to be abused.

In our community, police officers recently discovered a seven-year-old boy named Isaac who had been locked in a urine- and feces-laden closet for almost six months. His parents reportedly had denied him food for up to a week at a time. When discovered, Isaac weighed only thirty-six pounds and was so malnourished he was losing his hair and could barely stand. Officer Ben Baltzer, who found the boy, said that when he interviewed the parents, they acted as if Isaac had gotten what he deserved. Isaac's mother said she didn't like his attitude and so he was being punished.[12] One of the authorities interviewed about the case said Isaac should make a full physical recovery, but his emotional healing would take years. In particular, this little boy will need much help overcoming the shame transferred from his evil parents, who gave him "what he deserved."

Defense Mechanism

A second and closely related reason abuse victims have large amounts of shame is that absorbing undeserved shame is a natural defense mechanism for children who have been abused by their parents or caregivers. It's much easier for abused children to conclude that they are bad and defective than to accept the fact that their parents (who are all-powerful and beyond the scope of the child to change) are evil and their parenting is defective.

Children possess a God-given intuitive desire and expectation to be nurtured and loved by their parents, which reflects the relational aspect of the image of God. Psychological research on attachment theory has shown that the security of a child's attachment with his or her parents is of utmost long-term importance for the child's healthy development. In fact, the need and desire for love and nurture from parents is so great that if parents are abusive instead of loving, children resort to various psychological defense mechanisms to cope. They may deny the abuse, dissociate, or blame themselves (absorb toxic shame). Judith Lewis Herman explains this dynamic:

> When it is impossible to avoid the reality of the abuse, the child must construct some system of meaning that justifies it. Inevitably the child concludes that her innate badness is the cause. The child seizes on this explanation early and clings to it tenaciously, for it enables her to preserve a sense of meaning, hope, and power. If she is bad, then her parents are good. If she is bad, then she can try to be good. If, somehow, she has brought this fate upon herself, then somehow she has the power to change it. If she has driven her parents to mistreat her, then if only she tries hard enough, she may some day earn their forgiveness and finally win the protection and care she so desperately needs.[13]

Thus, abused children are put in an extremely difficult emotional bind, for they are dependent on one or more abusive adults. As a defense against the powerlessness and vulnerability that comes from acknowledging that their parents are evil, they instead blame themselves. In essence, they absorb their abuser's guilt and shame. The abused child's erroneous conclusion that his or her guilt and defectiveness are the causes of the abuse is further strengthened by the abusive parents' destructive verbal messages. This complex defense mechanism, combined with abusive parents' shaming messages, helps explain why shame is so deeply entrenched in abuse victims.

Susceptibility to Shameful Behavior

A third factor in the shame created by abuse is that the damage and emotional starvation suffered by abused children make them much more susceptible to destructive, often sinful behavior, which can in turn create more shame. In other words, Satan takes advantage of the impact of abuse to entice people into meeting their needs in inappropriate ways that often end up being very destructive. This does not justify destructive, sinful behavior, but we must understand this dynamic if we're going to minister effectively to broken people.

Some Christians are so concerned to uphold the doctrine of human depravity that they fail to recognize that broken sinners, especially abuse victims who are saturated with shame, are rarely motivated to repent simply by having their noses rubbed in their sin.[14] In fact, they often get entangled in destructive sin because they're convinced they are despicable, unredeemable sinners.[15] As a result, when shame-filled people hear sermons that merely focus on their sinfulness, their shame is intensified, they become more convinced of their irredeemabililty, and their sin is driven deeper underground. Yet, if the church is going to carry out its central mission of redeeming sinners, it must be, as author Philip Yancey observes, a place that offers "grace on tap."[16]

Lucy, a beautiful middle-aged woman who has been in vocational Christian ministry for many years, illustrates the manner in which abuse creates shame and emotional hunger, which leads to sinful behavior, which in turn creates more shame and further reinforces the core belief of worthlessness. Lucy is an expert on the destructive effects of a shame that nearly destroyed her life. As a young girl, she was molested by various adult men, including her stepfather, her pastor, and a family friend. In her teenage years, when her abusive stepfather found out she was sexually active outside the home, he told her she was a worthless whore.

Lucy describes the incredible damage and confusion created by the abuse and the resultant shame that led to destructive behavior:

> Just about every man I had contact with as a young girl eventually wanted sex. Older men told me they loved me and wanted to take care of me. I actually thought they meant it. I was so needy and in need of love—a father's love—that I accepted whatever I could get. When they left, I felt so abandoned and so ashamed that I had believed them. So I felt that it simply had to be me. This didn't happen with my friends, so it must be me. It's interesting that I was very smart. I was an A student. I was very talented—I danced, did ballet and jazz, sang, and played the piano. But I always felt it didn't matter what I could do; it was my body that people were interested in. That's where my worth was. I had the feeling that I somehow "owed" sex to men.
>
> The drinking began when I was very young, prior to being a teenager. I remember the first time I tasted alcohol. The feeling was "I'm finally OK." The feelings of fear and longing and self-consciousness and unhappiness left ... for that small amount of time. It was an escape from my feelings. It changed my reality for a while. As I got older, the alcohol allowed me to do things I would not have done sober. Then as the guilt and shame over what I had done overwhelmed me, I either drank more or I took Valium to quell the feelings of disgust and shame. It's such a vicious cycle. The abuse sets up the worthless feelings, the worthless feelings set up the need to escape, the need to escape sets up the destructive behavior and/or addictions, the behavior sets up the need to escape and hide in the addictions, and the addictions lead to more destructive behavior, which sets the entire cycle into motion again.

Lucy found Christ as a young woman, but she lived several more years of compulsive promiscuity and alcoholism before she was able to truly experience the love and grace of God, find strength and direction from Scripture, and overcome her destructive lifestyle.

I believe this cycle of abusive treatment; shame; sinful, destructive behavior; and more shame lies behind Jesus' treatment of the Samaritan woman in John 4:7–39. The fact that the Samaritan woman came to draw water in the middle of the day strongly suggests she was a social outcast, for water was normally drawn at sunset. While Jesus didn't overlook her sexual sin (John 4:17–18), he didn't start there. Rather, he met her where she was, and treated her with the love and grace her shame-filled soul craved.[17] He saw a needy woman engulfed with shame, who was trying to fill her soul by means of sinful sexual relationships. Knowing this, Jesus appealed to her inner longings by offering her living water that would quench her deepest thirst (John 4:10–14). The most amazing aspect of the Samaritan woman's conversion is the account she gives to her fellow Samaritans. She testified to the Christ by saying that he was the one who "told me all the things that I have done" (John 4:39)—a profound indication that Jesus had offered grace to a shame-filled sinner. She had tasted enough of the grace of God that she could allow her sins to be exposed, first to Christ and then to her neighbors.

Nature of Our Sexuality

Fourth, abuse victims are so filled with shame because of the nature of the abusive behavior itself, particularly sexual abuse. Our genitals are the most intimate and personal part of our bodies. Any inappropriate exposure, let alone contact with one's genitals, results in deep shame, which may explain why some of the Hebrew words for "shame" used in the Old Testament refer to the external genitals.[18] This isn't because the genitals are inherently shameful, but because they are so personal that they have a profound capacity to incite shame when inappropriately exposed. Furthermore, as noted in chapter 2, sex is the most powerful bonding activity one can engage in. Sexual sin forms a unique bonding that creates damage beyond that brought about by any other bodily activity (1 Corinthians 6:18). Thus, when one is violated sexually, it invariably results in tremendous shame.

✳

A final comment on the relationship between shame and abuse is in order. The exact manner in which abuse creates long-term damage is complex and inadequately understood. Recently some researchers have turned their attention to the precise mechanisms by which children adjust to the trauma of abuse. They have found that shame, not the severity of the abuse, has the greatest effect on adjustment one year after the abuse.[19] In other words, feelings of shame mediate (act as the intermediary agent for) the emotional trauma of the abusive event.[20] Shame resulting from childhood abuse has also been shown to be strongly associated with adult revictimization and adult depression.[21]

In summary, in a fallen world, all humans experience shame, but the dynamics of abuse are such that abuse victims' lives literally revolve around shame. Abuse produces shame, and then the more shame abuse victims feel, the more long-term damage they will experience. It's as though the shameful, corrupt things an abuser does penetrates below a victim's skin and alters his or her heart and soul. The shame of abuse often makes victims feel they have been permanently damaged and corrupted by the abuse. The things they hate and fear in the abusers seem to have sprouted in their own hearts like an alien parasite they cannot remove. This aspect of toxic abusive shame is eloquently voiced in the song "Figure .09" by Linkin Park, who describes internal pain and destructive thoughts that never stop. But abuse victims aren't able to let go of the pain or the shameful thoughts. Rather, the very thing they hate has become a permanent part of them. They lament regarding their abusers, "You've become a part of me. You'll always be right here. You'll always be my fear."

SYMPTOMS OF SHAME

While abuse victims and perpetrators ooze shame from every pore, shame manifests itself in very diverse and even contradictory ways. For instance, hair-trigger anger as well as servile passivity, debilitating depression as well as frenetic over-achievement, arrogance as well as inferiority, can all result from destructive shame.[22] Hence, it's helpful to mention some of the most telltale characteristics of shame:[23]

- *Chronic struggle with low self-esteem*. Shame-filled people do not accept their God-given worth. They feel inferior to others, inherently flawed, and unalterably defective.
- *Low-grade depression*. Those who view themselves as permanently inferior and defective develop a sense of hopelessness that often leads to depression.
- *Insecurity and jealousy*. Feelings of inferiority and worthlessness create great insecurity, which leads in turn to jealousy of others. When others succeed or are complimented, it triggers insecurity in a shame-filled person.
- *The need to compare and compete*. Shame-filled people constantly compare themselves to others and must compete to stay ahead.

- *Inability to accept criticism.* Because shame-filled people reject themselves, they assume everyone else rejects them as well. Even constructive criticism triggers self-rejection and is perceived as a wholesale attack. Shame-filled people cannot separate who they are from what they have done.
- *The need to blame others.* Insecurity and self-rejection cause shame-filled people to flinch from accepting blame for their mistakes. Thus, they constantly blame others for their own failures.
- *Feel they don't belong.* Shame-filled people feel as though they are defective and different from the rest of the world. In their minds, other people are "normal," but they are different and do not belong.
- *Self-focused.* Shame-filled people are so insecure they constantly focus on themselves. They overinflate their place in life. All comments are interpreted as being about them. If they are in a group, they assume everyone is looking at them. Thus, they are unable to freely love and serve others.
- *Externally focused.* Since shame-filled people are insecure about what's on the inside, they rigidly control what others see on the outside. They deeply fear that others will discover the truth about their inner defectiveness, and so they're desperate to create the appearance that everything in their life is OK.
- *Prone to become addicted.* Chronic shame is extremely painful and often leads to compulsive or even addictive behavior, which can temporarily anesthetize emotional pain. Shame can often lead to alcoholism, sexual addiction, and eating disorders.
- *Sabotage intimacy.* Shame-filled people long for intimacy but are deeply afraid their defectiveness will be exposed. Thus, they tend to sabotage relationships as they begin to get intimate.
- *Hypercritical.* Shame-filled people project their shame onto others by being hypercritical. They cannot accept God's grace for themselves, nor can they extend God's grace to others.
- *Unaware or dishonest with feelings.* Because shame-filled people are full of painful negative feelings, they detach from their own feelings. They don't know what they really feel. Emotions they find unacceptable are transformed into more acceptable emotions. For instance, a shame-filled man often has a hard time admitting he is disappointed or fearful, so he'll act angry instead.
- *Shallow.* Because shame-filled people intensely dislike themselves, they do not engage in healthy reflection or introspection. They constantly

hide from others, so they're typically unable to offer more than a shallow, surface-level conversation or relationship.

- *Tired.* Living a shame-filled life is tremendously draining. Great energy is expended to keep up a facade so that one's real self is never exposed. Shame strips people of hope, joy, and life and leaves them exhausted and spent.

THE BIBLICAL MEANING OF SHAME

While the secular literature on abuse frequently discusses shame, it is typically ignored in the biblical/theological literature.[24] Similarly, pastors rarely, if ever, preach sermons on shame, though sermons often trigger shame—especially for abuse victims. The failure of the biblical community to address the doctrine of shame is most curious, since it's such a profound human experience and since Scripture has so much to say about it. The English word *shame* and related terms *(ashamed, reproach, humiliate, nakedness)* appear approximately three hundred times in Scripture. These uses are translations of approximately ten different Hebrew and seven different Greek root words.

The basic biblical concept of shame is emotional humiliation due to sin, which results in human or divine disgrace and rejection. Shame in Scripture carries similar connotations to its modern usage—a painful emotional sense of guilt, unworthiness, and disgrace due to one's failure to live up to a standard. Furthermore, as does the psychological literature, the Bible speaks of the debilitating effects of shame—it breaks the heart and makes one emotionally sick (Psalm 69:20). But unlike secular psychological descriptions of shame that define it purely in terms of subjective human experience, biblical shame is ultimately defined by the character of God. Hence, the Greek and Hebrew words used in the Bible for shame sometimes refer not to human emotions but to *behavior* that is intrinsically shameful.[25] Thus, the key to overcoming shame is more than simply learning to love and accept oneself; it is to discern God's perspective on one's shame and guilt, and to let his perspective drive and reshape one's thoughts, actions, and, ultimately, one's feelings.

Biblically, shame is not just an emotional or psychological reality but a judicial one as well, for human emotional experience is not always concordant with one's spiritual condition. For instance, the Bible repeatedly speaks of hard-hearted evildoers, who are guilty but lack an appropriate sense of shame (Jeremiah 3:3; 6:15; 8:12). Likewise, the Bible speaks of the righteous, who are unjustly shamed by their abusive enemies (Psalm 22:6; 69:7–9, 19–21; Jeremiah

15:15). Biblical shame, especially in the Psalms and the Prophets, is often connected with God's judgment on unrepentant sinners, who often do not feel guilty or shameful.[26] Thus, the Bible treats shame as a common painful response to sin. But due to the warping effect of sin on the heart and mind, shame is not necessarily a reliable emotion. The Bible is quite clear that humans do not always feel shame when they are guilty, and they are tempted to feel shame when they are not guilty.

SATAN'S FOURFOLD STRATEGY FOR ENHANCING SHAME

Satan's work in the world has been compared to a burglar who breaks into a jewelry shop in the middle of the night. Instead of stealing the items in the jewelry case, however, the burglar merely swaps price tags. Cheap cosmetic jewelry is given a ridiculously high price tag, while a precious diamond necklace is priced at a pittance. In a similar manner, Satan cannot create a new world, but he can rearrange the price tags. In the case of shame, he overinflates and underinflates the appropriate value of shame based on guilt. Hence, humans attach more shame than they should to certain behaviors (especially those that God has forgiven), while attaching less than they should to other behaviors (especially those that have not been repented of).[27] Let's consider the various ways Satan plots to pervert the truth and ultimately to drive people away from God.

Deny or Ignore Guilt

Abusers are tempted to minimize or ignore their guilt so that they don't feel painful, appropriate shame. Zephaniah proclaimed judgment on evil, physically violent men who had no sense of shame (Zephaniah 1:9; 3:1, 5). Jeremiah also excoriates evil, ruthless abusers (Jeremiah 2:34; 7:6, 9) who were so hardened they could neither feel shame nor even blush (Jeremiah 6:15; 8:12). The inability to feel shame for real guilt helps explain the repeated prayer in the Old Testament that God would cover evil people—especially physical abusers—with shame (Psalm 35:4; 40:14; Jeremiah 3:25).

Modern authorities on abuse perpetrators note this same dynamic, and report that abusers rarely have remorse for their actions.[28] This might also explain why in one study of incarcerated sex offenders, 70 percent were not interested in participating in treatment programs.[29] The twisted logic goes like this: "If I do not feel shame, I am not really guilty; if I am not guilty, there is nothing to fix." Thus, failure to feel shame keeps sinners from being driven to the God who forgives guilt and heals shame.

A recent example of an abuser with no shame is professional boxer Mike Tyson. In 1992, Tyson was convicted and given a six-year prison sentence for raping a beauty pageant contestant. In a subsequent interview with Fox News reporter Greta Van Sustren in 2003, Tyson declared that he did not rape the woman but that she has so victimized him that "she put me in a state where . . . now I really do want to rape her."[30] Tyson also indicated he'd like to rape the woman's mother. A few weeks after doing the interview, Tyson was again arrested for physical assault. This illustrates how lack of shame takes away a God-given restraint on sin, so that those who have no shame pollute the land with their flagrant evil (Jeremiah 3:1–3).

Take Others' Guilt

The most common manner in which Satan distorts shame with abuse victims is to cause them to feel shame for their abusers' guilt. Children instinctively take their abusers' guilt. For instance, Antwone Fisher, whose memoir was recently made into an inspirational motion picture, experienced years of severe abuse of every kind before finally being abandoned to the streets by his foster parents as a teen. In his memoir he reveals that a neighbor woman first began to sexually molest him when he was three years old. He recounts the incident and his own reaction in which he innately blamed himself for the abuse:

> She has on the worst monster face you ever saw. Only this I didn't make up in my mind. It's too terrible to be true. But it is true. Then she's finished. Her voice lays flat as she says, "Where your clothes at? Put some clothes on." She sounds like it's my fault I don't have clothes on. She dresses, tosses my clothes at me, and says, "Go on outside in the shade and play. I think they makin' mud pies out there." For a second Wanda smiles. But then her face flashes a warning. She doesn't need to tell me in words. I know what it says—never, never, never tell, or something more horrible than you can even imagine will happen to you. And it wasn't really the fear of her punishing me that kept me from telling anyone all those years. It was the unspeakable shame I felt about what went on in the base-ment, and my unspeakable shame that maybe it was my fault.[31]

As I noted earlier, abuse victims also feel shame because abusers strategically shift the blame to their victims. In Bible times abusers (especially military and political leaders) would maim or disfigure their enemy so they'd experience long-term shame for the abusers' actions (Judges 1:6–7; 1 Samuel 11:2; 2 Samuel 10:4–5). Tamar is a tragic example of a sexual abuse victim whose life was ruined because of the shame she experienced due to her rapist. Amnon was guilty, but in essence she bore his guilt and shame (2 Samuel 13:13–20). Abuse victims can learn, by God's grace, to reject the guilt and the resultant shame they don't deserve. For example, the apostle Peter instructed his audience of Christians who were experiencing persecution—including verbal and physical abuse—"If you suffer as a Christian, do not be ashamed [feel shame], but praise God that you bear that name" (1 Peter 4:16 NIV).[32] In other words, abuse victims can learn to reject their abusers' guilt and not take on their guilt and shame.

Reclaim Forgiven Guilt

If I were to pick up tomorrow morning's newspaper and read an ad by a local home builder who was offering to give a brand-new 10,000-square-foot mansion in a luxurious gated community, along with full membership to the most prestigious country club, free of charge to any criminal convicted of multiple felonies who calls their toll-free number, I would assume the ad was a sick joke. Criminals deserve a prison cell, not a mansion. Their crimes deserve social stigma, not country-club prestige.

It's hard for us to accept the fact that God offers to remove all the guilt and stigma of our sin and to give us present and eternal blessings apart from any good deeds on our part but only through faith in Christ (Romans 3:21–24; Philippians 3:9). We have sinned, so we don't deserve God's favor and blessing. But this is exactly the meaning of grace—undeserved favor. Here's the truth that is so incredible to believe: When God removes the guilt of sin, it is completely and utterly removed (Psalm 103:8–12). The beauty of the gospel of grace is that God saves not the beautiful but "the lame" and "the outcast" and that he will "turn their shame into praise" (Zephaniah 3:19). Satan, the accuser, wants to keep believers from experiencing the joy of their salvation. He wants them to reclaim forgiven guilt—to continue to feel a sense of shame for sin God has forgiven. Abuse victims are particularly vulnerable to this satanic strategy and must resist it fiercely.

Take on Others' Harsh Judgment

A final way Satan distorts the truth regarding shame is to cause us to define ourselves based on others' low view of us. This shame is the rejection and disgrace others put on us because they find us unacceptable. Anyone who has endured junior high school understands the destructive power of social shame. Several of the Hebrew words for shame in the Old Testament highlight this aspect of shame.[33] One term comes from a root that means "to make a sound," and refers to scornful whispering.[34] Another word for shame comes from a word whose meaning is "to wound," but figuratively it means "to taunt or insult."[35] Another term for shame or disgrace comes from a root *(qālôn)* that means "the lowering of another's social position."[36] Many passages of Scripture speak of the unwarranted shame and dishonor that others heap on the innocent—shame the innocent must learn to reject. Often the Bible speaks of physical or verbal abusers who heap shame on the innocent (1 Samuel 20:34; Nehemiah 4:4; Psalm 22:6). Abuse victims are especially vulnerable to the effects of social shame, for harsh judgment from others can strengthen their erroneous core belief that they are defective and worthless.

Lucy, the woman whose story of abuse and alcoholism I shared earlier, demonstrates the potency of this aspect of shame. By the time Lucy was a teenager, she had been molested by several male authority figures in her life, including her stepfather. She had no healthy sense of boundaries or intimacy, and she became sexually active with her boyfriend. When her abusive stepfather found out she was having sex with her boyfriend, he told her she was a worthless tramp who so disgusted him that he ordered her not to use the hallway near his room so he wouldn't have to look at her. Lucy said this incident did more to infuse her with a sense of utter worthlessness than did the sexual abuse. Satan used the vicious, demeaning comments of Lucy's evil stepfather to drive her farther away from health.

STRATEGY FOR OVERCOMING DESTRUCTIVE SHAME

Since shame is such a pervasive, destructive force in the lives of abuse victims, a brief strategy for overcoming destructive shame is in order.

Clarify Ownership

Satan jumbles up shame so that perspective is lost with regard to what one should and should not feel shame for. Hence, when I work with male sex addicts (all of whom have massive amounts of shame, often including shame from being childhood abuse victims), I give them an exercise to help them sort out and respond to their shame. I ask them to write out their shame history—to prayerfully construct a detailed personal history of the times throughout their lives when they felt the greatest shame, listing the events that precipitated the shame. They then try to answer three questions about each shameful event: (1) What do I need to own? (2) What do I need to confess? (3) What do I need to make right?

The first question involves sorting out who was responsible for what happened. For example, one may have a shameful memory of being abused, but the abuse wasn't that person's fault. Abuse survivors should not own the abuse. Subsequent choices, however, are a different matter. With God's help, a person can begin to clarify which shameful events he or she must own (numbing the pain by getting drunk, acting out his or her abuse by abusing others, and so forth).

Once ownership for sin has been clarified, it's time to specifically confess to God the sins for which one is responsible (1 John 1:9). Confession of sin by a believer doesn't maintain one's salvation but strengthens one's walk with God and the sense of God's forgiveness.[37] After confession comes the final step of restitution. Restitution can be a counterproductive attempt to earn God's favor, but, properly done, it's a biblical concept that highlights ownership of both one's sin and the damage it has caused (Exodus 22:1–15; Leviticus 6:5; Deuteronomy 22:28–29). Biblical restitution flows from the experience of God's grace (Luke 19:1–8). Restitution might involve making a long overdue apology, offering to pay for counseling for someone you've deeply damaged, or even writing a symbolic letter to someone who can no longer be contacted.

Accept the Judge's Verdict: God Delights in His Children

Abuse victims experience overwhelming shame because of their abusers. One of the key steps to shedding this toxic, undeserved shame is to let God, not the abuser, define one's worth. It is surely one of Satan's greatest perversions that abuse victims ingest toxic shame and conclude that they are worthless scum, when the Creator and Judge of the universe allowed his own precious Son to be abused so he could have an eternal love relationship with them.

Abuse victims must learn to accept by faith the Judge's verdict. If we are believers, he declares that our sins are completely forgiven—removed as far as the east is from the west (Psalm 103:12). He declares that nothing can separate us from his love (Romans 8:38–39). He declares that he chose us for salvation before the world was even created, based not on our innate goodness but on his rich grace (Ephesians 1:4–7). He declares that all who have put their faith in Christ have been justified. This means that when he, the Judge, looks at us, he doesn't see our sin but the righteousness of Christ.[38] Thus, God does not look at his children with disgust but with delight (Zephaniah 3:17). Even when we fall into sin, he disciplines us out of his love; he does not punish us out of disgust (Hebrews 12:6–11).

Abuse survivors must learn to reject their abusers' judgments and rely on the true Judge's verdict—he delights in them![39] A practical way abuse survivors can learn to accept God's verdict is to compile a list of biblical descriptions of who they are and what they possess in Christ, and then to prayerfully meditate on each of these truths.[40] For instance, as a believer I am God's child, united with Christ, forgiven, reconciled to God, blessed with every spiritual blessing in Christ, and so forth. These descriptions tell me how God views me.

Prayerfully Hand Shame Back to the Abuser

One of the most empowering things an abuse survivor can do is to prayerfully hand shame back to his or her abuser. Theologians rarely discuss this concept, but it's a frequent biblical theme. Biblical writers often asked God to shame their abusive enemies.[41] Most likely, this meant asking God to do two things: (1) cause the abuser to be overwhelmed with shame for his or her sin so that they would repent, and (2) bring utter destruction on the abuser if he or she didn't repent.

Asking God to utterly destroy an unrepentant abuser is not an unchristian prayer.[42] Abuse victims experience tremendous injustice, but God is a God of justice. Humans long for justice and innately rebel with the cry "That's not fair" when they don't receive it. In fact, the Bible tells us that the prospect of God's bringing full and final justice on the heads of unrepentant evil people is what allows us to endure injustice in this life without becoming bitter (2 Timothy 4:14; 1 Peter 2:23). Christians are not to seek revenge, not because it's an inappropriate desire, but because they don't have the power or the authority to properly exact justice on abusers. Paul admonished the Roman believers not to take revenge on their enemies but to let God do it for them (Romans 12:19). His retribution on evildoers will be perfect and inescapable. Thus, it's biblical to pray that our abusers will be filled with shame so that they may repent and that they'll be punished and destroyed if they do not.

Practically, abuse survivors can apply this principle by writing down the name(s) of their unrepentant abusers. They should then regularly pray over the list, asking God to engulf these individuals with shame so that they will repent, and to bring divine judgment on them if they do not repent.

Choose to Reject

In a fallen world we can never stop people from shaming us, but we can refuse to accept the shame package they hand us. This step requires discipline and tenacious commitment to biblical truth, but with God's help we can choose to reject the shame that abusers and others keep trying to give us. Christ is our great example, for even though in his public torture and execution on a cross he experienced the greatest shame imaginable in ancient culture,[43] he focused on God and chose to disregard (ignore) the shame created by his abusers (Hebrews

12:2).[44] In other words, one must clarify the truth and deliberately reject illegitimate shame that others give.

The first step in carrying this out is to recognize the dynamics at play. Often we're so conditioned to simply accept shame from others that we don't question it. When others treat us shamefully, we tacitly assume they must be right—we *must* deserve it. Of course, this is hardly correct. It's particularly tempting to accept inappropriate shame from family members because we are so conditioned to accept their judgments.

Healing from toxic shame requires that we learn to carefully analyze shame messages and immediately reject the shame we don't deserve.[45] It's difficult but essential for abuse victims to do this. For instance, Jonathan, whose abusive father tried to kill both him and his closest friend, David, was shamed by his father for protecting David. Saul cursed Jonathan, called him a bastard,[46] and accused him of bringing shame on the family (1 Samuel 20:30). In truth, it was rebellious Saul who had shamed the family (15:28–35). Being told by an abusive family member that I am a shameful bastard does not make me one. Abuse survivors can learn to reject the illegitimate shame others want to give them.

A practical way abuse victims can apply this principle is to regularly journal the shameful implicit and explicit messages they receive from others. They should then prayerfully reflect on each message and write down what is false about each, based on biblical truth. If a given message is particularly difficult to shake, they should memorize a few Bible passages that refute the lies in that message.

Experience Authentic Community

Experiencing authentic Christian community is one of the most important ways shame-based lies about oneself can be challenged. In authentic Christian community we let people see who we really are: we confess our sins (James 5:16), we are emotionally honest about our joys and our sorrows (Romans 12:15), we give and receive love (Romans 16:16), we meet each other's needs (Acts 2:45; Galatians 6:2), we pray for each other (James 5:16), we challenge each other (1 Thessalonians 5:14), and we help each other when we fall into sin (Galatians 6:1). As we experience authentic community, we increasingly recognize the shame-based lies and learn to embrace the truth.

While authentic Christian community isn't always easy to find, it is what God has designed for the church (Acts 2:41–47). Shame isolates us from God, others, and ourselves; authentic community helps us to reconnect and to overcome our shame.[47] Thus, abuse survivors must make finding a healthy Christian community a top priority.

＊

We've seen in this chapter that abuse creates great clouds of toxic shame. But shame is not the only debilitating effect of abuse. There are other types of abuse damage that are just as damaging as shame, but they are in many respects more confusing. Hence, in the next chapter we'll explore two other primary emotional effects of abuse—powerlessness and deadness.

chapter 6

✳

powerlessness and deadness

Brianna came into counseling when she was twelve years old. She had not experienced physical or sexual abuse, but years of chronic emotional neglect by her alcoholic mother and emotionally paralyzed father had taken a heavy toll. In addition to the damage of neglect, her parents had divorced a few years earlier, and she blamed herself for their breakup. Her loving stepmother brought her into counseling because she was exhibiting sexually precocious behavior at school.

As part of her initial evaluation, the therapist asked her to draw a self-portrait. Brianna worked intently with the colored pencils and produced a smiling little girl onstage, "making people laugh" (see figure 2). She portrayed herself under the spotlights, entertaining her family and friends in the seats below. The therapist was intrigued by this depiction and asked Brianna if she always felt this way, as the drawing appeared artificial and contrived. Brianna shook her head soberly, turned the picture over, and began to draw again. Initially, she seemed to be drawing the same portrait, but new details made this one dramatically different. In this second picture, she drew her face saturated with sad, dark emotions (see figure 3). Small images depicting abandonment and traumatic memory obscured her facial features. In this picture, so contradictory to the first, she stood utterly alone in the darkness—no smile, no friends, no cheers.

How could a young girl viewed by her family as sweet and innocent be so sexually aggressive on the playground that school officials threatened expulsion unless she received professional counseling? Why would a young girl, in a span of less than twenty minutes, draw two antithetical self-portraits? The answer is that the trauma Brianna had experienced in her short eleven years of life had caused her to begin to split. She had developed two radically different personas.

Figure 2

Figure 3

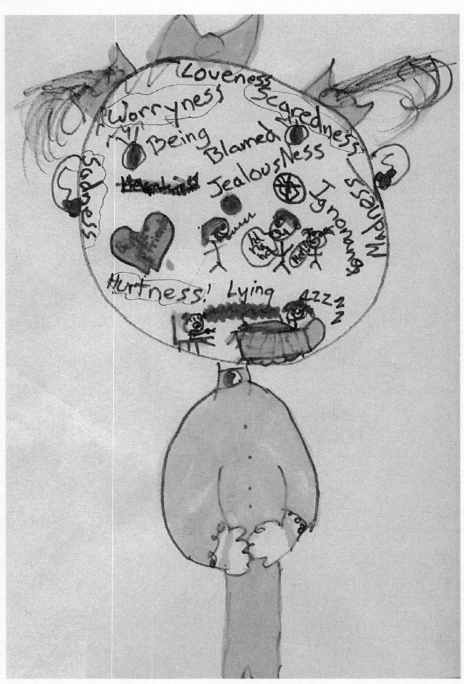

One was the acceptable, happy public self everyone loved and applauded; the other was the hidden, troubled self no one clearly saw, understood, or touched. Brianna was successfully able to dissociate (internally pull away) from her pain and loneliness to such an extent that she fooled everyone around her, including herself. In essence, Brianna learned to live by dying. But deadening ourselves to feelings, longings, and memories doesn't really kill them; they just become more invisible, more influential, and less comprehensible.

After several months Brianna's family discontinued her counseling. Tragically, three years later Brianna showed up in her counselor's office again. She had been involved in a nine-month sexual relationship with her thirty-five-year-old tennis coach. No one knew. Brianna's story illustrates the way abusive trauma creates shame and a sense of powerlessness, which in turn can create dangerous deadness.

TRAUMA: THE CREATION OF POWERLESSNESS AND DEADNESS

In the past few decades much fruitful research has enlarged our understanding of the effects of abuse. Research on the effects of trauma is especially relevant to understanding how and why abuse victims become the walking dead.

Modern trauma research actually began in the late nineteenth century when the French neurologist Jean-Martin Charcot began a formal study of the disorder called "hysteria."[1] The word *hysteria* comes from the Latin word for uterus and was thus believed to be an exclusively female psychological disorder characterized by bizarre symptoms such as extreme fear or anxiety, loss of memory, convulsions, extreme emotional excitability, and physical or emotional paralysis. Charcot's careful investigation led him to conclude that, although the symptoms of hysteria appeared to be of neurological origin, they were actually psychological. Two other notable physicians, Sigmund Freud and Pierre Janet, also began studying hysteria at that time and came to similar conclusions, namely, hysteria was caused by psychological trauma. Shortly before the twentieth century began, researchers discovered that the symptoms of hysteria could be relieved when women captured their traumatic memories and the feelings associated with them, and put them into words. This treatment became the cornerstone of modern psychotherapy.

After doing extensive case studies with women in Vienna, Freud reached the conclusion that hysteria was most often the result of a particular kind of trauma, specifically sexual abuse.[2] Before long, however, Freud shrank back in horror at the implications of his conclusion. The women he analyzed were consistent in their accounts of sexual abuse, so Freud had to somehow account for their stories and symptoms. He reasoned that surely upper-class men could not commit incest with their daughters, so he completely dismantled his theory of the origins of hysteria. He decided that these women had invented fantasies of sexual relations with their fathers.[3] This was the basis for Freud's famous "Oedipus complex theory" in which young children are said to innately desire erotic relations with their opposite-gender parent. Thus, women who suffered hysteria symptoms were ultimately to blame for their problems. It was all in their heads! Sadly, Freud, like so many others, decided in the end to blame the victims instead of the perpetrators.

While Freud and many fellow researchers reversed their theories and blamed women's fantasies, not trauma, for hysteria,[4] political events in the twentieth century would undermine their chauvinistic theories. During World War I thousands of soldiers had to withdraw from the battle lines due to hysteria-like symptoms (amnesia, physical or emotional paralysis, uncontrolled weeping, inability to speak), even though they didn't appear to be physically injured. One military psychologist coined the term "shell shock" to describe these symptoms, assuming that these soldiers were suffering from neurological damage caused by being close to exploding artillery. Further research showed that many of the men suffering from "shell shock" hadn't been subjected to artillery or other explosions; they had, however, experienced the trauma of war. Some medical authorities argued that these soldiers were moral invalids and cowards who should be dishonorably discharged. Other military psychologists recommended electric shock treatments and severe reprimands as "treatment" for these shell-shocked men.

Researchers debated the nature and origins of hysteria and shell shock for several decades, but a new consensus emerged by the mid-twentieth century. Particularly the symptoms of soldiers who returned from months of combat in World War II, as well as those of returning POWs and concentration camp survivors, made it increasingly clear that the symptoms were not the result of moral weakness. *Anyone* subjected to high levels of psychological stress could develop symptoms.[5]

Researchers have gradually come to understand that all forms of trauma, be it domestic violence, sexual abuse, war, or natural disasters, create extreme stress, which can result in a variety of debilitating emotional and physical symptoms. If the stress symptoms continue over the course of time, they can lead to a condition labeled post-traumatic stress disorder (PTSD),[6] in which the traumatic event is reexperienced through nightmares, flashbacks, emotional numbing, hyperarousal (rapid breathing, heart palpitations, and the like), and extreme avoidance of trauma reminders.[7]

Virtually everyone who experiences a traumatic event suffers stress afterwards. For some, the stress symptoms lessen with time, and the memory of the traumatic event is stored as an unfortunate event belonging to the past; for others, however, the memory and emotions connected with the trauma begin to take on a life of their own, and as the trauma is replayed over time, distress increases.[8] For these people, time does not heal all wounds. Why? Because extreme stress can produce physiological changes. God made our bodies in such a way that our hormonal and neurological systems (particularly the hypothalamic-pituitary-adrenocortical systems) automatically go into action in response to perceived danger ("fight or flight"), giving us the extra energy and alertness to act. For some, however, these bodily systems that were aroused by the trauma don't return to their normal state, resulting in long-term physical and emotional stress symptoms.[9] In other words, trauma can create long-term physical and emotional changes mediated by the abuse survivor's hormonal and neurological systems.

UNDERSTANDING THE EFFECTS OF TRAUMA

It's important to recognize the effects of trauma, for they are foundational to understanding the relationship between trauma, powerlessness, and deadness. Judith Lewis Herman identifies three primary trauma effects: hyperarousal, intrusion, and constriction (numbing).[10]

Hyperarousal

Hyperarousal, as the name suggests, is a condition in which the nervous system is perpetually aroused long after the traumatic event has ended.[11] This results in chronic hypervigilence, anxiety,[12] increased heart rate, sleeplessness, irritability, being easily startled, and even nausea.

What is particularly disconcerting about hyperarousal is that a seemingly endless number of events or experiences can unexpectedly (and often subconsciously) remind the brain of the trauma event and trigger a physiological response. For example, a woman walking down the street may suddenly experience a panic attack. Her heart begins to race, and she feels nauseous for no apparent reason. A particular cologne's scent, a stranger's face, or even a color in a shop window may have subconsciously reminded her brain of the man who abused her when she was a child, causing her body to instantly respond as though she were in grave danger. Hyperarousal trauma triggers can be very complex, bearing no obvious or logical connection to the trauma one has experienced. This makes hyperarousal even more frustrating for abuse survivors and tempts them to find ways to simply shut down emotionally so that they won't experience these symptoms.

Intrusion

Intrusion involves traumatic memories and is the reliving of the trauma event through flashbacks when one is awake or through nightmares when one is asleep. Most adolescent and adult abuse survivors report abuse-related nightmares in counseling.[13] Intrusion can also involve intense emotions such as panic or rage. In other words, the trauma memory of the past keeps "intruding" into the present, and abuse victims relive the past trauma over and over again. Intrusive memories can be profoundly traumatic, for they often have all the vividness and emotional intensity of the original trauma. Intrusion memory triggers, just like hyperarousal triggers, can be very complex and may bear no obvious or logical connection to the trauma one has experienced.[14]

Timmy was a young boy who was fondled by a male neighbor. In therapy he was asked to write a letter indicating what he wanted to happen to his abuser. His letter poignantly illustrates the link between powerlessness, hyperarousal (fear and nausea), intrusive thoughts (nightmares), and a desperate desire to regain power and safety:

> I feel that he should go to jail until he dies because I think that whoever touches children should be punished as worse as you can and that he should die. Because I hate him. It makes me afraid of other men. It makes me afraid to go to bed sometimes because I don't want to dream about him. He makes me cry every time I think about him. And his name now makes me want to puke.

Another aspect of intrusion is compulsive reexposure to or reenactment of the trauma. This behavior is a subconscious attempt to overcome the powerlessness experienced during and after the trauma. This behavior doesn't really give the child (or adult) the sense of mastery and power they desire, and so they keep engaging in the behavior, even when it becomes increasingly dangerous and harmful.[15]

Children often act out (reenact) their trauma experience over and over again in play. At the age of seven Gabriel began to see a counselor because he had developed severe stuttering soon after witnessing his father commit suicide. In the first several play therapy sessions, Gabriel would begin the session by elaborately setting up a train set. He would then pretend to run over his father, who was tied to the tracks, with the train's engine. In his play, he killed his father over and over again. This was done silently and methodically for six continuous sessions. During the sixth session he abruptly and permanently terminated the train executions of his father.

Gabriel loved his father, but his compulsive play was his attempt to gain mastery over the terrifying event that had made him feel so powerless. If his father had to die, then instead of helplessly watching him kill himself, Gabriel would be the one in control of his father's death, of his anger over his loss, and of his pain and vulnerability.

As Gabriel continued in counseling and learned to face his fears, emotions, and the dark traumatic memories, his stuttering improved dramatically. In his last therapy session, he was asked to draw one more picture (see figure 4). He depicted his fear in the form of a dinosaur, and said the dinosaur came into his room every night in his nightmares (intrusive traumatic memories) and was "scaring him to death." As he finished drawing the dinosaur, he looked up at his therapist with a smile and described himself standing over the dinosaur, picking it up by the tail, and throwing it "all the way to New York." God was healing Gabriel.

Figure 4

Adolescent girls who have been sexually violated may become highly promiscuous as a subconscious attempt to regain a sense of control. One of my parishioners in a counseling session told me how she had been raped at a party by her sister's former boyfriend. Then the boy began keeping track of when this girl's family was gone and repeatedly broke into her bedroom and molested her when her sister (who shared her bedroom) was out for the evening. This horrendous experience produced a profound sense of powerlessness, which helps to explain why she became so promiscuous that she'd often walk into a room at a party and decide which boy she would seduce into having sex with her that evening. After much counseling and healing, this woman has come to realize that this behavior had been her destructive (and sinful) attempt to regain a sense of control over the very act that had made her feel so powerless.

Numbing

Numbing (also called "constriction") is the emotional condition that results from overwhelming trauma. Internally, it involves the shutting down of all feelings so that, instead of feeling pain, one simply feels nothing. Externally, it has been described as a "reduced responsiveness to the outside world."[16] Sometimes abuse survivors are aware of shutting down emotionally, but in cases of extreme, particularly chronic trauma, children don't report going numb, for it's all they've known.

Numbing can take place at the time of the trauma itself, in which time seems to slow down, pain subsides, and a state of detached calm reigns. Numbing can also be experienced as pulling away from one's feelings and even one's own self (sometimes called "dissociation").[17] Abuse survivors, especially those who experienced chronic or severe abuse, often describe dissociation by recounting that during the abuse it felt as though they had left their body and were somewhere in the room, watching what was happening to them.

Numbing can also take place long after the original trauma, when abuse survivors shut down all feelings (pleasurable and painful). No feelings seem preferable to painful and confusing feelings.

Emotional numbing is complex—it can be a conscious choice, or it can be an automatic response to extreme stress.[18] For some victims of trauma, emotional numbing proves insufficient to ease their distress, so they resort to drugs and alcohol to numb their pain chemically.[19] While numbness or dissociation at the time of the trauma can provide immediate emotional protection, over the long term it comes at a high price. One abuse expert wisely observes, "Dissociation does not take the abuse away, it takes the person away."[20]

A more serious form of dissociation is amnesia, in which victims of trauma have no conscious memory of the traumatic event(s).[21] The past decade has seen considerable debate regarding the possibility and accuracy of repressed memories,[22] but it is simply irrefutable that extreme trauma can cause partial, as well as complete, blockage of memories. In other words, abuse can deaden not only one's feelings but also one's knowledge of the truth.

Lenore Terr, an expert on childhood trauma, has done extensive case studies of seven adults who had repressed memories of childhood abuse for years — abuse that was later confirmed — and her studies demonstrated that abusive trauma can create complete memory blockage that may last for decades. While she found that memories of abuse can be subject to corruption and are occasionally false, it was rare for spontaneously recovered abuse memories to be substantially false.[23]

One of the most powerful scientific validations of the reality and frequency of repressed abuse memories was conducted by Linda Meyer Williams. Williams obtained the records of 206 women who as children had received hospital treatment after being sexually assaulted. She was able to set up interviews with 129 of these women seventeen years after the abuse had taken place. The research method was rigorous: the interviewers didn't know anything about the circumstances of the women's abuse; they simply asked questions about their memories of abuse and recorded them. Williams found that 38 percent had no recollection of the abuse they had experienced some seventeen years earlier.[24] Other studies of contact abuse and neglect confirm this finding: a significant percentage of those who experience childhood abuse will experience partial or total memory loss of the abuse.[25]

The mechanism by which traumatic abuse memories are deadened is not entirely understood, as memory is a very complex process. There is some evidence that the hippocampus, one of the key parts of the brain that processes and records memories by putting them in their proper place in one's personal history "time line," becomes suppressed during traumatic events.[26] This suppression compromises the brain's ability to remember some traumatic events or to place them in the context of the rest of a person's life. The memories are still in the abuse victim's brain but aren't stored as a unitary whole that can be recalled as a historical event; rather, they're stored as fragments of sensations, which can then trigger PTSD symptoms, even though the person has no explicit memory of the abuse.[27] In some cases, abuse amnesia is only partial, and sometimes it results from the conscious decision of the victim to repress painful memories of abuse.

Traumatic amnesia is relatively rare for those abused in adulthood and for those who suffer a single-event (onetime) trauma. It's most often experienced by children, because they typically have the greatest sense of powerlessness, are most dependent on their abuser (especially if the abuser is an adult), and have the fewest cognitive skills to make sense of the abuse. In fact, after studying survivors of childhood incest, one abuse researcher concluded that "massive repression [of memory] appeared to be the main defensive resource available to patients who were abused early in childhood and/or who suffered violent abuse."[28] Sadly, some childhood abuse is simply too overwhelming for a child to deal with—and so this child survives by dying to the truth of his or her abuse.

The symptoms of trauma can be so severe that it's often easier for laypeople to accept their reality in veterans of military combat than in physical or sexual abuse survivors. For instance, when I was studying in Europe, I distinctly recall my sympathy for an elderly man in our congregation who had fought in World War II and had been imprisoned in Italy. By his account, his captors had treated him fairly well and had given him appropriate medical care for his injuries. After the war he finished college and became a sports reporter. However, he developed such severe stress symptoms (shaking, muteness, paralysis, and uncontrollable crying) that he had to resign from the radio station to take a lower-paying job as a truck driver. I had no problem recognizing and validating his long-term combat trauma symptoms. About the same time, however, I began to counsel a young woman in our singles ministry who was also exhibiting symptoms of trauma. When she told me her story of long-term childhood physical, sexual, and emotional abuse, I felt quite sorry for her but became impatient that she didn't just "get over it."

I later came to realize her experience and resultant damage were surprisingly similar to the combat veteran's, but her trauma symptoms were less socially acceptable (at least in my male world). Research on stress and PTSD does show, in fact, that the trauma effects of abuse and combat are strikingly similar. For instance, in one major study of eight survivor groups, the group with the highest stress response symptoms was Vietnam combat veterans; the group with the second highest symptoms was victims of sexual assault.[29] Furthermore, ten stressor variables that increase PTSD were identified. Vietnam veterans typically experienced nine out of ten of these stressors; victims of physical or sexual abuse also often experience almost all of these.[30]

Both combat and abuse can create long-term trauma damage. For instance, various studies show that up to fifty years after combat or POW imprisonment, many veterans still experience severe trauma symptoms.[31] Abuse can cause long-term trauma damage as well. In one major study of adults who had experienced documented childhood abuse, one-third of the adults fit the criteria for lifetime PTSD.[32] Prolonged or repeated trauma in particular, be it chronic childhood abuse, chronic domestic violence, or prison camp incarceration, can produce such long-term and pronounced damage that some experts have argued it deserves a new diagnostic category.[33]

It's important to note that one need not experience long-term trauma or actual physical injury to experience long-term emotional and somatic (body) damage. The key element in making an event traumatic (thus possibly creating long-term effects) is not actual threat or injury but the victim's *perception* of it. In other words, the victim's subjective assessment of how threatened and powerless they feel is what makes an event traumatic.[34]

Psychologist Dan Allender notes that child abuse often involves three forces that strip a child's freedom to choose and thus create a pervasive sense of powerlessness and hopelessness. Abused children often have an utter inability to (1) change their dysfunctional family system, (2) stop the abuse, and (3) eradicate the pain in their soul.[35] Because of their sense of stark vulnerability and powerlessness, abused children and battered women typically experience far more trauma than men—who can generally defend themselves and rarely feel physically threatened or helpless—can understand.

These principles can be clearly viewed in the effects of the Chowchilla school bus kidnapping in 1976. On a summer afternoon in Madera County, California, three men kidnapped a busload of twenty-six children ages five to fourteen, along with their bus driver, as they returned from a swim outing at the fairgrounds. The victims were driven around for eleven hours in two vans before being entombed in a moving van buried in a rock quarry. After sixteen hours underground in an eight-by-sixteen-feet space, the victims dug their way out and were found in a remote area near a park. They were taken to a nearby medical center, where they were all pronounced in good physical condition. None of the children had been physically harmed. They were welcomed home and supported by their community, and the entire ordeal had lasted less than forty hours.

In spite of the brevity of the experience and the lack of physical injury, the psychological effects on the children were devastating. Lenore Terr conducted a study of twenty-five of the twenty-six kidnapped children five to thirteen months after the ordeal, and again four to five years after the event.[36] The latter study revealed that, even five years after being kidnapped for less than forty-eight hours, all twenty-five children continued to exhibit post-traumatic stress symptoms, including somatic disturbances, nightmares, and extreme anxiety. Many of the children continued to experience profound embarrassment and humiliation for the extreme vulnerability they felt during the kidnapping. Thirteen suffered from an irrational fear that a fourth kidnapper was still at large, though there was never any evidence of this. Almost five years after the kidnapping, twenty-three of the twenty-five children suffered from severe pessimism, believing their futures would be greatly limited, and twelve children suffered nightmares of dying.[37] Other studies of long-term effects reveal similar findings.[38] Even short-term trauma that produces little or no physical injury can create long-term emotional and psychosomatic damage.

This history of trauma research is important for several reasons: (1) It helps us understand why people who have been abused sometimes can't just "get over it"; (2) it helps us understand why childhood abuse can continue to have major negative effects years later; (3) it helps us understand why abuse victims often deaden themselves emotionally, spiritually, and relationally, even though it can create even greater problems; and (4) it reminds us that we must be very careful to avoid blaming abuse victims for their trauma symptoms.

This isn't implying that abuse survivors have no responsibility for their behavior, but it's simply pointing to the truth that the effects of trauma are very complicated. Many of the effects of trauma are not consciously chosen by the victim. Abuse victims do not choose to have amnesia, nightmares, flashbacks, panic attacks, or increased heart rates. At the same time, as adults, we all must come to the point of taking responsibility for our unhealthy patterns of behavior. Abuse victims often *do* choose to deaden themselves in response to their pain instead of turning to God for strength and healing. Ultimately, abuse will often prompt survivors to trust in themselves and their own defenses instead of to put their trust in God. Hence, in time, abuse victims must come to recognize the unhealthy ways they've learned to cope with their trauma, and allow God to help them change their unhealthy responses.

DEAD MEN WALKING: IMAGES OF DEADNESS

The following verbal and visual images—all of which resulted from the trauma of abuse—further illustrate various aspects of powerlessness and deadness.

Jilian — Powerlessness

The college pastor in Jilian's church referred her for counseling after she began exhibiting out-of-control, self-destructive behavior that developed shortly after she had been abused. Jilian had a difficult time talking about her feelings with her counselor, but she was able to powerfully express them in this self-portrait done in therapy (see figure 5).

The colors in her picture reflected her mood—dark and flat (monochromatic). In her picture she is being pulled down into a huge whirlpool that threatens to engulf her frail body. The whirlpool is much bigger and stronger than she is, highlighting her powerlessness. She is completely naked, suggesting great vulnerability in the context of her powerlessness. Her only hope is seen in the black chain that surrounds her. Further counseling made it clear that the chain represented her parents' love and faith, which was the only thing keeping her from total destruction. The outcome of the conflict is ambiguous in the picture; it is unclear whether the chain will be strong enough to keep her from annihilation.

Figure 5

Abby — Death to Desire

Abby illustrates the truth that abuse and powerlessness kill desires. As a survivor of chronic neglect and spiritual abuse, she articulately described to me the gradual process of dying to desires:

> Growing up in a large blended family with a severely handicapped sibling, constant financial struggles, and frequent moves, there was no shortage of disappointment. My parents would tell me they were sorry and wished it could be different, but the unspoken message was "but it's not OK to feel sad about it."
>
> That shame message taught me early on that desire was a dangerous thing. I was an intense, driven child with great initiative and sky-high dreams. My dreams served as an escape from reality. In my late teens, however, the harshness of my reality became stronger than my dreams. Escape mechanisms only work for a period of time until, like a drug, one needs something stronger. When dreams couldn't provide an escape any longer, I turned to deadness.
>
> Soon after high school my parents convinced me to drop a college scholarship and stay home to support the family physically and financially. I convinced myself that it was actually what I wanted to do. At first I was happy. It was all in a spiritual context, and I felt like the family hero. I worked several jobs and was able to earn quite a bit of money. Every time my family had a financial crisis, they asked me for money, which soon turned into many thousands of dollars. Saying no was not an option. That meant an hour lecture from Scripture telling me how selfish I was.
>
> Eventually I became depressed. I stopped my pursuits and hobbies because I knew I could never pursue them anyway. I saw that there was no way out, and I felt trapped forever. I eventually reasoned that desire was my real enemy. I thought to myself, "If I don't desire, then I can't be disappointed." I was desperate to escape my misery, and I distinctly remember choosing to die to desire.
>
> A few years ago I began to realize just how dead I was. One Sunday after church, I saw a woman talking to a young mother and her baby. As the woman reached out to hold the baby, I could see tremendous desire and expression on her face. My next rush of thoughts shocked me. "Why would anyone feel excited about holding a baby?" I instinctively backed away. Strong desires felt threatening to me. Then I felt scared. Until then, deadness had been an attractive solution, a shelter to the relentless, unending pain in my heart. But was this the consequence? I had always loved children! How could I feel so turned off by someone who was excited about holding a baby? That night I learned that my deadness was a choice and that it was sin because it affected other people. It clashed with the very nature of what God had designed me to be.
>
> Today, desire versus deadness is still one of my biggest struggles. It often feels like desires and passions are dangerous things that should be avoided at all cost.

Yet God continues to work on me and show me more and more ways to repent. I know he can't use an Abby who is dead, so I'm willing to keep changing, even though it's painful.

Abby's story offers great hope because of the way she began to recognize and repent of her death to desire and of the way she experienced God's renewal of her heart. Sadly, this kind of experience is virtually impossible for children who lack the cognitive abilities to do the healing work Abby did. It's very difficult psychologically to live with no hope. As the writer of Proverbs warns, "Hope deferred makes the heart sick, but desire fulfilled is a tree of life" (13:12). Thus, hopeless people often become dead inside.

Johnny — Death to Hope, Death to Relationship

Johnny began to see a counselor because he was failing in school. He demonstrated no motivation and showed visible signs of depression.[39] His parents had recently divorced. Johnny experienced considerable traumatic stress as a result of their emotional neglect and his father's harsh, physically abusive methods of punishment. In therapy he drew a picture of a dejected, lonely boy with his hands in his pockets (see figure 6). He repeatedly drew himself alone, outside the circle of friends and family. The boy in the picture had no feet, evidencing an inability to act—probably reflecting Johnny's feelings of powerlessness. The caption read, "Here I am, just standing there." Clearly, this was a boy who had become dead to hopes, dreams, and relationships.

THE TRAGEDY OF POWERLESSNESS AND DEADNESS

The great tragedy of deadness is that we were created for life (John 10:10). The tragedy of feeling nothing is that God created us to experience joy and to delight in him (Psalm 34:8).[40] It's tragic to remember nothing when the truth is that God is the sovereign Lord of history. Jesus is truth incarnate (John 14:6). Death comes from hiding from the truth; life comes from embracing it (John 8:32–45). When we deaden ourselves to the truth, we are ultimately demonstrating that our God is not big enough for the real world in which we live.[41]

The tragedy of being dead to hope is that Christianity is rooted in the proclamation that the risen Jesus gives hope to the world (Matthew 28:5–10). The tragedy of feeling powerless is that God is the omnipotent ruler of the universe; nothing is too hard for him (Genesis 18:14). He delights in giving strength to the destitute (Isaiah 40:9–31). In short, God made us in his image so that we could be fully alive, delighting in him. He also made us to enjoy intimacy with other humans. Abuse threatens to maim and destroy the very purposes for which we were created.[42]

✳

In this chapter I've focused on the internal impact of abuse. We've seen how abuse deadens and destroys an individual's emotions, hope, and sense of being alive. But abuse has an impact that reaches far beyond the individual survivor. Thus, in the next chapter I'll evaluate the impact of abuse on a person's most important relationships.

Figure 6

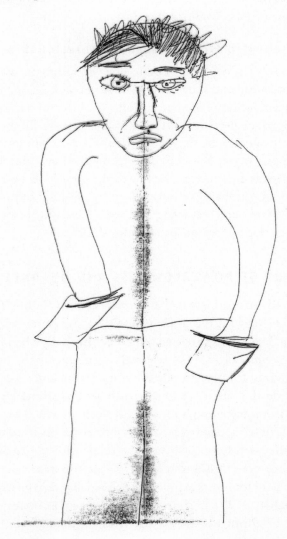

chapter 7

✳

isolation

ngrid is an articulate forty-year-old accountant who works for a Christian
publishing company. She is highly regarded by her coworkers and gets
excellent job reviews. While working for a Christian organization has been
very positive for her, it hasn't erased the dramatic impact of her childhood
abuse. Most of her coworkers would be flabbergasted to know how much
shame and isolation she experiences every single day. Ingrid was never beaten,
physically neglected, or raped, and yet the abuse she did experience was
astoundingly destructive. When Ingrid shared her story with me, I was struck
by the way her abuse had fragmented her most significant relationships, leaving her feeling isolated and often hopeless. She described her abuse and its
impact as follows:

> When I was a child, my mother was an alcoholic and extremely unstable. She
> wasn't a happy drunk. She was the kind of drunk who would pick a fight with
> my dad and end up crying and talking to me about her sex life. From the time I
> was seven, she was very sexually explicit when talking to me about my dad or
> about other guys she found attractive. At their drinking parties, she would flirt
> shamelessly with all the men. But when I became an adolescent and found pleas-
> ure in attracting boys of my own, she would call me a slut.
>
> My mother had insatiable intimacy needs that she has used me to fill all my
> life. Up until I was in high school, she would make me sleep in her bed when my
> dad was out of town. She would spoon with me and kiss me on my neck while
> she rubbed her body up and down my back. Whenever she found the opportu-
> nity, she would touch my clothed breasts (up to and including this past Christ-
> mas). From the time I was fifteen, I just tried to stay out of the house as much
> as possible. My skin crawls every time my mother touches me.
>
> My dad, on the other hand, was my "safe" parent. He was completely unin-
> terested in me or anything I did, and he let my mother rule the house. I think he
> wanted to be a good father, but he didn't know how to protect us from my

mother. Also, he was uncomfortable with any show of emotion whatsoever. As long as we kept the conversation light, and as long as everyone acted happy, he was fine. I haven't had any major trauma in my life. My parents took relatively good care of us, provided a nice house, took us on vacations, and bought us things when we wanted them. Even so, the abuse and neglect I experienced left me with a deep-rooted shame that I will probably never fully recover from.

The worst part, though, is that I picked up where my parents left off. I've abused myself in ways far worse than my parents ever did. For as long as I can remember, I've had this little voice inside me that cries, "Something is wrong here!" I have a sense of mournful sadness and a feeling of utter worthlessness. I have never felt like a woman or an adult. My life is a giant mistake, and I'm wasting precious oxygen. I loathe myself and have thought about suicide at least once a day for the past twenty years, because I believe it would be best for everyone concerned if I just went away.

At an early age, I discovered how to drown out that little voice while at the same time slowly killing myself from the inside out. At thirteen, I started sneaking booze from my mom's liquor cabinet. At fifteen, I became sexually active, and I started doing drugs. At nineteen, I had an abortion. When my mom found out, she called me a slut, and when she told my dad, he didn't bother to look up from the TV. By the age of twenty-three, I had slept with so many guys I couldn't count them anymore. I found it was even more of a thrill to seduce married men, and it became quite a hobby. I had sex with people whose names I can't remember and with people whose names I never knew.

I spend every minute of every day feeling like no one loves me, and that society in general is deeply disappointed with my mere presence. I want more than anything else to be completely invisible. When I'm sad, which is a lot of the time, I lock myself in my room and isolate myself from everyone, including my family. When I cry, I hide in my closet with all the lights off so no one can see me. Only during the last year have I been able to let Gabriel [my husband] see me cry, and I still feel selfish when I do. I don't feel like people should be forced to look at me, so during my everyday life I try to be as hidden as possible. I usually wear long sleeves so my arms don't show, and I wear my hair long so I can hide under it. I have yet to achieve invisibility, but I keep trying.

I have sabotaged most of my personal relationships. The only friends I still have are the persistent ones who don't take it personally when I don't call them. Ever. It is nearly impossible for me to believe that God loves me, even though I want him to. Most of the time I feel like he couldn't possibly have chosen me to be one of his children, and I won't be surprised if I die and find out my name isn't written in the Book of Life. I don't reach out to him for help because I'm convinced he wouldn't be interested. I love my family beyond words, but I find it hard to accept their love in return, because I don't feel like I deserve it. It's so hard, in fact, that up until recently, I became enraged inside when my daughter would pick up my hand and kiss it while we were driving in the car.

It's mentally and physically exhausting to constantly fight the lies that I've believed for so long they have become my truth. I don't know what, if anything, is left of the person I started out to be.

THE RELATIONAL IMPACT OF SIN AND ABUSE

Why would a woman like Ingrid, who has a loving husband and daughter and numerous close friends, pull away from the very people who mean the most to her? Why would she recoil from her daughter's affectionate kisses? After hearing several years of teaching and preaching on the love of God, why would she continue to believe that God didn't love her and that she would wake up on judgment day and find that her name wasn't written in the Book of Life? Why would a bright, talented adult woman have no clear sense of who she is?

While the specific relational effects of abuse vary based on the type and severity of abuse,[1] the simple fact is that abuse often produces profound long-term relational impairment. Research clearly shows that abuse survivors are much more likely to be in unhealthy relationships in which they are revictimized, have a harder time making social adjustments and experiencing satisfying relationships, and have a much more difficult time establishing relational trust than those who have not been abused.[2] Abuse survivors are also more likely to experience divorce or separation.[3]

The debilitating effects of abuse on relationships are apparent not only in adults but also in children. Research shows that abuse often leaves its mark sooner rather than later, for children and adolescents who have been abused are more distrustful and isolated and have less intimate friendships than their nonabused peers.[4]

Abuse creates further isolation for abuse victims because of the discomfort people often feel around abuse survivors. Nonvictims often don't want to be reminded of the unpleasant aspects of the world. They are uncomfortable facing overwhelming evil. They don't want to have to deal with the damaging effect abuse has on those around them. So they distance themselves from the subject of abuse and the victims of abuse.

The relational impact of abuse is so substantial and consistent that disconnection from other people is considered one of the primary effects of trauma.[5] When victims disconnect from others, they cannot enter into intimate relationships but instead keep others at a safe distance. I noted in chapter 2 that a major aspect of being made in God's image is that humans are created for intimate relationships. Unlike animals, humans simply cannot thrive in isolation; they were designed by God to bond with others. Humans long for and need intimate relationships. Thus, one of the great tragedies of sin in general and abuse in particular is that they undermine and shatter intimate relationships.

The most dramatic example of the sin-shattering effect on human intimacy is found in Genesis 3. Genesis 2 eloquently described the human need for intimacy and the beautiful way God designed this need to be met through loving relationships. In Genesis 2:18 we're told it was not good for Adam to be alone, so God made a helper to complement him as his equal.[6]

When God created the woman Adam longed for, God took her from Adam's rib, suggesting the most intimate kinship or connection between the man and the woman. Moses described the relationship of the man and the woman as a "one flesh" relationship—a relationship so intimate that Adam and Eve enjoyed complete physical and emotional oneness. They were naked in each other's presence, without the slightest twinge of shame (2:25). Their physical nakedness was surely indicative of complete openness and transparency with each other. Amazingly, this is the only Old Testament passage in which physical nakedness is unambiguously positive.[7] The creation account ends with a shout of delight over the intimacy Adam and Eve enjoyed as a divine gift.

The celebration was soon shattered the instant they sinned (3:6–13). All of the intimacy they had previously experienced unraveled, for instead of enjoying each other's bodies in a celebration of their love, they covered their genitals in shame.[8] Instead of the man and woman being intimate allies in ruling over creation, Adam blamed and attacked Eve for his own failure. Instead of experiencing delight in their intimacy with God, they hid from him in the bushes.

Sin disrupts intimacy and turns lovers into enemies. Abuse, more than any other type of sin, has a particularly menacing effect on relationships. By definition, abuse is the misuse of one's power to harm another person. Abuse is a frontal assault on another person's worth and dignity, and hence it can cripple one's ability to experience healthy relationships.

THREE DYNAMICS THAT LEAD TO ISOLATION

While past abuse predictably will have a deleterious effect on present and future relationships, this dynamic warrants exploration. Given the overwhelmingly negative effects of abuse on human intimacy, how does abuse specifically impair relationships?

Abuse creates several dynamics that fracture relational intimacy. In chapter 5 I delved into one of the most destructive results of abuse, namely, shame. Shame powerfully contributes to isolation, for it makes victims feel utterly defective and worthless and impels them to hide from others. We can hear shame dripping from many of Ingrid's statements at the beginning of this chapter. I'll now note three additional abuse dynamics that can lead to isolation.

Shattered Assumptions

Abuse shatters many of the false assumptions that give us security (for example, bad things do not happen to good people; God will never let evil people harm me; if I pray, the abuse will stop; most people are basically good). Abuse causes people to feel unsafe and powerless. The world is increasingly viewed as hostile and dangerous. Hence, abuse survivors feel safer and more powerful if they avoid the vulnerability that comes from trusting others. Furthermore, shattered assumptions about the world often cause abuse survivors to become disillusioned, which in turn fractures trust and intimacy. Judith Lewis Herman makes this observation:

> Traumatized people feel utterly abandoned, utterly alone, cast out of the human and divine systems of care and protection that sustain life. Thereafter, a sense of alienation, of disconnection, pervades every relationship, from the most intimate familial bonds to the most abstract affirmations of community and religion. When trust is lost, traumatized people feel they belong more to the dead than to the living.[9]

The prophet Jeremiah illustrates the way abuse can shatter assumptions and create relational disconnection. Jeremiah was a godly prophet with an extremely difficult assignment from God—tell a rebellious people who will not listen to you that they are about to experience inescapable divine judgment (Jeremiah 1:19; 11:6–13). Jeremiah knew intellectually that God is all-powerful, just, and worthy of praise (20:11–13). But after he experienced physical and verbal abuse by the high priest and others (20:1–2, 10), Jeremiah pulled away from God, complaining that God had deceived him (20:7). He cursed the day he was born, as well as the man who had told his father that Jeremiah had been born (20:14–18). Abuse shatters our assumptions about life and tempts us to defensively pull away from God and others.

Mistrust

Shattered assumptions lead naturally to mistrust. Mistrust is one of the most consistent consequences of abuse, and trust is the cornerstone of relational intimacy. All forms of abuse create mistrust, though sexual abuse, particularly incest—one of the greatest imaginable forms of betrayal—often produces the greatest level of mistrust and can significantly increase various trauma effects.[10]

Abuse victims' mistrust is often so pervasive that it outweighs other types of consequences. For instance, based on his extensive research with child sexual abuse victims, David Finkelhor makes this observation:

> [Abuse] victims report that the lasting trauma of incest is not so much sexual as emotional. The scar that stays the longest is a deep inability to trust others, particularly men. They find themselves suspecting others' motives, feeling that they are being used. They have a hard time opening up or getting close, because they fear all men want from them is sex.[11]

Trauma victims' mistrust often involves far more than mistrust of their abusers. In fact, abused children very often feel significantly more anger and mistrust toward the nonabusive parent for not protecting them than they do toward the abusive parent. For instance, women who in childhood were molested by their fathers often report much more anger toward their mothers than their fathers. They also often report some positive memories of their abusive fathers but virtually none of their mothers.[12] Abuse victims' mistrust is often globalized, infecting and undermining every single relationship.

Tineal illustrates this dynamic. A children's choir director had sexually abused her over a twelve-month period. In therapy she drew a two-framed picture of herself behind bars (see figure 7). In the first frame, she is turned away. She is bleeding from a knife stuck in her back. This symbolizes the horrible betrayal she had experienced by a "man of God" who was supposed to protect her but instead violated her. Her hands are tied behind her back, and a leg iron and weight is on her leg. These highlight her sense of powerlessness. In the second frame she stoically stares out from behind the bars, all alone.

The betrayal she experienced from one man—and the subsequent mistrust—had led to isolation from all others. The sad irony is that when Tineal drew this picture, her abuser was actually isolated behind bars in a state prison, and yet she was the one who felt isolated and imprisoned.

Numbing, or Constriction

Since one of the primary trauma effects is numbing (or constriction; see page 100)—shutting down emotionally—it's easy to see how abuse survivors often experience little or no relational intimacy. Numbing means that abuse victims

Figure 7

don't feel anything, be it pain or pleasure. They don't feel their own feelings, nor can they recognize and embrace the feelings of others.

In shutting down to avoid pain, abuse survivors also miss out on love. As C. S. Lewis so eloquently notes, those who shut down their emotions to avoid pain pay an astronomical price for emotional safety:

> To love at all is to be vulnerable. Love anything, and your heart will certainly be wrung and possibly be broken. If you want to make sure of keeping it intact, you must give your heart to no one, not even to an animal. Wrap it carefully round with hobbies and little luxuries; avoid all entanglements; lock it up safe in the casket or coffin of your selfishness. But in that casket—safe, dark, motionless, airless—it will change. It will not be broken; it will become unbreakable, impenetrable, irredeemable. . . . The only place outside Heaven where you can be perfectly safe from all the dangers and perturbations of love is Hell.[13]

Relational intimacy is built on emotional connection and risk taking. To form intimate relationships, one must first be aware of one's own feelings. Emotional constriction causes trauma victims to be estranged from their own past and their negative emotions. Hence, they cannot enter into deep relationship with others because their deepest self is locked away. Furthermore, their constriction makes it all but impossible for them to enter into the pain and feelings of others. Just as healthy marital sexual intimacy requires physical nakedness, so relational intimacy requires emotional nakedness (honesty and transparency).

Various Bible passages call believers to emotional connection with other believers. We see it, for instance, in the example and admonitions of the apostle Paul. Paul had very intimate relationships with his fellow ministers and with those he shepherded. He admonishes believers to "rejoice with those who rejoice, and weep with those who weep" (Romans 12:15); "bear one another's burdens" (Galatians 6:2); be "of the same mind, maintaining the same love, united in spirit" (Philippians 2:2); and "look out . . . for the interests of others" (Philippians 2:4). As long as abuse survivors remain shut down, they are not able to experience soul-satisfying intimacy.

Sandy illustrates the dynamics and the relational dangers of shutting down. Sandy grew up in a neglectful and emotionally abusive family. Sandy's mother would routinely share the graphic details of her sexual and marital struggles with Sandy. Sandy found these conversations to be extremely painful and emotionally paralyzing. Hence, in counseling she drew a picture of one of these conversations with her mother (see figure 8). Sandy pictured herself with adultlike clothes and makeup, but with the proportions of a small child. Her face is tense.

Figure 8

She is talking on the phone to her mother, who is yelling at her. She is simply agreeing with her mother verbally, saying "uh-huh" over and over. But she really wants to say two things to her mother: "shut up" and "good-bye."

Sandy was not allowed to express her pain or to say anything negative to her mother. She was not allowed to set limits around her emotional needs. Her real voice had been silenced. Thus, she had learned to shut down her painful feelings. She became very skilled at saying "uh-huh," regardless of how she really felt. Sadly, Sandy continued to shut down, and by adolescence, she had become promiscuous and had been abused by several different boys. Abuse victims who are shut down simply cannot experience healthy, intimate relationships; they often experience destructive relationships instead.

In the song "Easier to Run," the group Linkin Park describes the way abuse, shame, shutting down, and isolation are connected. They describe a dark secret they've kept locked away from everyone. They tell of wounds so deep they can't be seen by others—wounds that create a shame that makes them want to simply ignore their past. They sadly confess, "It's easier to run, replacing this pain with something numb; it's so much easier to go than face all this pain here all alone."

SABOTAGING THE MOST IMPORTANT RELATIONSHIPS

It's understandable that abuse survivors find it much easier to run and to replace the pain with something numb. But denying the past does not eliminate the past. Abuse survivors' tendency to run from the past and die to the future has a particularly destructive effect on the present. It sabotages their most important relationships.

God

Surprisingly few formal studies have been conducted on the spiritual impact of abuse, but those that have been done reveal that abuse seriously undermines religious faith. The first national random sample survey in the United States of sexual abuse showed that sexual abuse victims are far more likely to be nonpractitioners of religion than those who had not been abused.[14] In her large-scale study of incest victims, Diana Russell found there was no significant correlation between religious upbringing and incest victimization, but there was a striking relationship between incest victimization and adult religious practice. She found that 56 percent of adult Catholic and Protestant incest victims had defected from their religious faith.[15]

The impact of abuse on one's relationship with God is seen in three typical responses: rejecting, withdrawing, and cowering. While these responses look very different, the end result is quite similar—intimacy with God is shattered.

Rejecting

This is the response of abuse victims who conclude that God does not exist. Given the evil abuse they've experienced, some victims simply reject the notion that there is a personal, transcendent God with whom they can have an intimate relationship. I believe this is the least common and most extreme spiritual response to abuse, but it's still very significant.

In a stunning and terrifying account of the Holocaust that won a Nobel Peace Prize for literature, Elie Wiesel recounts receiving and witnessing unimaginable abuse in Nazi concentration camps in Auschwitz and Buchenwald. Wiesel was a young teenager when one day he and all the other prisoners were forced to watch the Nazis hang three fellow prisoners. One was a small boy who, because he was so light, did not die quickly when the chair under him was tipped over. Instead, he slowly choked to death for over a half hour while the other prisoners were forced to watch. One prisoner behind Wiesel kept asking, "Where is God?" "Where is God now?" Wiesel heard another internal voice answering, "Where is he? Here he is—he is hanging here on this gallows."[16] For some abuse victims, God died with their abuse.

One need not experience the extreme murderous abuse of Nazi concentration camps to reject God. The band Everclear articulates the way nonlethal abuse can also cause abuse victims to reject belief in God. In their song "Why I Don't Believe in God," they specifically mention childhood physical abuse and abandonment by a mentally ill mother as the cause of loss of faith. At the end of the song, they proclaim, "I wish I believed like you do—in the myth of a merciful god."

Rejection of God as a consequence of abuse isn't limited to adults and adolescents. The process of losing faith can begin in childhood. Wesley was molested by another boy when he was six, and then he began to initiate sexual behavior with other children. In therapy he drew a picture of what he was feeling when he initiated sexual activity (see figure 9). He said the picture was of his heart. He drew himself as a child with tearstains on his cheeks. His heart is black. He is alone, and God has vacated his heart. The caption reads, "Where's God when I'm scared?"

Wesley, as a young boy, had already begun to experience great pain over the sensation that God had not been there when he had been molested. A child who comes to believe God is absent from his or her heart may eventually come to believe God is absent from the universe. Amazingly, this was the relational pain Wesley felt when he was sexually acting out with other children.

Figure 9

Withdrawing

Withdrawing and cowering are far more common and insidious spiritual responses to abuse than rejection. Abuse survivors who withdraw still believe God exists, but they don't believe they can trust him. Instead, they withdraw from him so that they feel less vulnerable to being misused. They may reason that God did not stop their abusers from violating them, in spite of the Bible's testimony that God will protect his children (Psalm 27:1–3; 91:1–14).

Since abuse victims have experienced betrayal and harm from those who are more powerful than they are, God is particularly frightening to them because he is said to be all-powerful. When the abuser was the victim's father or spiritual leader, mistrust and withdrawal from God are particularly problematic. Individuals, particularly children, project their understanding of their earthly father onto God, their heavenly Father. They often reason that if their earthly father, who had limited power, abused them, then God, their omnipotent heavenly Father, might well do the same. So the only solution for many abuse survivors seems to be to limit their vulnerability to an unsafe God by withdrawing from him, by not completely surrendering to him.

Linda Katherine Cutting, a highly accomplished concert pianist and music professor, tells of growing up in a dangerous, abusive home. Her father was a minister, who reportedly chronically abused his children physically, sexually, and spiritually. Both of Linda's brothers committed suicide. As an adult, Linda suffered a nervous breakdown and completely lost her ability to perform music. Her father never acknowledged his evil behavior and continued for many years to serve as a minister in New England.

Linda lost her sense of relationship with God. She ended up becoming a Quaker and felt much more comfortable in a church with no pulpit, no cross, no preacher, and no emphasis on human religious authority. Sadly, through her minister father's abuse, these had become the very things that had caused her to withdraw from God. She recounts, "In my father's church, he always had the final word. At the end of each week, on the day after the beatings, he offered absolution. We could ask our Father in heaven through our earthly father to forgive us our sins. 'Our Father who art in heaven,' we'd begin. But as long as our father was leading it, the words seemed tainted."[17]

What is difficult about withdrawing from God is that it often takes place at a subconscious level. Many abuse victims believe in God and do all the things Christians are supposed to do. They worship, tithe, pray, and serve in their church. But they do these things out of religious duty, not heartfelt affection. Their relationship with God is not intimate, for they have withdrawn from him. They don't really trust him. In fact, their active Christian service is a hollow substitute for a personal relationship with a God who frightens them.

Cowering

A third spiritual response to abuse is to cower before God. This response may involve mistrust, but the emphasis here is not so much on something being wrong with God but on everything being wrong with oneself. Cowering is a shame-based response in which abuse survivors feel they are so defective that God will never really love or accept them. They believe that God exists and that he probably loves some people, but he could never love them. They are too disgusting.

In one sense, cowering is a reliving of the abuse. Just as abuse survivors had cowered before their abuser and had come to believe they deserved the abuse, so they cower before God and come to believe they deserve to be rejected by him. This is precisely what Ingrid articulated in her story when she confessed, "It is nearly impossible for me to believe that God loves me, even though I want him to. Most of the time I feel like he couldn't possibly have chosen me to be one of his children, and I won't be surprised if I die and find out my name isn't writ-ten in the Book of Life."

As with other aspects of abuse, cowering is intensified if the abuser was the victim's father. Linda Cutting testifies to her own cowering response to her min-ister father's abuse:

> The thing that's kept me spiritually alone all of these years was somehow equat-ing God with my father's church and, most of all, with my father.... In Sunday school we used to sing "Jesus loves the little children, all the children of the world." It listed the colors "red and yellow, black and white." For some reason I never felt I was on the list. I'd sing as loud as I could, so that God would hear my voice, and I'd look over at the mural of Jesus' gathering the children into his lov-ing arms and wish I could be one of them.[18]

Spouse

Since God intended the husband-wife relationship to be the most intimate of all human relationships (it alone is to be a "one flesh" relationship), abuse dam-age is often seen most acutely in marriage. Marriage should involve the greatest level of long-term trust, for in a healthy marriage, couples share that which is most precious—their bodies, their wealth, their homes, their children, and their dreams. Sadly, many abuse survivors have experienced such profound betrayal that they conclude, "If I couldn't trust my family, whom can I trust? No one is trustworthy."[19] This can then become a self-fulfilling prophecy as abuse sur-vivors refuse to trust even a loving spouse, and their marriage crumbles.

There are many specific ways in which the damage of abuse impacts marriage and creates isolation from the survivor's spouse. Abuse affects a couple's ability to communicate. In one study, 23 percent of abuse survivors reported they had no meaningful communication with their partners, whereas only 6 percent of nonabused adults said this.[20] Abuse survivors often have a difficult time confid-ing in others, including their spouses—due in part to a difficulty trusting others and possibly also because childhood abuse survivors are conditioned to keep secrets, which can become an ingrained pattern on into adulthood.

Abuse survivors' difficulties with marital communication are often the result of residual shame. Shame-filled people want to hide; they don't want to bare their souls, not even to their spouses. For survivors of physical and verbal abuse, conflict avoidance is a huge factor that affects marital communication. These individuals learned as children to avoid conflict at all costs, for conflict was inherently dangerous. Hence, they became conditioned to avoid any per-ception of conflict, even in a safe relationship. Thus, real communication becomes virtually impossible, because the moment potential conflict is perceived (no matter how mild), the abuse survivor shuts down emotionally and verbally, and genuine communication ceases.

Sexual intimacy is one of the most important ways by which married couples reenact their marriage vows and express and strengthen their intimacy as a couple.[21] Sadly, abuse survivors, especially female sexual abuse survivors, are particularly prone to sexual dysfunction in marriage.[22] Interestingly, childhood sexual abuse does not have the same impact on adult men, for overall it is not an accurate predictor of adult male sexual dysfunction.[23] For men, childhood *emotional* abuse seems to have the greatest impact on adult sexual health.[24]

For women, there are many factors in childhood sexual abuse that may help bring about adult sexual dysfunction. To begin with, sexual relations with even a loving husband can be a trauma trigger that evokes memories and sensations of childhood abuse. Any number of marital behaviors or experiences, from a hug in the middle of the night to the actual position of intercourse, can trigger childhood sexual trauma. Also, since sexual abuse creates distrust, the most intimate physical act—sex—often is simply too intimate to be enjoyed. Additionally, a female sexual abuse victim often develops great dissatisfaction about and even antipathy toward her body and its sexual urges. Her abuser's interest in her body had been the source of great pain, so subconsciously her body has become the enemy.

Victims of nonviolent sexual abuse also struggle with accepting sexual pleasure, for in the process of being abused, they may have felt a mixture of sexual pleasure, shame, and revulsion. Thus, nonabusive sexual pleasure becomes connected with prior abuse and shame, so the adult survivor is automatically repulsed by and seeks to shut down all feelings of sexual pleasure. This dynamic helps explain why female sexual abuse is especially related to the inability to achieve orgasm in adulthood.[25]

A final way in which abuse inhibits marital closeness is by undermining the sense of self, thereby causing victims to feel worthless, powerless, and inferior to others. Female abuse victims often feel this most keenly, as they become unable to set healthy boundaries, make appropriate requests of their partners, or expect to be treated with respect. This helps explain why women who experience violence in childhood are more likely to marry violent men.[26] Furthermore, women who have experienced violence in childhood or in their marriage often develop trauma bonds with violent men. They become so conditioned to being physically abused and develop such cognitive distortions that they come to believe an abusive relationship is quite acceptable. It must surely be what they deserve.[27]

In short, when abuse undermines a woman's sense of self, it keeps her from being able to function as an equal partner in marriage. A woman can only be the complementing helper God intended (Genesis 2:18) when she perceives herself as her husband's complete spiritual equal. Only then can a married couple experience deep intimacy.

Family and Friends

Abuse fractures intimacy not only with one's spouse but with other family members as well. Children who grow up in abusive families are traumatized and shamed. They aren't consistently loved and nurtured and don't learn conflict resolution skills. Hence, all relationships in abusive families are weakened.

Girls who experience incest from their fathers often report intense conflict with their mothers and other siblings, who resent the special attention they are being given by their father.[28] Boys who have been abused tend to externalize their pain, and they often express a desire to hurt their siblings and peers.[29] Girls, on the other hand, tend to internalize their abuse damage. This most often results in depression, which can also impair relationships with siblings.[30] In short, abuse isolates family members.

Kay grew up in a sterile, neglectful family. Her mother hadn't dealt with her own childhood pain, so she was completely disconnected from her own feelings and from her own children. Kay's father was a good provider but was very disconnected as well. Kay's physical needs were met, but she was emotionally starved. In therapy she drew a picture of her family (see figure 10). Everyone is in a black box that isolates them from each other. Kay commented that the blackness came from her father. Kay felt no intimacy with anyone in her immediate family. Her family members were each in their own isolated world, emotionally disconnected from each other.

The impact of abuse is particularly salient in the abuse survivor's relationship with his or her children. One of the key abuse dynamics that negatively affects parenting is shame. We see this dynamic in Ingrid's confession (see the beginning of this chapter):

> I love my family beyond words, but I find it hard to accept their love in return, because I don't feel like I deserve it. It's so hard, in fact, that up until recently, I became enraged inside when my daughter would pick up my hand and kiss it while we were driving in the car.

Ingrid became enraged because her daughter's spontaneous affection triggered shame. Ingrid didn't feel worthy of love, so she'd instinctively and aggressively

Figure 10

reject it from her own child. This shame/rejection dynamic causes a mother to feel guilty for being a terrible mother and harming her child.

As a result of this shame, abuse-surviving mothers are often guilt-ridden and unable to set healthy limits on their children's behavior. Due to the emotional impact of abuse, particularly numbing (constriction), these moms are often distant and emotionally unavailable to their children. And, at times, the experience of abuse has a detrimental effect on the parent-child relationship when parents visualize their abusers in their own children—when, for example, a child's physical appearance, personality, or behavior resembles that of the parent's abuser. For instance, a mother may become hostile toward her son who looks like her ex-husband who had beaten her. A father, without consciously realizing it, may become cold and neglectful toward his daughter who has his own abusive mother's personality.

Abuse also has a dramatic impact on peer relationships. Consider these important research findings:

- Children who have been physically abused tend to be more aggressive, experience more conflict, have lower peer status, and show less positive reciprocity with other children than their nonabused peers. In fact, one of the most extensively documented consequences of child physical abuse is heightened aggression, especially toward peers.[31]

- Abused children may have as many friends and the same frequency of contact as do their nonabused peers, but they experience more conflict, especially during play, and enjoy less intimacy in their peer friendships.[32]
- Neglected children tend to be less aggressive toward peers than physically or sexually abused children, but they also tend to be more passive and withdrawn and to have fewer friendships.[33]
- Sexually abused children also tend to be more aggressive than their nonabused peers and are particularly characterized by increased sexual behavior with or toward other children.[34]

Sexualized behavior often continues and even increases as the child gets older. One of the most notable characteristics of opposite-gender relationships among adolescent and adult survivors of sexual abuse is increased sexual activity and promiscuity, often leading to revictimization.[35] In terms of dating relationships, adolescent abuse survivors report significantly more verbal and physical abuse toward and from their partners.[36] Due to self-blame and shame, survivors of sexual abuse are also less confident in establishing same-gender friendships, which are important developmentally for overall relational skill building.[37]

RECONNECTING AND HEALING

The bad news—and the good news—about being a human made in God's image is that we are profoundly affected by our relationships with other humans. When people misuse their power and abuse others, tremendous long-term damage is created. Abuse damage is particularly evident in abuse victims' relationships. Abuse creates shame, mistrust, and emotional constriction, all of which undermine abuse survivors' relationships. Abuse isolates victims. The good news is that *healthy* relationships have tremendous power to nurture the soul and heal the wounds of abuse.

The power of human relationships to heal is an expressly biblical concept. It was a loving relationship with his new bride that healed and comforted Isaac after he lost his mother (Genesis 24:67). It was David's intimate relationship with his friend Jonathan that helped him endure physical abuse and attempted murder by King Saul (1 Samuel 19–20). It was Barnabas and the disciples at Damascus who took the risk to love and disciple Saul, the very man who had been persecuting Christians (Acts 9:1–30). Shortly before the apostle Paul (the man formerly called Saul) was executed, it was Timothy and Luke who brought him help and comfort when others had abandoned him (2 Timothy 4:9–17).

God has designed the church, the body of Christ, to be the matrix in which healing and sanctification take place. Believers are to love, restore, and care for each other because they are all part of the same spiritual body through Christ.[38] This is a particularly powerful principle for those who have experienced abuse by family members because, in spite of what one has experienced from his or her physical family, God has given a spiritual family of fellow believers who can love and nurture and aid in the process of healing.

There are two principles that come into play as we encourage abuse victims to reconnect with others. *Friends and family members of abuse victims must recognize the critical role they play in preventing and healing abuse damage.* Their response to abuse will largely affect the extent to which the abuse will create long-term damage. For instance, parents' and caregivers' harsh, disbelieving, or apathetic responses to a child's abuse disclosure can be as damaging as, or more damaging than, the original abuse, whereas supportive responses can mitigate abuse damage.[39]

This principle is true for adult survivors of abuse as well. One of the strongest findings in a large-scale study of female sexuality and abuse was that women who were raped as adults were far less likely to destructively seek to control their sexual desires (shut down, etc.) if they had felt very close to at least one immediate family member in childhood.[40] In another study of adult rape survivors, the reported length of time required for recovery was directly related to the quality of intimate relationships the women experienced in the present. Survivors who had a supportive, stable relationship with a spouse or partner recovered more quickly than those who did not.[41]

Friends and family members of abuse survivors must be patient, recognizing that shattered trust is rebuilt very slowly. They must also be strong and gracious, for in the early stages of recovery abuse survivors often lash out most severely at their closest allies. It's very helpful for loved ones to realize that much of the abuse survivors' rage is displaced rage at their abusers.

The second principle is this: *Abuse victims must, with God's strength, learn to develop safe, intimate relationships.* They must learn to resist the temptation to hide and pull away. They must learn to give God and the healthy people he puts into their lives a chance to love them. They, in turn, must learn to love others, in spite of the fact that the world is not always a safe place. They must learn to resist distrusting God and good, safe people because of what an evil, unsafe person did to them.

Lori Tapia illustrates this principle as she summarizes the lessons she learned in her journey of healing from incest. In particular, she notes the way God healed her sexuality and her marriage after several years of complete shutdown, isolation, and rage:

> All our hard work and perseverance in the flow of God's presence had paid off. The fruits have been profound joy, hope, true faith, and yes—great sex! Not only did genuine intimacy become possible for me—it even became enjoyable.... Learning to trust has been the most important step for me. I didn't know how. Step by excruciating step, I learned to trust [my husband] more each time.... The process has convinced me of the capacity of the human heart to respond to persistent love. I believe we want terribly to believe that love is real and that we are loved. Maybe we've just never seen it lived out. Or maybe we have, but our souls were so wounded that we could not receive it. At some point I had to choose to believe. The payoff has been worth the risk.[42]

Lori's comments set the stage for the next and final section of *Mending the Soul*. Now that we've surveyed the profound soul damage created by abuse, we need to discover the process of healing. In the next three chapters, I'll map out a path so that those ravaged by abuse can experience emotional, spiritual, and relational healing.

part 3
the healing path

chapter 8

✳

facing the brokenness

n the first two sections of *Mending the Soul,* we evaluated the nature and impact of abuse. In particular, we noted that, as a result of human depravity and satanic strategy, abuse is rampant throughout human society. We also saw that abuse perverts various aspects of the image of God in humans and consequently creates long-term soul damage. Thus, it's particularly important in this last section that we sketch out a plan for healing.

A little girl named Latisha beautifully illustrates the spiritual necessity of healing the wounds of abuse. In her first counseling session, Latisha, painted a watercolored heart (see figure 11). The image ran on the paper, depicting the deep sorrow and shame of her soul. Her painted heart was punctuated with black and gray holes, visualizing the hurt and damage done by the sexual abuse perpetrated on her and by the sexual touching she had done to other children. Latisha was a sweet Christian girl who felt tremendous guilt for her actions. "Please," she begged, reaching for the Scotch tape, "help me tape up the holes; if you don't, the devil will crawl in!" This young girl intuitively knew that the soul damage of her abuse had to be healed, or else Satan would use it to generate more damage to herself and to others. Let's see what it would take to develop a path for healing the holes of the soul, beginning with the emotional damage that needs to be healed.

LANCE'S STORY

I met Lance at church when I was doing graduate work in Europe, and I was impressed with his confidence, drive, and life experience. I enjoyed spending time with him. Lance's father had been a career military officer who had been stationed in various bases around the world. Lance entertained us with lively stories of childhood adventure. He spoke of his parents, especially his father, in

Figure 11

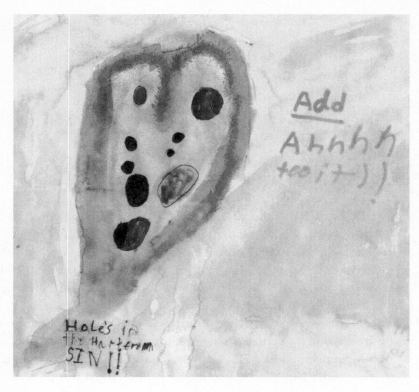

glowing terms. He explained that his parents currently lived in Asia, for his father had left the military and had been a pilot for a Christian relief agency for the past twelve years. Lance gave the distinct impression that his father was a combination of Hudson Taylor, Chuck Yeager, and John Wayne.

I was delighted to get the chance to meet Lance's parents, Don and Mindy, when they came to the area for a conference. I was surprised to find Don quite nervous and reclusive. I found Mindy even more puzzling. She was obviously a talented and dedicated aid worker. She had recently been appointed as the women's director for their entire region. I had heard she was greatly valued by her agency for her organizational skills and efficiency. Thus, I found it unsettling that in personal conversation Mindy was so emotionally flat and disconnected that it was painful to carry on a five-minute conversation with her.

The next time I saw Lance's mother was at Don's funeral. Lance's family told everyone Don had suffered a fatal allergic reaction to a medication his doctor had prescribed for him. The vicar performing the funeral service spoke eloquently of Don's faithful service for the Lord. Mindy was the rock of Gibraltar.

She assured everyone that God was good and was in control, and that she would be fine. Somehow it seemed rather surreal to me.

Lance and Mindy were not telling the real story of Don's death. Shortly after the funeral I received one of the greatest shocks of my life when a friend, who was an administrator in the same aid agency as Lance's parents, told me what had really happened. Don did not die in his bedroom of an allergic reaction. He had been murdered in a prison cell—where he had been placed the day before for molesting the four-year-old son of a local political official.

Worse yet, an investigation revealed that Don had been molesting little boys for years. The relief agency had received numerous reports of Don molesting both missionary children and local children. The agency had merely shuffled him around to new relief teams in new locations. It was also discovered that for years Mindy had known her husband was molesting boys, but Don kept saying he was sorry and promising he wouldn't do it again. She kept accepting his promises and refused to think about the past.

Mindy also refused to process her anger, hurt, and terror at Don's behavior. She had learned this strategy for coping with pain long before she had met Don. Her own father was an alcoholic who died when she was young. Mindy had learned as a young girl to deaden herself to the truth and to the pain. She had passed this strategy on to her son, who would, in turn, perhaps pass it on to his son.

Lance's response to his father's murder was incredible. He kept saying what a great father Don had been. Lance, like his mother, indicated that he was trusting the Lord and that he was doing fine. In fact, Lance went back to work two hours after the funeral was over. One of the last things Lance told me after the funeral was that his father was a great man.

Lance found it impossible to face the truth and the painfulness of his father's sin, so he molded the facts and his feelings into something more manageable and sanitary. Sadly, assiduous refusal to face the brokenness was exactly how his mother and the relief agency had dealt with the horror of Don's sin. It did not eradicate the ugly truth; it just drove it underground, where it grew in the darkness.

FACING THE BROKENNESS: REASONS TO LOOK AT ONE'S PAST

Some Christians argue that we need not understand our painful past to move victoriously into the future. Looking at past pain is said to be little more than an exercise in blame shifting, which only creates destructive bitterness.[1] Others

suggest that revisiting the painful past only serves to perpetuate the pain—
"What's done is done. Why stir up the past? It can't be changed. Just focus on
obedience to God in the present." Several times I've heard Christian leaders use
Philippians 3:13 to prove these points ("forgetting what lies behind and reaching forward to what lies ahead"). Such wholesale rejection of looking at past
abuse and brokenness is utterly misguided. The painful events of our past create deep-seated trauma, shame, and cognitive distortions that negatively shape
the present until they are exposed and challenged.

Facing the reality and impact of our past is implicit in Philippians 3:13.
When Paul tells the Philippians that believers should forget what lies behind,
he isn't saying we should simply put the past behind us, forget about it, and
focus on the future. He can't be saying this, because just a few verses earlier he
gave a detailed account of his past (3:1–7), including his previous abuse of Christians (3:6). It must have been very painful for Paul to reflect on the fact that in
the past he had personally abused Christians, but he doesn't shrink back from
such reflection and confession.[2]

It's also clear that Paul had reflected deeply enough on his past that he could
identify unhealthy, harmful beliefs and emotional responses that needed to
change. Most specifically, he came to realize that his preconversion behavior,
including his abuse of Christians, was grounded in the misconception that he
could gain God's favor through strict adherence to the law. It was Paul's horribly misdirected attempt at self-righteousness apart from Christ that provided
the immediate context of "forgetting what lies behind" in Philippians 3:13.[3] Paul
had a clear grasp of the scope of his sinful past, the lies that had fueled his sin,
and exactly what he needed God to help him change. In other words, we cannot
put the painful past behind us until we have fully grappled with it.

There are four main reasons believers should face their brokenness—take an
honest look at their past abuse and pain—as they seek to become spiritually and
emotionally healthy.

A Way to Express Faith

Facing our brokenness is a breathtaking act of faith in the living God; refusal to
face our brokenness is a tragic denial of his existence, power, and goodness.
Because the denial of painful reality comes so naturally, it is rarely labeled as
sinful. Nor do we recognize how much it dishonors the God who loves us. The
Bible says that God is a God of truth (John 14:6). God is the Lord of history,
who will ultimately triumph over all human evil (1 Corinthians 15:25–26; Revelation 20:7–15). Scripture declares that nothing, not natural disaster, abuse,

or demonic powers, can separate us from the love of God (Romans 8:38–39). Thus, refusal to face the truth about our brokenness is no trivial matter. Dan Allender puts it succinctly: "Denial is an affront to God. It assumes that a false reality is better than the truth. It assumes that God is neither good nor strong enough to help during the recall process. Ultimately, the choice to face past [abuse] memories is the choice not to live a lie."[4]

Stated positively, as we refuse to deaden ourselves to the truth and to the pain of our past abuse, we throw ourselves into the arms of the only one who can heal us. This is why Jesus pronounces a blessing on those who are willing to mourn (and to keep on mourning);[5] they are the ones who will experience divine comfort (Matthew 5:4). As long as we minimize the ugliness of our lives, we short-circuit the divinely ordained means of grace. We also short-circuit the experience of God's power and sufficiency. It is only when we stand naked and broken before him, refusing to ease our pain by lying to ourselves, that we fully taste his sweetness.

Over and over again the psalmist admonishes us to cry out to the Lord in our brokenness so that we can taste God's power and beauty: "The LORD is near to the brokenhearted and saves those who are crushed in spirit" (Psalm 34:18). "This poor man cried, and the LORD heard him and saved him out of all his troubles" (34:6). "Turn to me and be gracious to me, for I am lonely and afflicted. The troubles of my heart are enlarged" (25:16–17). "How long shall I take counsel in my soul, having sorrow in my heart all the day? ... But I have trusted in Your lovingkindness. ... I will sing to the LORD, because He has dealt bountifully with me" (13:2, 5, 6). "God is my helper; the Lord is the sustainer of my soul. He will recompense the evil to my foes" (54:4–5). As we are willing to face and taste our brokenness we will be able to taste God's sustaining power.

A Way to Live in the Truth

Facing our brokenness forces us to live in the truth and helps us to identify and extinguish the destructive lies created by the shame of our abuse. Thus, looking at our painful past is necessary for correcting the distorting effects of shame. Anna Salter states this point well: "Those negative parts of the self that remain totally hidden will remain totally shame-based. Darkness produces good mushrooms, but poor flowers."[6]

In particular, the vast majority of abuse victims inappropriately blame themselves for their abuse, which in turn creates numerous emotional and relational problems.[7] This dynamic often begins in childhood, for abused children are dependent on their parents and long for a close relationship with them. So they instinctively minimize and take responsibility for the evil of the abusive parents.[8] The lie that the child is responsible for the parents' abuse is perpetually reinforced by the abusive parents' blame shifting.

This destructive distortion of reality continues on into adulthood. Thus, I often hear adult survivors of childhood abuse make statements such as, "My father didn't really molest me; he just touched me inappropriately a few times." "Overall my parents really took pretty good care of me." "My home wasn't nearly as bad as others." "No wonder my parents got so angry with me; I was a hard child to raise." These self-protective statements serve to lessen the painful acknowledgment that their parents did not love them as they should have. They also serve to perpetuate destructive shame by minimizing the reality of their parents' evil behavior and by shifting responsibility for it. God calls us to walk in the truth (John 8:31–32; Ephesians 4:25; Titus 1:1). As we face the reality of our brokenness, we can begin to embrace the truth and reject the lies.

A Way to Heal

Facing the truth of past abuse and damage is necessary to mitigate and heal the ongoing effects of trauma. I noted in chapter 6 that unresolved past trauma often intrudes into the present through hyperarousal, intrusion, and numbing. These trauma effects are complex and involve largely involuntary responses to conscious and subconscious stimuli. These posttraumatic symptoms may continue for years, even decades, unless trauma and brokenness are faced. In the case of trauma, out of sight is not out of mind. Just because one has been able to repress past trauma doesn't mean it is no longer embedded in the brain, having a significant impact. As one trauma expert notes, "[Unresolved] trauma continues to intrude with visual, auditory, and/or other somatic reality on the lives of its victims. Again and again they relive the life-threatening experiences they have suffered, reacting in mind and body as though such events were still occurring."[9]

One of the axioms of trauma therapy is that healing from long-term trauma effects requires survivors to face the reality of the trauma and the way it affected them (their brokenness).[10] Hence, the goal of facing our brokenness is not to wallow in the past but to reclaim it in such a way that it loses its destructive grip on the present. In short, trauma symptoms are not healed by ignoring past trauma but by facing, processing, and reinterpreting the trauma.

A Way to Experience Healthy Relationships

Facing the truth and the pain of our past is also necessary in order to experience appropriate, healthy relationships. In other words, we must be honest about others' sins against us in the past in order to experience appropriate relationships in the present. As we relate in an appropriate manner with abusive people—setting boundaries, reconciling only when they have repented, and so forth—we minimize the risk of additional abuse to ourselves and others, and we increase the likelihood that they will be convicted of their sin. For instance, when Mindy kept denying the reality of Don's sexual abuse and the pain and loss she felt, it made it much easier for Don to continue to molest children.

VICTIMS AGAIN!

One of the many hard realities about abuse is that it is far more likely for abuse victims to be victimized again than for those who have never been abused to suffer abuse in the first place.[11] There are many dynamics that cause abuse victims to be more vulnerable, including shame that makes victims feel unworthy to set boundaries or to have relationships with healthy people; a sense of powerlessness that makes victims feel unable to challenge others' hurtful behavior; emotional numbing, or constriction, which makes it difficult for victims to recognize internal signals warning them that another person is unsafe. Healing from all of these unhealthy dynamics requires abuse victims to face their brokenness, for only then will they begin to come alive, to overcome shame, and to hear and respond appropriately to their feelings.

Recently in our community we had a tragic example of these dynamics.[12] A couple was honeymooning at an upscale resort hotel in Scottsdale. In the middle of the night, the couple reportedly got into a fight, and the groom strangled his new bride to death with his bare hands. The groom was said to have fled to Las Vegas, leaving his wife's body in the hotel room. He was tracked down the next day by police and charged with second-degree murder. The irony of this horrible crime is that the day the couple flew to Arizona to begin their honeymoon, the groom was to appear in court in Michigan on charges of domestic violence against this same woman he had just married. While it's inconceivable that a woman would marry a man who only a month before had been arrested for assaulting her in her apartment, it is consistent with the fact that women who have not faced the brokenness of past abuse often aren't able to think or feel in a healthy manner and thus end up placing themselves in grave danger.

Additionally, parents who themselves were victims of childhood abuse compromise their ability to protect their own children unless they have dealt forthrightly with their own abuse.[13] While we must be careful not to blame mothers for their husbands' abusive behavior, many researchers note that the wives of incestuous men are often described by their daughters as weak and sickly, with no sense of power or boundary setting with regard to their abusive husbands. This is often due in part to their own histories of physical or sexual victimization, which they haven't fully faced or overcome.[14]

In essence, women who were victimized in childhood can get locked into a long-term victim role that can keep them from having the courage, strength, and insight to protect their own children. Sadly, denial of one's own victimization will often increase the likelihood of victimization in the next generation. Anna Salter brilliantly describes the ways a mother's denial can put her own children at risk:

> The impact of denial will often affect not only the survivor's life but her attitude toward any molested child with whom she comes into contact. Her own children are particularly at risk, given that she is likely to identify with them and project her defenses onto their situation. If she dissociated during her own abuse, she may dissociate upon evidence of her child's. If she did not report her own, she may equate reporting with public shame and be furious at her child for reporting. If she insisted that her own abuse was not abuse and that her perpetrator was not really an offender, she may mislabel and rationalize her child's abuse. If she denied the impact of her own abuse, she may follow suit one generation later.[15]

In short, unless we face the pain and truth of our past victimization, we will not be able to experience healthy relationships in the present.

BIBLICAL EXAMPLES OF FACING BROKENNESS

The story of Joseph powerfully models the importance, for both personal and relational health, of facing the brokenness of abuse. After God miraculously delivered Joseph from prison and gave him an exalted position in the Egyptian government, Joseph did not simply ignore his painful past. Rather, he honestly faced the past abuse he had suffered some fifteen years earlier. He didn't deny or repress his emotional pain, but he entered into the ache of his brothers' past abuse and present distrust by weeping bitterly (Genesis 45:2; 50:15–19).

Furthermore, Joseph repeatedly orchestrated events to force his brothers to come to grips with their abuse (Genesis 42:14–20; 44:1–5). Joseph didn't execute his plan (hiding a cup in Benjamin's grain sack and accusing his brothers of stealing, making them leave Benjamin behind) simply to torment them; rather, he sought to force them to come to grips with the reality of their sinful behavior, a reality he had not repressed or minimized. Joseph's boldness in facing the truth of his brothers' abuse and its personal impact prompted his brothers to do the same, causing them to repent.

Similarly, the apostle Paul didn't deny or repress the way a man named Alexander had harmed him, but he was honest about how he had been harmed. He warned Timothy, "Alexander the coppersmith did me much harm. . . . Be on guard against him yourself" (2 Timothy 4:14–15). In being honest about how he had been painfully mistreated, Paul was able to protect Timothy. Godliness requires that we face the truth of our past abuse. It is only then that shame and distortions can be healed and appropriate relationships can be established.

THE DYNAMICS OF DENIAL

We tend to come up with different ways to avoid facing the truth of our past abuse and resultant damage. Since facing our brokenness is necessary for spiritual, emotional, and relational health, any technique we consciously or unconsciously utilize to avoid the truth of our abuse must be identified and rooted out. Anna Salter provides a helpful continuum to explain the abuse denial techniques commonly employed by victims (see below).[16] The continuum moves from left to right from greater to lesser levels of denial.

Amnesia	Does not admit event	Event was not abuse	Event was not important	Event is not important

At the extreme end of the denial continuum is traumatic amnesia, in which abuse victims have no conscious memory of the abuse.[17] While some find the concept of blocked memories too incredible to accept, this is, as I noted in chapter 6, a real phenomena that has been irrefutably documented. It is most common in childhood abuse victims who are experiencing ongoing abuse, but it can also occur in adult victims of trauma, including those who experience combat, prison camp internment, accidents, and natural disasters.[18] Traumatic amnesia is technically not a denial technique, for "technique" typically denotes a conscious, deliberate strategy; by definition, amnesia is a lack of memory, and hence doesn't involve fully conscious, deliberate denial. Nevertheless, it is a form of denial in that it involves experiences too traumatic to be remembered.[19]

Next on the denial continuum is remembering but not admitting the event—a state of great denial but less than amnesia. Victims who employ this technique have memories of abuse, but they refuse to admit those memories into their world; they reject them by pretending that these incidents happened to someone else or by so compartmentalizing their abuse experiences that it is as though they happened in another life.[20]

The next technique is admitting that the event happened in your world but relabeling it as nonabusive. Survivors who employ this technique say such things as, "My father didn't abuse me; he was just physical with me sometimes," or "My uncle didn't molest me; he just touched me sexually." Denying that an abusive event was really abusive is so common that abuse counselors are advised not to just ask their counselees if they were abused in childhood but to ask such questions as, "As a child, were you ever touched in such a way that made you feel uncomfortable?" "As a child, did anyone ever ask you to do something sexual, such as [identify a specific action] ?"[21]

The next technique, involving less denial, is admitting that the event happened and was abusive but asserting that the event wasn't really important. Abuse survivors who admit they were abused will often distance themselves from the pain by confidently maintaining that they weren't really affected by the abuse; they see themselves as resilient. I've heard several abuse survivors employ this denial technique, acknowledging how their abusive homes had created long-term damage in their siblings while denying it had a negative impact on them.

The final step on the continuum is admitting that one was abused and that it had an impact in the past but denying that it is significant in the present. Individuals who experienced chronic abuse in childhood will often acknowledge they had a horrible, painful childhood, but they'll assert that their past abuse has little impact on their current personal or interpersonal life.

All of these denial techniques allow an abuse victim to deny the full painful reality of their abuse and thus impede their healing and growth.[22]

A HEALING MODEL

I'll use the following model (see page 141) to frame the path to healing in the rest of *Mending the Soul*. The bottom tier of this model represents the most unhealthy, destructive state. Here we find the greatest amount of hiding. In this domain, one is thoroughly disconnected in all relationships (with God, self, and others), which is often reflected in abusive and addictive behaviors.

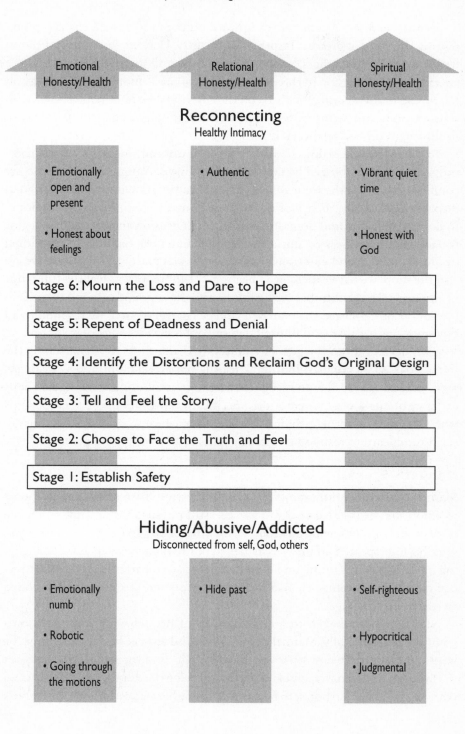

Emotional Honesty/Health

Relational Honesty/Health

Spiritual Honesty/Health

Reconnecting
Healthy Intimacy

• Emotionally open and present

• Honest about feelings

• Authentic

• Vibrant quiet time

• Honest with God

Stage 6: Mourn the Loss and Dare to Hope

Stage 5: Repent of Deadness and Denial

Stage 4: Identify the Distortions and Reclaim God's Original Design

Stage 3: Tell and Feel the Story

Stage 2: Choose to Face the Truth and Feel

Stage 1: Establish Safety

Hiding/Abusive/Addicted
Disconnected from self, God, others

• Emotionally numb

• Robotic

• Going through the motions

• Hide past

• Self-righteous

• Hypocritical

• Judgmental

Health increases as one moves upward on the model, with the top representing the state of greatest health and maturity. Here we find a reconnection with God, self, and others, reflected in healthy and satisfying intimacy. I've charted this progression in three key domains of life—emotional, spiritual, and relational. In this chapter, I'll focus on the emotional realm. Chapter 9 will concentrate on reconnecting with God (spiritual realm), and chapter 10 on reconnecting with others (relational realm).

In the emotional realm, the state of greatest unhealthiness is a state of thorough denial characterized by emotional numbness. Among believers who are conditioned to "do the right thing," this unhealthy state is often evidenced in dispassionate, robotic behavior in which individuals "go through the motions" to do their spiritual and domestic duty but lack passion and joy. As one begins to face the brokenness of abuse and to grow in emotional health, emotional deadness recedes, and emotional vibrancy takes its place. The healthier we are and the more we have experienced healing, the more we will feel the full range of emotions. The healthy believer is able to acknowledge and respond to the feelings of his or her heart. Ultimately, as image bearers of God, we respond to all our emotions because God himself demonstrates a wide range of emotions.

This doesn't mean the goal of counseling is simply to feel. That's only the initial goal. As we grow in emotional health, we *will* feel more, and as we do so, we'll increasingly be able to recognize what our emotions are telling us about the state of our souls. Our emotions specifically tell us about our relationships with God and with other people.[23] Healthy people hear what their emotions are saying and learn to respond to these insights in an appropriate manner.

Manuel's Story

Manuel offers a helpful example of the progression from emotional deadness to emotional health. Manuel was a successful physician who came to see me after he was caught having an affair with a nurse in his office. Manuel, who had been having repeated affairs, was ashamed but had no idea why he kept engaging in them. He was numb and evidenced almost no emotions in the first several counseling sessions. He had little motivation and wasn't sure he intended to stay in his marriage.

Slowly Manuel began to face the reality of his behavior and of his own painful past. Gradually, Manuel began to feel and to hear his heart. In time, he wept, not just over being separated from his wife and three children, but over the fact that he had never felt like a real man during the duration of their fifteen-year marriage. He also began to realize that his father's physical and verbal abuse had created deep insecurities regarding his masculinity, and that getting drunk and having affairs was his subconscious attempt to bolster his fragile male ego. Furthermore, he gradually began to feel how much he had distrusted God, who seemed just as whimsical and unsafe as his abusive father had been.

As Manuel began to face the impact of his father's physical abuse on his view of God and himself, the lights started to go on. He came to recognize how he had pulled away from God and from his wife. For the first time, he recognized that, when he felt contempt toward others, he was ultimately displaying his own insecurities about his competence and worth. He learned to go to his heavenly Father with these insecurities and ask forgiveness for his sinful cruelty to others. Manuel learned to recognize feelings of fear and distrust toward God, and he repented of his attempts to "bargain with God." Eventually, Manuel learned to share his true self, including his insecurities, with a small circle of trusted friends. He found this gave him the sense of connection he had always longed for but could never find in alcohol, pornography, or affairs.

In time, Manuel learned to hear the faintest stirrings of his heart and to listen to what they were telling him. One breakthrough came as he watched an elderly couple in a park sharing a cookie. He wept as he told of seeing this couple in the sunset of their life enjoy such a simple pleasure together. It stirred in his heart a longing to experience more of God's gifts and helped him realize how much he had missed by numbing his emotions.

That year Manuel experienced more joy and intimacy than he had known in his previous forty years of life combined. He also experienced more sorrow, but his emotional pain no longer drove him to destructive addictions but to his heavenly Father and to his accountability partners. Manuel still mourns the loss created by his abusive father, but in coming alive and facing his brokenness, he's no longer driven by the impact of his father's abuse. Rather, by God's grace, the pain of his abuse was used to drive him to a new level of intimacy and emotional life.

Walking in the Truth: Stages in Healing

Walking in the truth is much easier said than done, so some specifics should be helpful. I'm framing the path of walking in the truth in six specific stages. These stages are roughly, but not strictly, sequential. As one begins a particular stage, a previous stage(s) must often be solidified.

Stage 1: Establish Safety

It is exceedingly difficult for abuse victims to give up their defense mechanisms and come alive to healthy intimacy when their safety is still threatened.

Powerlessness makes deadness and denial extremely enticing—particularly for those who have experienced chronic abuse. Thus, the first step in trauma recovery is establishing safety.[24]

It's hard for those who haven't lived with an abusive husband or parent to appreciate the emotional and psychological toll of chronic abuse. Imagine the child who goes to bed every night wondering if tonight will be the night her father will fondle her. Imagine the wife who never knows when her husband will come home from work in a blind rage. Imagine the families who can never relax on the weekends or the holidays because that's when Mom or Dad gets drunk and abusive. Even if the abuse only takes place a fraction of the time, the abused child or battered spouse is constantly on the alert, never knowing when the next eruption will occur. Thus, parents and church leaders must be particularly sensitive to the need for abuse victims to have a safe environment in which they can begin to heal, where they can regain that crucial sense of power and control over their lives that abuse strips them of.[25]

While God can and does use suffering to build character, there is no virtue in enduring avoidable suffering. In fact, the Bible teaches that we should avoid abuse and seek safety whenever possible. Jesus repeatedly avoided physical assault and sought safety by hiding (John 8:59), by maintaining physical separation from his abusers (Matthew 12:14–15; John 11:53–54), and by eluding them (John 10:31, 39). Other godly individuals in the Bible, such as David and Paul, also repeatedly fled from physical abusers (1 Samuel 19:12; 27:1; Acts 9:22–25; 14:5–6; 17:8–10, 14). Creating safety for those traumatized by abuse has a strong biblical basis. The Bible frequently instructs those in positions of power to ensure the safety and protection of those who are vulnerable (Psalm 82:3–4; Proverbs 24:11–12; Isaiah 1:17).

Mary, the missionary daughter whose story was told at the beginning of chapter 1, wrote a poem two years after her initial abuse disclosure. At this point, Mary had only begun to heal, but her poem articulates the importance of safety in her healing journey. She wrote the poem to thank her immediate family members and close friends, who had repeatedly protected her from the family members who were denying the cousin's sexual abuse.

The Starting Place
I have finally found a place to start over,
When I thought that there was no way
And nobody would love me again
Because of what I'd done

And what he did to me.
I have found it.
I'm still not beautiful,
I'm still not smart,
I still don't know how to trust or how to love you,
But you have given me the chance I wanted,
The chance I needed,
When nobody else cared
To let me start over.
You saw me and loved me
Just the way I am.
I have found a shelter in you.
I have found a best friend in you.
I have found hope in you.
I have found a love in you.
Thank you for giving me a place to start over.

When she wrote this poem, Mary had much yet to sort out. She still didn't feel beautiful or smart. She didn't yet know how to trust others, but the safety her loved ones offered opened the way for her to begin to heal and grow.

Stage 2: Choose to Face the Truth and Feel

After establishing safety, one of the first things abuse victims must do to begin to heal is to decide that, based on the truth of Scripture, it's better to face the pain than to numb it, and it's better to face the truth than to distort reality. This is a preliminary stage to emotional vibrancy and cognitive health.

Abuse victims cannot choose, by an act of the will, to immediately eradicate emotional numbing or mental distortions. Even if they are convicted that they need to stop numbing and denying, they cannot simply conjure up feelings or establish clear perceptions of reality. In the early stages of healing, abuse victims rarely comprehend how deeply abuse has influenced their perceptions and their feelings. Consequently, this healing stage involves *choosing to begin the journey* of emotional life and truth. It involves a deliberate choice to no longer suppress the truth and a willingness to enter into whatever feelings surface as one abandons denial of past abuse. For many survivors, it's the most terrifying step imaginable, for they have spent their entire lives and enormous amounts of psychological energy keeping the gnawing truth and painful feelings at arm's length. They fear that once they start processing and feeling the painful feelings, it may unleash an emotional avalanche that will never stop.

Thus, choosing to face the truth and feel involves a deliberate act of worship based on God's trustworthiness and the recognition that our own human resources are utterly inadequate to heal us. We see this in Proverbs 3:5–6, where the writer admonishes us to "trust in the LORD with all your heart and do not lean on your own understanding. In all your ways acknowledge Him, and He will make your paths straight." As we begin to lean on God and not ourselves, he promises to provide "healing to your body and refreshment to your bones" (Proverbs 3:8). The Hebrew word in Proverbs 3:5 for "trust" *(bāṭaḥ)* indicates complete reliance, which results in security and confidence.[26] It is often contrasted with the false security that comes from trusting in humans, riches, idols, military powers, religion, or one's own righteousness.[27]

The following picture drawn by an adolescent boy describes his emotional and spiritual condition after being exposed to sexual abuse in a church (see figure 12). It vividly illustrates both the tendency of abuse victims to lean on themselves for their healing and the inadequacy and futility of such a strategy. The picture is titled "Weathered and Tired." Written on the boy's face and body are various phrases that articulate drastic reliance on self for healing and protection: "I *have* to hold back the darkness." "I must endure." "I have to be strong." "I have to withstand." "I cannot fail." Around his heart is written "Make the hurting stop!" Sadly, no matter how much energy he puts into this effort, he cannot endure, he cannot be strong enough, he cannot hold back the darkness, and he cannot heal his hurting heart. Only God can!

Denial and deadness may provide temporary relief, but they can never heal us or make us feel secure. They are feeble substitutes that will only make us more tired and more disconnected from God and others. Healing requires that, in an act of faith, we turn from reliance on human strategies for healing and turn to God by choosing to face the truth and feel.

Stage 3: Tell and Feel the Story

This stage is one of the most extensive and demanding aspects of walking in the truth. Abuse survivors generally have finely honed skills for avoiding the painful truth about their abuse. Thus, sorting out the truth is difficult because a survivor's life story often tends, as one abuse expert puts it, "to resemble a fairy tale rather than history."[28]

Getting at the truth is often a multilayered process. One of the best ways to begin the journey is to start constructing and telling one's own abuse story. This is often done in a clinical setting with a professional counselor,[29] but telling one's story to safe, mature nonprofessionals can also be very beneficial. This is affirmed

Figure 12

by Galatians 6:2, which says that in the body of Christ, we are to "bear one another's burdens." If revisiting one's abuse becomes too overwhelming—triggering unmanageable trauma symptoms—professional counseling is in order.

    There's no single correct way to construct a person's abuse story. A good starting point is to build a timeline of abuse events, recounting what happened at what age by whom. This list should then be fleshed out by noting the responses of family members and caregivers to the abuse, since this is a crucial element to one's story. If family members perpetrated abuse or contributed to the damage (which is often the case), then a major part of constructing the abuse story is to fashion a family history, noting not only family members' roles in the abuse but also other patterns of destructive behavior they engaged in.

Abuse survivors often tenaciously resist constructing a family history. After all, abusive families vigorously indoctrinate and intimidate abuse victims into keeping family secrets. Furthermore, Christians often feel that chronicling family dysfunction and sin is disrespectful and mean. But clarifying the truth about one's family is neither inherently disrespectful nor mean. Only when abuse survivors see the truth can they reject unwarranted shame and guilt, recognize lies, awaken emotionally, and take appropriate responsibility for their own behavior.

Unless we prayerfully reflect on the truth about our own families, we'll most likely repeat the dysfunction. This principle is found in psychological research literature, but, most important, it's found in the Bible. The clearest example is seen in the history of the Hebrew kings, most of whom were ungodly and led Israel and Judah into idolatry and evil. They had not only a broad societal influence for evil but also an immediate familial influence. For example, we read, "[King Abijam] walked in all the sins of his father" (1 Kings 15:3). "And [King Amon] did evil in the sight of the LORD, as Manasseh his father had done. For he walked in all the way that his father had walked" (2 Kings 21:20–21). Other passages highlight the intergenerational nature of family sins, noting that kings did evil according to all that their fathers (plural) had done (2 Kings 23:32, 37).

The rare kings who broke from the ungodliness of their fathers had to consciously assess the family history, sin, and dysfunction and, with God's help, choose to go against the family traditions and influences. King Hezekiah's father was Ahaz, a very wicked man. Hezekiah broke from the family behavioral patterns he had seen modeled and called the nation to do the same: "Do not be like your fathers and your brothers, who were unfaithful to the LORD" (2 Chronicles 30:7). Godly king Asa actually deposed his own mother from the position of queen due to her practice of idolatry—a practice she had learned from her ancestors (1 Kings 15:12–13). In short, it is not unkind or ungodly to thoroughly assess the truth about one's own family.[30] It is necessary for emotional and spiritual health.

Abuse survivors need to do more than just tell the facts of the story; they need to feel the appropriate emotions as well. This is best done with the help of a safe listener who can reflect back to the abuse survivor an appropriate emotional response to the abuse story. For the survivor, the initial processing of abuse memories tends to be more factual than emotional—at least in part because abuse constricts and distorts emotions that were too terrible and overwhelming to feel at the time of the abuse. In the early stages, one often hears survivors tell their tragic stories of abuse with little or no emotion, recounting the facts of their abuse as though they were reading a weather report. Sometimes survivors even smile or laugh as they tell of being raped or beaten.

Speaking the facts is an essential first step, but healing comes as one tells the facts and then integrates that truth with the appropriate emotional response.[31] One of the best ways to do this is through journaling the abuse event(s), with the purpose of entering into the feeling associated with the past abuse. In other words, survivors need to reflect on the abusive event and on what they were feeling when it happened. Dissociation and emotional constriction may have taken place so quickly and thoroughly at the time of the abuse that a survivor may find it nearly impossible to identify those past emotions. In this case, it may help to picture a child the same age he or she was when the abuse took place, to imagine what that child would feel if he or she experienced the same abuse, and to share their reflections with a safe, empathetic listener.

Samantha was a forty-five-year-old professional musician who entered counseling for relational and sexual struggles that had haunted her for years. She desperately wanted to find victory over her shameful sins that seemed so intractable. In spite of her natural beauty and warm personality, she had never experienced healthy, intimate friendships, and she couldn't embrace her God-given femininity because of the overwhelming shame.

Samantha found it difficult to process her feelings about her family history. She was finally able to recount the abuse she had experienced from her father, but she was disconnected from her emotional response. She experienced a huge breakthrough when her counselor asked her to collect pictures of herself when she was a child. She was then asked to reflect on what she felt as she looked at her childhood pictures and to think about what that child went through. Looking at a cheerful picture of herself at three years of age, Samantha began to experience deep emotion for the cute little girl who had subsequently been abused. This allowed her to begin to come alive emotionally and to identify the shame that had been cemented into her heart as a result of the abuse.

As Samantha continued to emotionally process her abuse history, she wrote the following poem about the little girl she saw in the portrait. She titled the poem "Reaching Out" because, as she began to connect with her feelings surrounding her childhood abuse, she came to realize she had been a vulnerable little girl with emotional needs as a child. She came to realize her abuse had caused her to feel shame and self-loathing for the very needs that came from being made in God's image.

Reaching Out

Who will cry for this little girl?
Who will quiet her tears of pain?
Who will reach for this little girl?
Who will shelter her from the rain?
Please won't you hold me and just let me cry,
Say words of comfort and wipe my sad eyes?
Please won't you play or just spend some time,
'Cause just being with me would be very fine.
I hear words of anger and I try ways to hide,
But the words are so cutting and they hurt deep inside.
I long for attention and for someone to care,
I feel like that's bad, so I hide away in despair.
I've learned to be strong, but I feel very weak.
O Lord, help me find the wholeness I seek.

In writing this poem, Samantha validated the painful feelings of her childhood abuse that had been locked away. She also began to validate her own self-worth and to shed the toxic shame created by the abuse. At this point, Samantha could move toward the next stage of facing the brokenness—the stage that involves correcting the distortions created by abuse.

Stage 4: Identify the Distortions and Reclaim God's Original Design

Satan uses abuse to create hideous distortions in our hearts and minds. It is understandable that children are unable to discern truth about their abuse, for they don't have the mental or emotional resources to do so. But God calls his adult children to boldly identify lies and not allow themselves to be led astray (Mark 13:5; Titus 3:3; 1 John 3:7). It's difficult for abuse victims to identify shame-based lies because they are so deeply embedded, have often been present for years, and rarely operate at a conscious level.[32] These lies are difficult to identify, let alone combat. Often abuse victims need the help of pastors, mature Christians with abuse experience, or even professional Christian counselors to identify their shame-based lies and distortions.

Most abuse survivors have come to believe numerous shame-based lies about God, themselves, and others.[33] Common shame-based lies about God include "I can't trust God because he didn't stop my abuse"; "God hates me"; "God is disgusted with me"; "God is punishing me for being such a horrible person." Common lies about others include "If others really knew who I am, they would reject me"; "You can't trust anyone; people will only hurt you"; "Men are all alike; all they want to do is use women"; "No decent man will ever want me." Abuse victims often believe lies about themselves such as "The abuse must have been my fault; I must have deserved it"; "I am permanently defective"; "My sexual urges show that I am disgusting and perverted"; "I don't deserve a decent guy; I would just ruin the relationship." All such lies are very damaging. Once the abuse survivor begins to identify the lies created by his or her abuse, the Bible can be used to challenge these lies.[34]

It's important to recognize that Satan creates distortions from abuse that revolve around our original (image of God) design. These distortions are often identifiable through shame and self-contempt. We noted in chapter 2 that being made in God's image creates powerful longings. Because one aspect of the image of God is the capacity for intimate relationships that mirror the Trinitarian relationships, when abuse fractures relational intimacy, victims' longings for relationship often cause them to conclude that *they* are the problem—that something defective in them must have caused their abuse.

Integral to the relational aspect of the image of God is our sexuality as male or female. Sexual abuse horribly distorts our sexuality, so that normal sexual urges are given a shameful interpretation. Abuse victims often find marital sexual relations to create shame. They often experience body loathing—rejecting the very body God gave them. Bodily sensations feel unsafe and dirty, so all physical pleasure is rejected. They may even become destructive to their own bodies through self-starvation or self-injury. Abuse victims must come to the point where they can accept that their longings for relationships and for love, their sexuality, their bodies, and their longings for affectionate touch are all beautiful aspects of God's original design. Under the lordship of Christ, each is sanctified and to be embraced.

Celestia has ministered to hundreds of men and women for the past thirteen years as a professional counselor. She often observes that when she encourages her clients to uncover the specific shame-based lies they've struggled with, they find that the lies are direct perversions of the best of their original design—the persons God had gifted them to be. For example, a thirty-year-old single professional woman described many shameful childhood memories involving public humiliation and verbal assault by her father when she "hammed it up" for the camera. As a child, she had an effervescent and vivacious personality easily detectable in the childhood pictures she brought to counseling. By age thirteen, this had all changed. She had become reclusive, and she no longer tried out for cheer squads or school sports teams. By age twenty-six, she was a hundred pounds overweight and completely shut down. She couldn't keep a job due to uncontrollable angry outbursts. She had never dated, and she hated her femininity—a fact she successfully hid. What impressed Celestia the most about this woman was her underlying beauty, sense of humor, and love of movement.

Celestia described their counseling sessions as a work of "finding buried treasure." Underneath the layers of shame was a cache of gold. As this woman began to grow and to reclaim God's original design, she took dance classes and volunteered to direct the church play. She began to unlock a door that had been shut for a very long time. She was undertaking a process of embracing those aspects of her personality and gifting that had previously been shamed. She was discovering her best self, created by God for his glory and her joy.

Stage 5: Repent of Deadness and Denial

We saw in chapter 6 that some aspects of stress trauma are automatic—not conscious—choices, especially in the early stages after the abuse. As abused children grow up and become adults, however, the psychological mechanisms they automatically employed in childhood to cope with the overwhelming trauma of abuse begin to become destructive patterns for which they must take moral responsibility. Dan Allender clarifies this progression from child self-protection to adult deadness and the resulting need for repentance:

> The function of self-protection must be seen in light of both dignity and depravity. The victim, at age nine, who learned to tune out the abuse by staring at a spot on the wall, must not be told with an insensitive snarl that her choice was self-protective and wrong. I affirm her choice to survive. I am proud that she found a way to minimize the damage and survive to the next day. Honesty, however, acknowledges that her adult adaptation of the child pattern is an outworking of her depravity, not her dignity. When, as an adult, she protects herself in relationship by tuning out, stiffening, detaching, or fleeing in connection between herself and another that deepens the potential for intense enjoyment (and thus vulnerability), she does more than assure her own survival. She sins against another and dismisses God's right to use her as His instrument of love and grace in the world.[35]

Abuse victims are tempted to deny and repress the truth about their abuse instead of taking the truth to God. They are tempted to cut themselves off from others, even though God has ordained the body of Christ to be a place of healing. They are tempted to deaden their feelings and hopes instead of worshiping and trusting the God who holds the future. Deadness and denial often become such ingrained patterns of behavior that abuse victims must carefully and prayerfully reflect on the ways they've sought to manage life on their terms. They must honestly assess how they've sinfully chosen denial over truth and death over life—and then choose to repent.

In noting that repentance is an important part of the healing process, I'm not saying 100 percent of all emotional numbness and denial is sinful. These are profoundly pervasive, innate defense mechanisms that are rarely developed consciously. Early on, they often provide a necessary defense from the overwhelming evil we have experienced. Clinicians Katherine Steele and Joanna Colrain explain how this happens in terms of dissociation (emotional shutdown):

> Dissociation is a universal survival response. When an experience is more than a child's mind can tolerate, he or she must escape. The human instinct to survive is paramount. When a being is small in size; dependent on others for nurturance, protection, and connection to the world; and unequipped to integrate abusive traumatic experiences (because of lack of experience and inadequate cognitive schema), he or she is left with no alternative except to dissociate. For survivors, dissociation is the way in which they have survived the intolerable.[36]

But what begins as a necessary defense mechanism will in time turn into a crutch, and a crutch can quickly turn into a sinful idol—anything to which we give our trust and allegiance other than the Lord God. While only God knows precisely where the lines are drawn for any given individual—lines that distinguish a necessary defense mechanism from a crutch or idol—the important thing is to recognize that such lines do exist. The Bible asserts that all humans are sinful and are naturally inclined to trust themselves, not God. Thus, we must ask God to show us how in our pain we have failed to trust him and have resorted to denial and deadness. As he reveals these patterns to us, we must turn from them, confess them as sin, and choose to embrace truth.

One of the great ironies of the Christian life is that the path of life is the path of death to self (Matthew 16:24–25). The way to save one's life is to lose it (Matthew 10:39). In Jeremiah 17:5–8, judgment is pronounced on those who put their trust in humans instead of in God. The prophet warns that those who rely on human strength in the day of trouble will be like a scraggly bush in the barren desert; they won't even be able to recognize prosperity when it comes. They may be able to survive, but just barely. They will not experience life, vibrancy, or fruitfulness. What an accurate description of those who, in the midst of their pain, decide to manage the pain on their terms instead of turning to their Creator! In our effort to shield ourselves from pain, we end up shielding ourselves from life, joy, and intimacy with God and others. In the midst of trying to run our universes, we won't be able to recognize prosperity when it lies at our feet. Self-protective deadness keeps us from tasting God's sufficiency and goodness.

The path to overcoming deadness is the recognition of our utter spiritual impotence. Deadness is the reaction to a trauma that feels so overwhelming the only way we know how to deal with it is to retreat and pull away from ourselves and our longings. Denial is the reaction to a world too dark and painful to face. So through denial we create a pseudoworld, a pseudohistory, and a pseudo-family we can live with.

We *do* face overwhelming forces. Evil *is* too big for us—both the evil around us and the sin within us. But this is exactly where faith comes in. Instead of trying to manage on our own terms a world that feels out of control, in faith we turn to God. Recognizing our spiritual poverty, we cling to Jesus as our only hope for life and health (John 6:68). We cling to the promises that he is the deliverer and the redeemer (Colossians 1:13–14). We cling to his assurance that he will finish the good work he began in us (Philippians 1:6). In short, abuse survivors must dare to hope on the basis of naked faith in Jesus Christ, who died to give abundant life to the dead (John 10:10).

Stage 6: Mourn the Loss and Dare to Hope

One of the surest signs an abuse survivor is healing and coming alive is that, after staring straight into the ugly vortex of his or her past trauma and pain, he or she can mourn the losses and yet look toward the future with hope. Mourning the losses occurs throughout the healing process, as well as at the end of the process.[37] Daring to hope, however, occurs in the latter stages of healing. As abuse victims continue to grow, come alive, and avoid denial, they increasingly have an accurate sense of their losses. Denial, on the other hand, causes victims to minimize the nature and damage of abuse.

Mourning loss is an honest response to what has actually happened, and it's also necessary for thorough healing. Only as we admit and mourn the losses can we continue to walk in truth. Back at the beginning of this chapter, we saw that, because Lance and Mindy didn't acknowledge and mourn the many losses created by Don's pedophilia, they continued year after year in denial and deadness.

Because abuse creates such deep wounds in so many areas of life, there are many losses for survivors to recognize and to mourn. For instance, survivors often need to mourn the loss of their innocence, their virginity, their parents' love, their childhood, their glowing image of their family, intimacy with other family members, their spouses' love and fidelity, and their reputations.

The propriety of mourning the losses of abuse is nowhere seen more clearly than in the book of Lamentations, one of the darkest, rawest reflections of grief in all of Scripture. This short book consists of five poems of lament in the form similar to funeral dirges. It begins with an emphatic expression of grief ("How lonely sits the city that was full of people!") and ends with an unanswered implied question about whether God had permanently rejected his people ("Restore us ... , unless You have utterly rejected us and are exceedingly angry with us").

While for many Christians, Lamentations is an obscure little book in the Old Testament with no modern relevance, it has played a very important role in Jewish religious practice. In particular, it has helped people deal with overwhelming losses caused by evil and abuse. In Jewish tradition, from ancient times until the present, Lamentations is read on Tisha b'Av, the annual day of fasting that commemorates the destruction of the temple by the Babylonians in 586 BC. In fact, it may well be that Jeremiah wrote this short book specifically for this annual day of fasting and mourning.[38]

It's hard for modern-day Gentiles to appreciate the depth of loss experienced by Jeremiah when the brutal Babylonians besieged Jerusalem, starved its inhabitants so that parents were reduced to eating their own children, tore down the city walls, demolished the temple, raped the women, publicly executed the civic leaders, and deported most of the remaining Jews to Mesopotamia, hundreds of miles away.[39] This was literally the loss of everything the Jews held dear and sacred. In the face of devastating, incalculable personal and national loss caused by evil abusers, the godly response was not to deny but to acknowledge one's grief and to mourn the loss.[40] This is exactly why Lamentations was inspired by God as sacred Scripture—it teaches us how to mourn overwhelming losses and yet find hope in God.[41]

Throughout this little book Jeremiah is unabashed about his grief and his anguish: "My eyes fail because of tears, my spirit is greatly troubled; my heart is poured out on the earth because of the destruction of the daughter of my people, when little ones and infants faint in the streets of the city" (2:11). He is very specific in recounting and mourning Israel's many losses, including the loss of their ability to worship, the loss of dignity before their enemies, children's loss of parents, the loss of city and homeland, the loss of freedom, the loss of virginity, the loss of peace and happiness, the loss of health, and the loss of life.[42]

Yet, interestingly, it is after some of his fiercest laments against God ("He has broken my teeth with gravel; He has made me cower in the dust"—Lamentations 3:16) that Jeremiah finds hope. In the midst of facing his grief and mourning his losses, Jeremiah suddenly declares, "This I recall to my mind, therefore I have hope. The LORD's lovingkindnesses indeed never cease, for His compassions never fail. They are new every morning; great is your faithfulness" (3:21–23).

It is only when we have the courage to truly face the hurt, disappointment, and loss created by abuse that we meet God face-to-face. Ironically, mourning the losses from past abuse allows us to meet God in the present and provides hope for the future.[43] As abuse survivors learn to face their brokenness, they can meet God in the midst of their pain and loss, and in meeting God, they can find miraculous hope for the future.

chapter 9

※

rebuilding intimacy
with God

In 1880 the immortal Russian novelist Fyodor Dostoyevsky penned *The Brothers Karamazov*, a literary masterpiece described by many as the greatest novel ever written. It's a complex tale of a troubled family with a "wretched and depraved" father who is eventually murdered by one of his sons. Dostoyevsky used this novel to probe some of life's most vexing questions, particularly the question of how a good, all-powerful God could allow widespread, hideous child abuse.

In this novel, Dostoyevsky expresses many of his own spiritual struggles. Given the fact that Dostoyevsky's father had been an abusive alcoholic surgeon who was so cruel that his serfs murdered him, it's no wonder that Dostoyevsky agonized over how one who had witnessed or experienced child abuse could ever become intimate with God.

Dostoyevsky employs two of the novel's main characters—rationalistic, skeptical Ivan and his idealistic, religious brother, Alyosha—to articulate this dilemma. In a chapter titled "Rebellion," Ivan mercilessly presses Alyosha with the horror of rampant abuse. First he recounts how the Turks ravaged villages, raped women, and bayoneted live babies while their mothers watched in horror. Then he tells the story of a "well-educated, cultured [European] gentleman" who sadistically beat his seven-year-old daughter with a rod from a tree. The man was delighted the rod still had knots in it. He proudly declared that the knots would "add to the stinging effect" and proceeded to beat the little girl for one, then five, then ten minutes straight. The pitiful little child screamed and screamed until she was gasping for air and could only whimper, "Ah, papa, papa, papa dear." The father was prosecuted for assaulting his daughter but was acquitted by a jury that declared flogging a child to be a private matter.

Ivan later tells the story of an eight-year-old Russian boy, who, while playing in a courtyard, accidentally hit a general's dog with a rock and injured its leg. The general responded by setting his hunting dogs on the boy, killing him in front of his own mother. Ivan ends his discourse by boldly declaring that if the suffering of innocent children is the price, or "ticket," for a relationship with God, then he will have to pass. He issues this protest:

> We cannot afford to pay so much for a ticket [for admittance into heaven]. And so I hasten to return the ticket I've been sent. If I'm honest, it is my duty to return it as long as possible before the show. And that's just what I'm trying to do, Alyosha. It isn't that I reject God: I am simply returning Him most respectfully the ticket price that would entitle me to a seat.[1]

Few who have experienced abuse are as bold as Ivan Karamazov in declaring their unwillingness to relate to God. But as I noted in the previous chapter, while abuse victims tend to respond to God in three different ways (rejecting, withholding, or cowering), the end result is quite similar: intimacy with God is shattered.

The estrangement from God that abuse victims experience need not be final, however. As vehemently as Dostoyevsky protested the injustice of child abuse and as graphically as he reflected on its horrors, he eventually overcame this obstacle to his faith. In fact, as one of Dostoyevsky's biographers recounts, it was while Dostoyevsky was suffering abusive imprisonment and exile in Siberia that he had a dramatic and intimate encounter with Christ that remained with him for the rest of his life.

Dostoyevsky had been arrested on political charges, convicted, and sentenced to die. He was forced to dig his own grave and then was ushered to the place of execution. Seconds before he was to be executed, his sentence was commuted, and he was sent to prison in Siberia where he witnessed and experienced widespread human misery. Dostoyevsky ended up spending almost a decade in Siberia in prison and then in exile. Instead of driving him away from God, these experiences drove him to God. His biographer summarizes the spiritual result of Dostoyevsky's experiences in Siberia: "Amidst inhuman sufferings, in a struggle with doubt and negation, faith in God was won."[2]

Fyodor Dostoyevsky demonstrates that while abuse often shatters intimacy with God, its effects need not be permanent. Even victims of severe, chronic abuse can rebuild intimacy with God.

THE SATANIC STRATEGY

Spiritual reconnection is a process that typically takes much time and energy. I want to note four foundational activities for abuse survivors to reconnect with God. To put these strategies in their proper context, I must briefly reflect on

Satan's strategy. We saw in chapter 1 that abuse has been rampant throughout history largely because Satan is the most powerful evil being in the universe. He does not have the power to create, but he delights in destroying and perverting all of the good things created by God. He particularly takes pleasure in distorting and destroying faith in God. This was seen in the very first human sin recorded in Genesis 3:1–5.

Here's Satan's cunning, three-pronged temptation strategy:

The Tactic	Biblical Dialogue
Question God's word	"Did God really say ... ?"
Discredit God's word	"If you eat the fruit you won't die."
Malign God's character	"God knows if you eat you'll become like him."

Adam and Eve took the bait, distrusted God, and shattered the relationship with their loving Creator. In the case of abuse victims, Satan continually seeks to corrode spiritual intimacy by applying this threefold strategy:

Tactic	Internal Dialogue
He uses the damage of abuse to cause victims to begin to doubt God's word.	"Surely the Bible doesn't teach you can't have sex with your boyfriend. After all, that's all you're good for."
He plays on the effects of trauma to discredit God's word.	"John 3:16 isn't true for you. You're too disgusting for God to love you."
He delights in using the evil that abuse survivors have experienced to malign God's character.	"You can't trust God. He is either impotent or mean—or maybe both. After all, he didn't stop your father from raping you. Maybe God doesn't even exist."

Satan uses the specific effects of abuse trauma to facilitate his three-pronged spiritual disruption strategy. He especially uses emotional numbing (constriction), powerlessness, shame, and a sense of betrayal as ways to disconnect survivors from God.[3] People who are emotionally constricted have great difficulty being intimate with God (or humans) because they are shut down. Those who have a great sense of powerlessness are often afraid of God, fearing he can't be trusted. Those who are filled with shame have such a warped view of God's character that they hide from him and cannot become intimate. Those who feel deeply betrayed are drawn to protect themselves by withdrawing; they don't trust or give themselves to others. Thus, Satan uses all of these trauma effects to keep people from understanding, loving, and trusting their heavenly Father.

In view of Satan's strategy and the specific effects of abuse, the following four activities are essential.

ESSENTIAL ACTIVITIES FOR RECONNECTING WITH GOD

Wrestling with God

As a pastor and more recently as a seminary professor, I've spent much of my adult life trying to help people deepen their walk with God. In my early years of ministry, I believed the spiritual growth process was quite simple. Teach people to have regular devotions, to pray, to build spiritual accountability and Christian fellowship, and—presto—they will soon grow to love and trust God. Much like planting seeds in the springtime, as long as the right nutrients, water, and sunshine are present (Scripture, prayer, Christian fellowship), spiritual growth is predictable and imminent. My spiritual growth formula was straightforward and foolproof. If the formula didn't work and an individual who was given the ingredients didn't soon experience the "abundant spiritual life" but continued to have doubts and struggles, the only logical conclusion was that he or she was rebellious or sinful.

But that was then. Two-plus decades of life have stripped me of pat formulas and easy answers. I've buried too many godly people who prayed for healing, counseled too many devastated abuse survivors who experienced unspeakable horrors, and watched far too many evil abusers escape earthly justice to accept an easy, painless formula for spiritual growth. Over twenty years ago, in my last semester of seminary, Celestia suffered a catastrophic ski injury that drove both of us to the depths of depression. Since then, she has endured seventeen major surgeries and lives with a chronic, incurable genetic disorder (which had led to her ski injury). I've often pled with God to heal my dear wife. I have agonized over Celestia's physical pain and over loved ones' emotional pain resulting from abuse, while questioning why many abusers seem to beat and molest for decades with impunity.

I now realize spiritual growth is often a very messy process. From a human perspective, God can be utterly confusing and downright hurtful. His actions can prompt fear and anger just as surely as they can prompt love and trust. But he is a good God who wants nothing more than to bless his children. Over the years I have watched God shatter my expectations and my comfort, but I have also tasted more of his goodness and sweetness than I imagined possible. Our spiritual pilgrimage will often lead us through dark valleys of doubt and frustration—and that's particularly true for abuse survivors. In fact, when survivors begin to grow and heal, they often find that their doubts, frustrations, and anger toward God intensify. Survivors who haven't yet begun to heal are often so emotionally numb that they do not have negative feelings in general or negative feelings toward God in particular.

I'm aware that the paragraph I've just written will make some readers nervous. Am I just projecting my own negative experiences? Have I been unduly influenced by secular abuse literature? While I would be dishonest if I said I'm completely objective and my personal experiences of suffering, abuse, and evil haven't influenced me (surely they have), I now realize that my tidy spiritual growth formula was quite unbiblical. If some of my attempts to become intimate with God have become rather messy because abuse and suffering has raised painful doubts about God, I stand in good company. David, Jeremiah, Job, and Habakkuk were among the godliest people described in the Bible.[4] They suffered excruciating verbal, physical, and spiritual abuse. They walked with God. They became intimate with God. But their path to spiritual intimacy led through dark valleys of doubt and struggle. Fyodor Dostoyevsky articulated a similar spiritual pilgrimage, stating that his faith was not a naive, boyish faith but rather the result of "passing through a great furnace of doubts."[5]

Notice the following inspired statements of godly believers who voiced deep frustration, disappointment, and confusion toward God:

> *How long, O LORD? Will you forget me forever?*
> *How long will you hide your face from me?*
> *How long must I wrestle with my thoughts*
> *and every day have sorrow in my heart?*
> *How long will [you allow] my enemy [to] triumph over me?*
>
> Psalm 13:1–2 NIV

> *My God, my God, why have you forsaken me?*
> *Why are you so far from saving me,*
> *so far from the words of my groaning?*
> *O my God, I cry out by day, but you do not answer.*
>
> Psalm 22:1–2 NIV

God has turned me over to evil men
  and thrown me into the clutches of the wicked.
All was well with me, but he shattered me;
  he seized me by the neck and crushed me.

Job 16:11–12 NIV

Look around and see.
Is any suffering like my suffering
  that was inflicted on me,
that the LORD *brought on me*
  in the day of his fierce anger? . . .
Without pity the Lord has swallowed up
  all the dwellings of Jacob. . . .
Like an enemy [God] has strung his bow;
  his right hand is ready.
Like a foe he has slain
  all who were pleasing to the eye. . . .
Like a bear lying in wait,
  like a lion in hiding,
[God] dragged me from the path and mangled me
  and left me without help.

Lamentations 1:12; 2:2, 4; 3:10–11 NIV

These are raw passages that tend to receive little attention in many Christian traditions. It's difficult to acknowledge that godly believers can have such dark feelings. The truth that the path to spiritual intimacy often involves deep disappointment, pain, and frustration is foreign to a modern Christianity often fixated on a more palatable religion centered on feeling good, not on becoming truly godly.

One of the greatest emotional difficulties faced by abuse survivors is coping with shattered expectations and assumptions.[6] Abuse survivors who believe in a good, loving God face agonizing struggles to understand why God allowed their abuse, why he did not intervene, and why in his justice he did not annihilate their evil abusers. Those who have no belief in God experience no such spiritual turmoil.

We see this agonizing struggle in David, Job, and Jeremiah when they experienced evil and abuse. They were devastated and frustrated because God did not act as they had expected him to. But instead of withdrawing and giving up on God, they voiced their lament to him. In short, they wrestled with him.

It has been wisely stated that the opposite of love is not hate but apathy. Thus, when abuse victims refuse to shut down emotionally and to ignore their anger and frustration with God and instead insist on wrestling with God until he responds, they are on the path to rebuilding spiritual intimacy. Jacob's refusal to let go of the angel until God blessed him, even though it meant wrestling all night long and ultimately experiencing a dislocated hip, is a wonderful paradigm for abuse survivors to follow (Genesis 32:23–32).[7]

We must keep wrestling with God, refusing to be content with a shallow relationship. This doesn't mean, of course, that a person can expect to wrestle with God until God answers all questions and solves all problems to his or her complete satisfaction. It simply doesn't work that way. The Lord of the universe does not answer to his creation; nor could we comprehend many of the answers if he were to give them to us. But he is a God who desires to be pursued and who desires an intimate relationship with each of us.

Thus, wrestling with God means we refuse to give up on him. Giving up on God is what Job's wife suggested he do: "Curse God and die!" (Job 2:9). Rather, we keep coming to God over and over, articulating our hurt and frustration, straining to hear his response, and refusing to stop wrestling until he responds. This includes taking the risk that his response may well create new questions and frustrations.

We set the stage for reconnecting with God when we value our relationship with him so much that we refuse to pretend everything is OK when it is not. We refuse to pretend we trust him when we do not. We refuse to pretend we are happy with him when we are infuriated by his actions. Author Philip Yancey describes the process of wrestling with God, particularly as it is modeled by Job:

> One bold message in the Book of Job is that you can say anything to God. Throw at him your grief, your anger, your doubt, your bitterness, your betrayal, your disappointment—he can absorb them all. As often as not, spiritual giants of the Bible are shown *contending* with God. They prefer to go away limping, like Jacob, rather than to shut God out. . . . God can deal with every human response save one. He cannot abide the response I fall back on instinctively: an attempt to ignore him or treat him as though he does not exist. That response never once occurred to Job.[8]

When abuse survivors express negative feelings—especially about the God they want to love and trust but cannot—they are often shamed and told, "You shouldn't feel that way." Nothing could be farther from the truth. These biblical examples of godly individuals wrestling with God teach us we must not ignore God in our frustration. Wrestling with God is an express attempt to reconnect with God by being honest with him about our feelings and perceptions—not to indict God (which would be sinful) but to engage him, to communicate with him in the most honest manner so that trust and intimacy can be reestablished.

Thus, Job repeatedly stated that he longed to plead his case before God (Job 13:3, 15; 16:21; 23:3–4). In spite of the fact that God seemed to be strangely silent, Job was committed to keep wrestling, to not be silenced by the darkness, and to speak what he believed to be the truth as long as he had breath in his nostrils (23:17; 27:3–6). What was the result of this agonizing process of wrestling with God? Job himself acknowledged that, at the end of this painful ordeal, intimacy with God was graciously restored: "I have declared that which I did not understand, things too wonderful for me, which I did not know.... I have heard of You by the hearing of the ear; but now my eye sees You" (42:3, 5). In other words, he had moved from knowing about God intellectually to knowing and experiencing God personally.

Similarly, the Hebrew prophet Habakkuk provides us with a specific biblical example of what the process of wrestling with God looks like. Habakkuk was shocked and dismayed at the gross wickedness and abusive violence rampant in his society. Instead of simply backing away from a God who didn't seem to care about abuse and abuse victims, Habakkuk cried out, "How long, O LORD, will I call for help, and you will not hear? I cry out to You, 'Violence!' yet you do not save.... The wicked surround the righteous; therefore justice comes out perverted" (Habakkuk 1:2, 4).

God's answer to this cry for justice seemed to create even more injustice (Habakkuk 1:5–11), for God told the prophet he would judge the wicked Judeans by allowing the Babylonians (who were even more brutal and wicked) to invade and conquer Judah. After hearing God's confusing answer to his complaint for justice, Habakkuk refused to back away or to deaden his feelings. He kept bringing his confusion and hurt in full vintage to God: "Your eyes are too pure to approve evil.... Why do You look with favor on those who deal treacherously? Why are You silent when the wicked swallow up those more righteous than they?" (1:13).

At the end of his brief prophetic book, Habakkuk unabashedly experienced deep emotional pain at the impending judgment: "I heard and my inward parts trembled, at the sound my lips quivered. Decay enters my bones, and in my place

I tremble" (3:16). But in the midst of his wrestling—refusing to back away, being honest about his dark feelings—he encountered God, and God gave him hope: "I must wait quietly for the day of distress, for the people to arise who will invade us. Though the fig tree should not blossom and there be no fruit on the vines, though the yield of the olive should fail and the fields produce no food, though the flock should be cut off from the fold and there be no cattle in the stalls, yet I will exult in the LORD, I will rejoice in the God of my salvation. The Lord GOD is my strength" (3:16–19).

Habakkuk was not expressing a pie-in-the-sky, sappy religiosity. He had faced head-on his fears and his emotional pain, and God had met him in the crucible. Much like Dostoyevsky, Habakkuk came to develop deep faith in and vibrant intimacy with God, not by ignoring his hurt and frustration, but by actively wrestling with God. Wrestling with God is ultimately predicated on the conviction that he is a living, personal God who speaks to his children (John 10:3–4, 14–16, 27). Thus, as abuse survivors wrestle with God to rebuild intimacy with him, they should persistently and specifically ask him to communicate with them so that they can rebuild their shattered faith.

The story of Elenore provides an excellent example of this process. Elenore experienced horrible, chronic childhood abuse that resulted in disrupted adult relationships with family members, friends, and God. Elenore's progress in counseling had been very slow, as her abuse had created some of the most intense shame and self-loathing her therapist had ever witnessed. In counseling, Elenore was challenged to specifically ask God to communicate to her. She did so, and a few nights later she had a dramatic dream that proved to be the turning point in her healing. She recorded her experience as follows:

> It was three o'clock in the morning, and I was wide-awake, thinking about all the things that had happened to me. My thoughts were interrupted by what I can only describe as a vision of God. God with outstretched arms was beckoning me to come to him. At first I was hesitant, feeling inadequate and insignificant. But as God called out to me, my heart melted, and I finally surrendered. I was irresistibly pulled toward God—I ran toward him. God swooped me up and sat me on his lap and embraced me.
>
> I could not see God's face, but he kept embracing me, holding me, and I felt the warmth of God's love and his compassion. I found myself crying—crying for the first time, and asking God's forgiveness for being so angry with him, for doubting him, and for keeping him out of my life. God just continued to embrace me; he did not let go of me. Amazingly to me, God started to cry. God

was crying with me. His tears were huge, and as they fell on me, they soothed and comforted me. The tears spoke volumes, but most of all they healed.

For the first time, I had hope. I knew that things would work out. The road would be long, but God reassured me that he would never let go of me. I hung on to those words of God. I just wanted to sit in God's lap, being comforted and loved by him. I must have fallen asleep, for I woke up in the morning feeling like I could face the future with God by my side.

Elenore's experience is certainly unique in that God deals with his children individually, but it offers an intimate example of a survivor wrestling with God, hanging on, asking God to speak and then experiencing his personal and loving response.

Reimaging the Fatherhood of God

Elenore's story also illustrates a second essential activity for abuse survivors in their journey to reconnect with God, namely, reimaging the fatherhood of God.[9] Until Elenore had this dream, she had fiercely resisted intimacy with God and with men. She was a highly educated professional woman who perpetually stayed in control. God had always seemed as dangerous as her abusive father. Her dream, for the first time, gave her a glimpse of God as a loving, safe heavenly Father. A reimaging of God marked the beginning of her spiritual healing.

Abuse dangerously distorts victims' perceptions of the character of God. As we'll see later in this chapter, abuse perverts and distorts virtually every aspect of God's character, so that abuse survivors can't recognize, let alone embrace, their awesome, loving Creator. These distortions often center around the fatherhood of God, which is a logical dynamic. At the heart of all abuse is the misuse of one's power so as to manipulate, dominate, and damage another human being. Since God is the ultimate power and authority in the universe, he represents abuse victims' greatest fears. If human authority figures (often males) used their limited power to harm them, abuse victims instinctively sense that God (portrayed as male) will use his unlimited power to harm them too. At best, they sense they must not give themselves to God; he is unsafe, just as other authorities in their lives have been unsafe.

For men or women who experienced abuse from their fathers or father figures, the problem is greatly magnified. Children develop their sense of God as a heavenly Father from their experiences with their human fathers. The Bible refers to God as our heavenly Father (Matthew 6:9, 32). So people who experienced abuse from earthly fathers find it terrifying to hear that God is a heavenly Father. By the same token, if mothers perpetrated the abuse, the fatherhood of God can be problematic as well. In this case, the survivors do not fear that their heavenly Father will *actively* harm them but that he'll do so *passively*. Again, this is logical. If earthly fathers didn't stop the abuse but allowed it to continue, then they intuitively conclude the heavenly Father must also be dangerous in his passivity. He won't intervene to offer protection, and ultimately he cannot be trusted.

In chapter 7, I mentioned Linda Cutting, who suffered chronic physical and sexual abuse from her father—which was doubly damaging to her concept of God, because her father was a minister. She tells of her spiritual decline in which she lost her connection with God because of her father. She begins by reflecting on her childhood:

> I am thinking about God—how I used to pray. I have this clear memory of believing in God, even when I was little and all the bad things with my father were happening. For so many years I prayed. . . . I stopped praying after Paul [her abused brother who committed suicide] died, after hearing my father say at his funeral, 'the Lord giveth and the Lord taketh away.' . . . The thing that's kept me spiritually alone all these years was somehow equating God with my father's church and, most of all, with my father.[10]

How can abuse survivors change their image of God as an unsafe father? The first step is to reflect on the negative lessons their abusers taught them about fatherhood, authority, and relationships. This is best done as a reflective journaling exercise. Once some of these negative messages are identified, an abuse survivor can consciously and deliberately embrace the fact that God is not his or her abusive father. God hates abuse and promises to harshly judge abusers.

For Linda Cutting, this distinction between God and her earthly father occurred in a dramatic way when she finally gathered the courage to contact the denomination that had ordained her father to inform them that he was an unrepentant child abuser. In spite of considerable evidence that could have been evaluated, a denominational official informed her there was nothing they could do. He furthermore told Linda about a similar case in which two adult daughters had reported that their minister father had raped them for years, and in spite of the substantiation of those abuse claims, the congregation had refused to remove the minister until he lost a civil suit filed by the daughters.

Linda was devastated to realize that her father's denomination would do nothing to remove him from ministry, but it precipitated a spiritual breakthrough: "After hearing how the church responded to the minister's daughters who were raped, I see that God is not the church, God is not the National Association of

Congregational Churches, and God is certainly not my father. At least not my biological father."[11] The manner in which these Christian leaders failed to challenge
an abuser forced Linda to recognize that they didn't really reflect God. And most
important of all, they forced her to recognize that her human father did not reflect
God. As she was able to separate her earthly abusive father from her heavenly
Father, she began to reconnect with God.

One of the most helpful ways abuse survivors can begin to separate God
from their earthly abusers is to clarify from the Bible their understanding of the
fatherhood of God. The Bible teaches that God is a loving heavenly Father whose
fatherhood is expressed, not in brutally using his power to oppress and abuse,
but in using his power to love and nurture. Specifically, God is a heavenly Father
whose fatherhood is described by the following actions:

- He feeds and cares for the birds of the sky and has infinitely more
  loving concern for his children than for the birds (Matthew 6:26).
- He delights in giving good gifts to his children, much more so than do
  human fathers (Matthew 7:11).
- He knows and notices when a tiny sparrow falls from the sky. He knows
  and cares when his children suffer (Matthew 10:29).
- He so actively and passionately loves his children that no trivial detail of
  their lives is overlooked or ignored. He even keeps track of the number
  of hairs on their heads (Matthew 10:30).
- He tenderly loves the powerless and the vulnerable. He delights in
  hiding truth from arrogant power brokers and graciously revealing it to
  those who resemble little children (Matthew 11:25–26).
- He specifically delights in being a Father to the fatherless and an
  advocate for vulnerable single mothers (Psalm 68:5).

Thus, God as the heavenly Father is an important biblical image that needs
to be clarified, not rejected out of hand.[12] John Cooper acknowledges that God
as Father can be a difficult concept for those who have been abused or neglected
by their earthly fathers, but he argues that we must not eliminate this image of
God. He notes the importance of the fatherhood of God for all humans, including abuse survivors:

> It is also true that many people in our culture (and others) have difficulty relat-
> ing to a Father God if they lack the experience of a good father. . . . But for most
> people, the need, desire, and ability to relate to a father figure is still strongly
> present. Many people who lack good human fathers gladly and readily receive
> God the Father as their ultimate security and source of healing. Eliminating the

heavenly Father is neither necessary nor helpful for dealing with the sins of their earthly fathers.[13]

As significant as the fatherhood of God is biblically and practically,[14] it is not the only biblical image used of God. Thus, abuse survivors need to enlarge their understanding of God. In the early stages of healing, a survivor may be unable to focus on God as Father without picturing an abusive father. So it's important to see that the Bible uses many other images to describe God, including some images that are feminine in nature.[15] As survivors reflect on these images of God and allow them to clarify and correct distortions about God's character, they can in time embrace God as their tender, loving heavenly Father.

For instance, God's tenderness, love, and creative power are illustrated by likening him to the images in the chart below:

Image	Scripture Passage
A mother who gave birth to the world	Psalm 90:2
The one who bore and nursed Israel	Numbers 11:12; Deuteronomy 32:18
A mother whose young toddler rests against her to receive comfort	Psalm 131:2; cf. Isaiah 66:13
A nursing mother who has compassion on her child	Isaiah 49:15
A mother who tenderly, graciously feeds her child with nutritious milk	1 Peter 2:2–3
A mother bear that zealously protects her cubs	Hosea 13:8
A hen that shields her chicks from danger under her wings	Luke 13:34; cf. Deuteronomy 32:11

Finally, abuse survivors must focus on the character of Jesus, for he reveals the Father. Jesus said that one who has seen him has seen the Father (John 14:6–11; cf. John 1:18). If abuse survivors want to correct and enlarge their understanding of God the Father, they should look at the words and acts of Jesus. Furthermore, while God is not a sexual being, the incarnate Jesus in his humanity was a male. Thus, focusing on the acts and character of Jesus can bring great healing to distorted images both of God and of human masculinity. For instance, in seeing how Jesus treated women, children, social outcasts, and their powerful male abusers, abuse victims see what divine and human power should really look like.

Jesus exhibited extravagant love and compassion toward women, children, and social outcasts. Jesus loved children. He held them, prayed for them, and said that the kingdom of heaven belonged to such as them (Matthew 19:13–15). Jesus was willing to be slandered by the religious leaders for eating with tax collectors and immoral sinners; in fact, he declared that he came to heal the morally sick (Matthew 9:9–13; cf. Luke 19:1–10).[16] That was the essence of his mission.

When Jesus looked at the needy crowds that followed him, he looked past their sin and "felt compassion for them, because they were distressed and dispirited like sheep without a shepherd" (Matthew 9:36). When Jesus was dining in the home of a religious leader, a well-known sinful woman, possibly a prostitute, entered uninvited. Jesus allowed her to scandalously kiss his feet, anoint them with costly oil, and dry them with her hair. When Simon the Pharisee criticized Jesus for allowing such shameful contact from a sinful woman, Jesus rebuked him and publicly praised the woman for her faith and her passionate love (Luke 7:36–50).

Over and over Jesus demonstrated compassion on the broken and the needy, healing the crippled, the blind, and the mute (Matthew 14:14; 15:30–31). In an outrageously chauvinistic culture that demeaned women, Jesus treated women with incredible respect and dignity. He allowed women to sit at his feet and receive his teachings and to travel with him in public ministry; he even chose women to be the first witnesses of his resurrection (in a Jewish culture that didn't even allow a woman to give testimony in court).[17]

In terms of Jesus' use of power and his posture toward males who abuse power, the gospel record is unequivocal. Jesus used his power to heal and liberate the needy and to rebuke the arrogant power brokers. On one or two different occasions Jesus physically drove money changers out of the temple, for they were desecrating the house of God while making a profit from poor people who sought to worship God (Matthew 21:12; John 2:13–16). Jesus repeatedly healed the sick on the Sabbath and verbally excoriated the Pharisees for their hypocrisy and lack of compassion (Luke 6:6–11). When his disciples argued over who was the greatest, Jesus called over a child and said that greatness is not about power but about becoming like a child (Matthew 18:1–4). Furthermore, Jesus promised to use his power to judge all who harm children, stating that if someone causes a little child to stumble, it would be better if the offender had a millstone hung around his neck and was dropped into the sea, compared to what Jesus would do to him on the day of judgment (Matthew 18:6–10).

Jesus' posture toward the vulnerable, the outcasts, and the broken stands in stark contrast to the behavior of abusers. Jesus' posture also stands in stark contrast to the attitudes of many modern-day church leaders who gather power and prestige by catering to the wealthy and the beautiful and who fail to love and nurture broken outcasts. Thus, the biblical images of the loving nature of God as Father; of God's tender, maternal-like love and nurture; of Jesus' love for broken sinners; and of God's judgment of abusers should allow abuse victims to see how different their heavenly Father is from their abusers. This awareness can allow them to be drawn to God and to look to him in the midst of their suffering.

Jessie's Story

As a young girl, Jessie had been molested for several years by one of the pastors in her church. When she came into counseling, she was asked to paint herself as a flower (see figure 13). The picture she drew surprised and amazed her therapist. Jessie lifted her brush and painted a small rosebush "without any thorns" in the middle of a meadow. A shadow was cast over the rosebush by a giant foot suspended in midair above the flower, ready to crush it at any moment. A car was parked nearby, and a bicycle was propped up against the rosebush.

Jessie's curious therapist was eventually able to decipher the meaning of the picture. Jessie was the rosebush. She had beautiful flowers, but she was very vulnerable. She was thornless in the middle of an open field. With no warning a shadow would emerge near the rosebush, and she would be crushed by the giant foot. This was her youth pastor, who would isolate her and molest her without

Figure 13

"Jesus wept."

warning. Those in the car and on the bicycle who came every day to visit and play with the rosebush were her parents and a friend who loved and cared for her but who could not eliminate the shadow.

The watercolor picture powerfully portrayed Jessie's fear, sadness, and vulnerability. But it portrayed much more. When the therapist asked her to make up a title for her picture, she replied without hesitation: "Jesus Wept." In the face of her abuse, this little girl had a brilliant insight into the character of God. As she sat ready at any moment to be crushed by her abuser, she realized that her loving heavenly Father wept at her abuse. He hated it, because he loves little children, just as he loves all who are vulnerable.

Understanding and Embracing the God of Scripture

Because Satan seeks to distance us from God by distorting all of his wonderful attributes, it's essential for abuse survivors to clarify who God really is.[18] In a world of horrible abuse, evil, and brutality, there is little hope apart from the promises and the character of God. Gary Haugen, a devout Christian who worked in the civil rights division of the U.S. Department of Justice, directed the United Nations genocide investigation in Rwanda. He has witnessed and investigated unfathomable incidents of abuse around the world. His experiences have not destroyed his faith in God but have forced him to clarify his convictions. Having experienced the putrid depths of human depravity and cruelty, he declares there is still hope, but it's found only in the compassionate, just God revealed in Scripture. Haugen makes this observation:

> As one who has with his own hands sorted through the remains of thousands of slaughtered Tutsi corpses, as one who has heard with his own ears the screams of boys being beaten like dogs by South African police, as one who has looked with his own eyes into the dull blank stares of Asian girls abused in subhuman ways, I hope in the Word of God. For in the Scriptures and in the life of Jesus Christ, I have come to know God—my Maker, the Creator of heaven and earth, the sovereign Lord of the nations. It is through his Word that God reveals his character, and it is God's character, and God's character alone, that gives me hope to seek justice amid the brutality I witness.[19]

Abuse survivors who have experienced human depravity and evil and have had hope stripped away need to rediscover the character of God. As they discover what the Bible says about his various attributes, they can consciously choose to reject the distorted images of God created by their abuse and perpetuated by their abusers. The following chart helps to clarify some of God's attributes.

Attribute	Definition/ Description	Biblical support	Common distortions created by abuse	Truth about this attribute
Love	God's love is the sum total of his goodness toward his creation. It includes compassion—his mercy shown to those who are suffering.	Exodus 3:7; Deuteronomy 7:7–8; Psalm 136; 145:8–9, 14–17; Hosea 11:9; Matthew 9:36; Romans 5:8; 8:31–39; 1 John 4:8–10	God loves other people but he couldn't love me. God's love must be earned. God's love is fickle and ephemeral. If I don't perform and measure up, God will no longer love me. God does not care about human suffering.	God loves his children unconditionally and eternally. Sinners are not loved by God because they are beautiful; they are beautiful because they are loved.[20] God is deeply grieved by human suffering.
Omniscience/ Wisdom	God knows all things actual or possible—past, present, and future.	1 Samuel 16:7; Psalm 37:18; 139:1–6; Isaiah 40:12–14, 27, 42:9; Jeremiah 1:5; Ephesians 3:9–11	I can't be honest with God or his people. God is disgusted with me because he knows all of my secret sins. My abuser will never answer for his/her evil. No one believes my story; the truth will never come out.	God loves me in spite of knowing everything about me. God knows and cares about all of my hidden struggles. No abuse is ever hidden from God's sight or escapes his justice.
Sovereignty/ Omnipotence	God has absolute, unhindered rule over all of creation. His sovereignty is governed only by his good character.	Genesis 50:20; Psalm 103:19; Isaiah 40:26; Jeremiah 29:11; 32:27; Romans 8:28; Revelation 19:11–21	God is a heavenly despot who cannot be trusted. God is just waiting to smash me. God isn't good because he didn't prevent my abuse.	God can and will bring good out of human and satanic evil. I can trust God's work in my life. God is bigger than my abusers and the damage they created; he can heal me. God will ultimately triumph over all evil.

Attribute	Definition/ Description	Biblical support	Common distortions created by abuse	Truth about this attribute
Holiness	God is distinct and separate from the created world. He is morally pure (separate from sin).	Leviticus 20:23, 26; Isaiah 6:1–7; 40:18–22; Habakkuk 1:13; 2 Corinthians 6:16–17; 1 Peter 1:15–16; Revelation 4:8	God is too pure to ever want someone like me as his child. I'm just a slut. God is like my abusive earthly father and cannot be trusted.	God is different from and greater than anything in creation. God has nothing in common with an abusive earthly father. He is loving, and far too pure to let unrepentant abusers go unpunished.
Righteousness/ Justice	God is morally perfect. He always conforms to what is right (based on his perfect character).	Psalm 58:10–11; 119:137; 145:17; Romans 2:9; 8:32–34; Hebrews 10:1–18; Revelation 16:5	There is no justice in the universe. Look what my abusers got away with. Those with the most power always win by crushing the weak. God will eventually crush me. I deserve to burn in hell.	No one can ever condemn God's children because Christ's perfect sacrifice satisfied the justice of God. God is a just judge; he will never allow unrepentant evil to go unpunished.
Faithfulness	God is absolutely loyal and dependable. He fulfills 100 percent of his promises.	Psalm 25:10; 119:89–91; Hosea 11:8–9; Philippians 1:6; 1 Thessalonians 5:14, 24; 2 Thessalonians 3:2–3; Hebrews 10:23	No one can be trusted, not even God. Everyone lies. The Bible works for some people, but not for me. God won't keep being patient with me. He will eventually give up on me like everyone else has.	God will *never* give up on his children. No matter how many people betray me, abuse me, or don't believe me, I can trust God. God *always* does what he says; I can trust his promises.
Eternality	God is free from all succession of time. He sees everything past, present, and future with perfect clarity. He has no beginning or end.	Exodus 3:14; Psalm 90:2; 102:12; Isaiah 46:10; 2 Peter 3:8; Revelation 4:8; 22:13	There is no hope; I could never have anticipated this horrible abuse, and I can't deal with it. I will never heal. I can't trust God's promises; they haven't worked yet, and they never will.	I can trust God because he always sees the big picture. I can trust God to fulfill his promises according to his timetable, not mine. No trial in my life catches God by surprise. He has a perfect plan for my healing.

Embracing the Cross

The most painful, vexing questions I've had to field as a spiritual shepherd have come from men and women who had been physically or emotionally broken by suffering and evil. No human will ever have a satisfactory answer to the weeping young woman who asks why God allowed her to be molested. Such a question simply cannot be answered to anyone's satisfaction.

God didn't choose to explain the mystery of suffering and evil to righteous Job, and he hasn't chosen to explain it to us either. But neither has he left us fumbling alone in the dark. The longer I study abuse and minister to victims, the more convinced I am that the fullest divine response to suffering and evil is the *cross of Christ*.

As abuse survivors learn to appreciate and embrace the cross, they will be drawn to a loving God. The life of the apostle Paul provides a great example. In spite of intense and repeated persecution throughout his ministry and physical abuse that ultimately cost his life, Paul's spiritual strength and equilibrium came from his fixation on the cross.[21] As he states, "I determined to know nothing among you except Jesus Christ, and Him crucified" (1 Corinthians 2:2), and, "For the word of the cross is foolishness to those who are perishing, but to us who are being saved it is the power of God" (1 Corinthians 1:18).

There are three reasons why embracing the cross helps abuse survivors reconnect with God.

The Cross Declares God's Compassion for Human Sufferers

When abuse survivors wonder if God is indifferent to human suffering and misery, they need only look at the cross. The cross declares, indeed it shouts, of God's compassion in action. On the cross Christ suffered the most excruciating physical, emotional, and spiritual torture to deliver us from the curse of sin. As Paul observes, "Christ redeemed us from the curse of the Law, having become a curse for us—for it is written, 'CURSED IS EVERYONE WHO HANGS ON A TREE'" (Galatians 3:13).

Unlike the dispassionate ancient Greek gods who were said to cavort on Mount Olympus, utterly unaffected by human misery, God responded to human suffering in the most dramatic manner possible. He allowed his own Son to enter the human race solely to suffer and die. Thus, we now have an answer to Elie Wiesel's haunting question posed as he watched the young boy slowly choke to death in a Nazi death camp: "Where is God now." The answer is that God is on the cross.[22]

The cross doesn't answer all of our questions about human suffering, but it assures us of God's compassion for human misery. As the German pastor Dietrich Bonhoeffer, who was murdered by the Nazis, wrote from his prison cell, "Only the suffering God can help."[23] In the cross of Christ we see a suffering God who can help those who suffer from evil and abuse.

The Cross Connects Jesus with Our Suffering

Those who suffer often feel isolated and disconnected from others. They often feel no one really understands what they are experiencing. This is true for many abuse survivors. The beauty of the cross is that it connects Jesus with our suffering, particularly the suffering produced by abuse.

The writer of Hebrews tells us that Jesus is our great high priest and urges us to go to him in prayer in order to receive mercy and grace. Our motivation is that, as a result of his earthly experiences, Jesus experientially relates to what we endure. The writer of Hebrews declares, "For we do not have a high priest who cannot sympathize with our weaknesses, but One who has been tempted in all things as we are, yet without sin" (Hebrews 4:15). The prophet Isaiah declared that the Messiah would be a man of sorrows who, because of his experiences of abuse, would be well acquainted with grief (Isaiah 53:3–5).

Thus, Jesus personally understands the horrors of abuse. He was verbally abused, mocked, slapped, beaten, spit on, violated (publicly stripped and hung naked), shamed, and tortured to death, and he experienced a hideous sense of separation from God the Father. Jesus understands what abuse victims suffer because he too was abused. Amazingly, he did so voluntarily in order to deliver sinners from death. Thus, abuse survivors can look to Jesus for mercy and grace. He understands and relates to the pain of abuse, and he cares about it. This truth is often overlooked by abuse survivors, but it is extremely helpful.

Corrie ten Boom was a young Dutch Christian who was imprisoned by the Nazis because her family had sheltered Jews. She and her sister, Betsy, were eventually shipped to Ravensbruck, a Nazi death camp. Corrie recounts the humiliation of regular "medical inspections" in which she and the other prisoners were forced to strip naked and walk single file past a "phalanx of grinning guards." In the middle of one of these abusive ordeals, God brought to her mind the precious truth that her Savior was crucified naked. He personally understood the abuse she was suffering.[24] This gave her great strength and comfort.

The Cross Breaks the Power of Evil and Seals Satan's Fate

For abuse victims, it feels as though evil has won and hope is lost. But the Bible declares that, through his death on the cross, Jesus broke the back of Satan and triumphed over evil. Paul tells the Colossian believers regarding Jesus' crucifixion that "when He had disarmed the rulers and authorities [demonic spirits], He made a public display of them, having triumphed over them through Him" (Colossians 2:15). This is the language of a triumphal military procession in which the defeated enemy is forced to march through the streets.[25] In other words, through the cross, the demonic forces have been defeated and publicly humiliated.

John makes a similar claim about the power of the cross over Satan: "The Son of God appeared for this purpose, to destroy the works of the devil" (1 John 3:8). Thus, the writers of Scripture, particularly Paul, teach that the overthrow and redemption of evil have already begun through the cross.[26] But our challenge is that, from a New Testament perspective, while the cross marks the beginning of the end for Satan and his demonic legions, God's final triumph over evil is yet to come. The crucifixion and resurrection of Jesus Christ assure us that the final triumph over evil *will* come. Through the cross it has already begun. Thus, it's not surprising that over half of the New Testament uses of the Greek words for "victory" appear in the book of Revelation, which tells of the end of the age and the final battles between the forces of God and Satan.[27]

What is most amazing is that God used evil itself (the abuse of the Son of God by crucifixion) to triumph over evil. Theologian Henri Blocher makes this comment:

> Evil is conquered as evil because God turns it back upon itself. He makes the supreme crime, the murder of the only righteous person, the very operation that abolishes sin. The maneuver is utterly unprecedented. No more complete victory could be imagined. God responds in the indirect way that is perfectly suited to the ambiguity of evil. He entraps the deceiver in his own wiles. Evil, like a judoist, takes advantage of the power of good, which it perverts; the Lord, like a supreme champion, replies by using the very grip of the opponent.... It is exactly this, the sin of sins, the murder of the Son, which accomplishes this work.[28]

Thus, in the greatest reversal in the history of the world, in the cross of Jesus Christ evil and abuse were used to secure the utter defeat of evil and abuse. We can now see why the cross was of such singular importance for the apostle Paul. The cross demonstrates God's mercy. It connects Jesus with human suffering. It breaks the back of Satan. It spells the eternal defeat of evil. For all of these reasons the cross should be central to our lives. For abuse survivors, embracing the cross is one of the most important ways they can begin to reconnect with God.

SONIA'S STORY

I was recently privileged to interview Sonia, a person who, like Fyodor Dostoyevsky, developed a deep intimacy with God in spite of having experienced abuse so horrific that it threatened to annihilate her faith. Sonia is a confident, middle-aged woman who exudes love for her family, her church, and, most important of all, her Savior. But the first two decades of her life were so dark that her faith and confidence are hard to comprehend.

Sonia was born to a father who was a sick pedophile and to a mother who was weak, powerless, and unwilling to protect Sonia. When Sonia was just three years old, her father began molesting her—and did so for the next ten years. Then when Sonia was thirteen, he began selling her as a prostitute to his friends. This continued for several years. To the day he died, Sonia's father maintained his innocence. He self-righteously proclaimed that the abuse was good for Sonia; it was healthy sex education, he claimed. Furthermore, her father professed to be a Christian and expressed faith in Jesus Christ as his Savior.

Hearing about what Sonia suffered, many people would assume she could never entrust herself to a heavenly Father. But that's hardly the case. In fact, Sonia's deep love for God is unmistakable. Sonia can't give a formula for how her faith developed, but she did share several things that were most important in this process:

- First of all, when she heard the gospel for the first time as a teen, she embraced the biblical truths that God loves sinners and wants to help us in the midst of our pain and that Jesus will never leave his children. She clung to these biblical truths in the dark days to come.
- Second, even as she continued to be abused, she cried out to God. While he didn't seem to immediately answer her prayers and stop the abuse, he did begin to work. He eventually gave her the strength to confront her father—and the abuse came to an end.
- Third, she worked hard to not allow her evil father to cause her to indict God or other men. She reflected on the fact that God put other men in her life who were good and pure, like her dear husband and her uncle.
- Finally, with the help of her loving husband and a godly pastor, she eventually learned to forgive her abusive father—to let go of hatred

toward him and entrust him to God. Sonia says this was the most important aspect of her spiritual healing. Once she forgave her earthly father, she became more intimate with her heavenly Father.

*

Since forgiving abusers, especially unrepentant abusers, is so complex and difficult, I've devoted my final chapter to this important subject.

chapter 10

✳

forgiveness

The well-dressed professional woman sitting across from me had requested a session to discuss her marriage. She had recently separated from her husband but was haunted with the moral propriety of her decision. As a pastor, I was often asked to assist with difficult marriage problems.

This woman had come because her therapist had suggested she contact me. She had some specific biblical questions her therapist felt would be best answered by a trained pastor. Knowing she was coming to talk about the biblical doctrine of marriage and divorce, I began by asking about her marriage. But this woman's situation had a decidedly ugly twist. As I probed deeper, she impassively acknowledged that her abusive husband had given her numerous sexually transmitted diseases over the course of several years, and he had continued his profligate behavior up to the present moment. Her husband's infidelity was a matter of public record. In fact, he openly flaunted his present mistress, but amazingly, he also wanted to stay married to his wife. Though he refused to give up his illicit lover, he battled fiercely for his wife not to divorce him. Repeatedly he hurled what he knew to be the ultimate barb at her: if she was really a Christian, she was obligated to forgive him and take him back, since Jesus said we must forgive seventy times seven (Matthew 18:21–22).

This dear woman desperately wanted to obey God, but reconciling with an unrepentant, abusive husband did not seem healthy. She agonized over knowing what Christian love and forgiveness really demanded of her. Did it mean she had to simply pray for her husband and overlook his immorality? Did it mean she had to lovingly welcome him back, even at the risk of contracting a potentially life-threatening STD? Further complicating matters, this woman's own family and church friends sided with the immoral husband in rejecting divorce as a moral option. They admonished her that she was obligated to forgive and reconcile.

This chapter is a modification of an article that was previously published as "Sexual Abuse and Forgiveness," *Journal of Psychology and Theology* 27 (1999): 219–29.

In subsequent years, I've heard abuse victims recount similar stories over and over, illustrating the widespread confusion in the Christian community about the relationship between forgiveness and abuse. Religious leaders and even family members are often quick to tell victims they must forgive, regardless of the circumstances of the abuse or the posture of the abuser.[1] Sadly, insensitivity to the complexity of the biblical doctrine of forgiveness and ignorance of the dynamics of abuse often lead Christian leaders to inflict much additional damage on survivors of abuse.[2]

Abuse victims need clear direction about the biblical doctrine of forgiveness and what it means for their relational healing. More specifically, they need to know what Christian forgiveness means for their relationships with their abusers, particularly if an abuser is unrepentant. This is what I seek to provide in this chapter.

In view of common misperceptions and the complexity of the issue, the best way to begin is by clarifying the nature of biblical forgiveness. One of the first problems one notes when researching this topic is that much of the religious literature implores forgiveness but never clearly defines it. It is widely known that the primary Greek verb in the New Testament used to indicate "to forgive" is αφιημι, which in general terms conveys the idea of "letting go." Sadly, many Christian leaders who address forgiveness fall into the trap of oversimplification and only define forgiveness as "letting go."

What does this mean for the little girl who disclosed to me that her teenage cousin had been molesting her, along with other neighborhood children, during the past year? Does it mean (as the molester's parents proclaimed) the girl and her parents should simply "let it go" and not notify the authorities? Does forgiveness mean this family must "let go" of their anger toward an adolescent sexual predator who brags about the number of children he has raped? Does it mean (as the extended family insists) the parents must "let go" of their refusal to bring their daughter to family functions if the teenage molester is in attendance? If forgiveness doesn't necessarily mean letting go of everything, then just what is it that is let go?

HARMFUL MODELS OF FORGIVENESS

We'll move toward an explanation of forgiveness by first noting some of the most inaccurate and harmful models. For survivors of abuse, the most damaging definitions of forgiveness are those that conflate forgiveness, trust, and reconciliation and eliminate the possibility of negative consequences for the offender. Sadly, this is a common mistake. For example, in a two-volume work that received a Book of the Year award, a respected evangelical states that, by definition, forgiveness involves a restoration of trust and a letting go of all negative emotions, including fear, anger, suspicion, alienation, and mistrust.[3] As if this definition fails to be difficult enough for abuse victims, who have every reason in the world to fear and mistrust their unrepentant abusers, the author keeps reminding readers that if we don't forgive others, God won't forgive us. By this logic, virtually all abuse victims are damned by their inability to trust their abusers.

While some may contend these views are imprecise due to a practical, nonacademic writing style, other scholarly writers make similar assertions. One of the most respected academic Bible dictionaries defines forgiveness as "the wiping out of an offense from memory" so that once the offense is eradicated, "the offense no longer conditions the relationship between the offender and the affronted, and harmony is restored between the two."[4] Again, by this definition, the majority of abuse victims could not practice forgiveness.

Inaccurate and harmful models of forgiveness may provide a partial explanation for the extreme antipathy of many abuse counselors toward forgiveness. A popular secular abuse healing manual states this sentiment most vividly:

> Never say or imply that the client should forgive the abuser. Forgiveness is not essential for healing. This fact is disturbing to many counselors, ministers, and the public at large. But it is absolutely true. If you hold the belief survivors must forgive the abuser in order to heal, you should not be working with survivors.[5]

FORGIVENESS AND CONSEQUENCES

Given such strong reactions against the forgiveness of abusers, it's imperative to clarify biblical forgiveness. One of the most important observations to make is that, while the Bible does describe forgiveness as the removal or letting go of a debt (Matthew 6:12), forgiveness does not necessarily remove negative consequences for the one forgiven, nor does it automatically grant trust and reconciliation.

One of the clearest examples is found in Numbers 14:20–23, where God declares that he will forgive the Israelites for their rebellion, but that not one of the adults will enter the land he had promised them. More relevant for abuse is King David's sexual violation of Bathsheba and murder of her husband. Once David repented, Nathan declared that God had forgiven him and taken away his sin, and yet a series of harsh consequences was meted out by God ("I will raise up evil against you from your own household" [2 Samuel 12:11]). Similarly, when the prophet Hosea took back his adulteress wife, Gomer, by God's directive he forgave her, but she was to remain in seclusion for two months and forgo sexual intimacy with her husband (Hosea 3:1–5). Trust is earned. Forgiving evil does *not* eliminate all negative consequences.

THE BIBLICAL NATURE OF FORGIVENESS

In classical Greek, αφιημι was used widely and consistently to mean "to release." This meaning is carried over into the New Testament, where αφιημι is used over 125 times and has different nuances of meaning. It is used to mean "to let go, to send away" (Matthew 13:36; Mark 4:36); "to cancel, to remit" (Matthew 18:27; Mark 2:5); "to leave" (Matthew 4:11; John 10:12); "to give up, to abandon" (Romans 1:27; Revelation 2:4); and even "to tolerate, to permit" (Acts 5:38; Revelation 2:20).

Clearly, in defining forgiveness, one cannot simply appeal to the root meaning of αφιημι as "to let go." The only way to accurately determine the biblical meaning of forgiveness as it relates to abuse is to look at a broad range of Bible passages that deal with forgiveness and malevolent evil and then draw pertinent principles. In doing so, one will quickly observe the complexity of biblical teaching on the subject and the inappropriateness of much of the evangelical rhetoric on forgiveness.

THE COMPLEXITY OF BIBLICAL FORGIVENESS

The biblical doctrine of forgiveness is surprisingly complex, a fact that seems to escape the notice of many Christian leaders. At first glance, many passages dealing with forgiveness appear to be patently contradictory:

- In Colossians 3:13 and Mark 11:25, believers are seemingly commanded to forgive others without qualification, whereas in Luke 17:3 (and inferentially in 2 Corinthians 2:7), forgiveness is entirely contingent on the repentance of the offender.
- In Ephesians 4:32, believers are commanded to forgive without qualification based on God's forgiveness, and yet in Hosea 1:6 and Deuteronomy 29:20 (also Joshua 24:19; 2 Kings 24:4), God himself staunchly refuses to forgive.

- Jesus and Stephen prayed that God would forgive their murderers (Luke 23:34; Acts 7:60), yet Nehemiah and Isaiah specifically prayed that God would not forgive evil people (Nehemiah 4:5; Isaiah 2:9).
- In Matthew 18:21–35, the disciples are taught they must forgive those who sin against them in an unlimited fashion and thus manifest God's mercy, and yet in the previous paragraph (18:15–20), Jesus says those who refuse to repent of their sin are to be excommunicated and treated as Gentiles and tax collectors.

Again, in order to build a coherent model of forgiveness, it's important to draw principles from a broad range of Bible passages.

These apparent contradictions suggest one of two things: either (1) the Bible's teaching on forgiveness is patently contradictory, and a harmonious biblical doctrine of forgiveness cannot be constructed[6]—a conclusion that flies in the face of the biblical doctrine of the divine inspiration and authority of Scripture—or (2) forgiveness does not always mean the same thing in the Bible.

I believe the latter explanation does justice to the biblical evidence. Careful examination of the Bible's teaching on forgiveness reveals very different kinds of forgiveness described within its pages. I believe it is most accurate and helpful to recognize three different categories, or types, of biblical forgiveness that must be distinguished if we are going to do justice to the Bible's teaching.

Judicial Forgiveness

Judicial forgiveness involves the remission or pardoning of sin by God.[7] It pictures a complete removal of the guilt of one's sin (Psalm 51:1–9), and it's available to abusers and all other categories of sinners (Psalm 32:1–5; 1 Corinthians 6:10–11). The judicial forgiveness of sin by God lies at the very heart of Christianity and the salvation experience.

God's desire is unequivocally to forgive and to heal those labeled by society as the worst, the most hopeless, and worthless sinners, a prospect that was as odious in the first century (Matthew 9:9–13) as it is today. Modern society's repulsion toward abusers, particularly toward child molesters, is well-known and in many respects quite logical. I vividly remember calling a close friend to inform him that a mutual friend had been discovered to be a molester, and that he should take extra precautions to protect children from this man. Upon hearing that this man was a child molester, my friend's first words to me were, "As far as I'm concerned, Bill can't die and burn in hell soon enough." I certainly understand my friend's visceral reaction to this shocking discovery, but as soon as we consign abusers to the ranks of the irredeemable, we distort the message and ministry of Jesus. What's more, we threaten to impale ourselves on our own sword of justice, for those of us who have never molested children are surely in need of God's mercy and his forgiveness for other kinds of malicious acts, as well as other kinds of sexual sins (Matthew 18:21–35).[8]

However, judicial forgiveness is contingent on confession (Psalm 32:5; 1 John 1:9), the acknowledgment of one's sin, and repentance (Luke 24:47; Acts 2:38; 5:31)—adopting a radically different attitude toward one's sin.[9] Since judicial forgiveness of sin is granted only by God, families and churches cannot give it. Hence, it's absurd for abuse victims to be pressured into forgiving their abusers so such abusers can go to heaven.[10]

While humans cannot offer judicial forgiveness, they can hinder abusers from finding God's forgiveness when they fail to press offenders for full ownership of their behavior or when they misplace blame for the abuse.[11] Sadly, the Christian church has quite a history of blaming the victims of abuse, especially when the abuser is a male church leader.[12] More insidiously, judicial forgiveness is hindered when churches or families press for premature reconciliation, which, in addition to reabusing the victim, often serves to validate and solidify the offender's denial of wrongdoing, thus preventing him or her from experiencing God's forgiveness.

Psychological Forgiveness

Psychological forgiveness is the inner, personal category of forgiveness, and it has two aspects: negatively, it involves letting go of hatred and personal revenge; positively, it involves extending grace to the offender.

Letting Go of Hatred and Revenge

Some philosophers have persuasively argued that bearing resentment against those who maliciously harm us is necessary to maintain the moral order and to maintain respect for the victim.[13] Furthermore, resentment often feels psychologically necessary for abuse victims. Letting go of resentment toward an unrepentant abuser feels like letting go of justice; it may also feel like letting the abuser win and may appear to justify his or her evil.

These arguments against psychological forgiveness cannot lightly be brushed aside. I'm clearly not equating all anger with undesirable hatred or resentment, nor am I letting go of justice. Anger can be a healthy and appropriate response to evil, for Jesus himself became very angry, particularly at those who defamed God and hurt humans made in God's image (Matthew 21:12–17; Mark 3:5).

Many of the psalms contain vivid expressions of anger toward evildoers (Psalm 5; 10; 69). Abuse victims can and should be angry at abusers, whose evil also angers God. The kind of anger prohibited in Bible verses such as Matthew 5:22 is the "deliberate harboring of resentment" with a view toward personal revenge.[14] Hence, Paul in Ephesians 4:26 indicates that one can be justifiably angry but must be careful not to let this disposition turn into sinful resentment.[15]

Thus, forgiving abusers at this level means letting go of settled bitterness and rage and committing abusers to God, who is both loving and just. The way victims are able to do this is by entering into God's point of view, for all humans—abuse victims as well as abusers—are individuals for whom Jesus Christ died.[16] At the same time, God will execute justice against all evil. This approach to forgiveness overcomes the objection that letting go of resentment demeans the victim and undermines justice.

At a practical level, letting go of bitterness means letting go of the right to personally exact revenge.[17] In other words, forgiveness is letting go of my right to hurt another person for hurting me. This is a cardinal element of forgiveness. Letting go of personal retribution, however, doesn't mean letting go of justice or the desire for it. Rather, justice is intensified. By letting go of my right to take personal revenge on my abuser, I am relinquishing the roles of judge, jury, and executioner over to God. His judgment toward unrepentant evil will be perfect and indomitable, making my feeble attempts at revenge appear quite puny. At the same time, in letting go of my right to hurt the offender for hurting me, I am implicitly expressing the desire that he or she would repent and experience God's forgiveness and healing, so that eternal judgment might be precluded.

Dan Allender and Tremper Longman helpfully observe that victims of evil should be greatly heartened by God's promise to exact retribution on all unrepentant evil, and they can and should long for the day of God's judgment on their abusers if they don't confess and repent of the sin of abuse.[18] I believe this is precisely Paul's point in Romans 12:17–21, for in verse 19 the believers are told not to take personal revenge but to leave room for the wrath of God, for vengeance is a divine prerogative.[19] We personally are not to take revenge because God will someday do it, and his revenge will be perfectly just and absolutely thorough. Peter encouraged Christians facing persecution with this same truth (1 Peter 2:23; also 2 Timothy 4:14–15).

We should also note Jesus' words about what God will do to abusers who cause children to stumble: they'd be better off if a large millstone were hung around their necks and they were dropped in the sea (Matthew 18:6). Interestingly, this verse appears in the same section as the famous parable of the servant who refused to forgive. Apparently, though Jesus implored his disciples to forgive those who sinned against them, he viewed this in concert with the promise that God will mete out severe judgment on those who practice evil in general and on those who harm children in particular.

Thus, in the final analysis, forgiveness is an act of faith, for when one forgives, he or she is trusting that God can and will bring judgment and create justice for all the wrongs committed against him or her.[20] By faith we let go of our attempts to exact revenge from abusers, trusting that God will carry out precisely the right inescapable vengeance that justice requires.

Extending Grace

It is not enough, however, simply to define psychological forgiveness in negative terms as the withholding of retribution, for there is a positive side to this as well. One of the Greek terms used for human forgiveness in the New Testament is χαριζομαι (2 Corinthians 2:7, 10; 12:13; Ephesians 4:32; Colossians 3:13), which means to extend grace. Thus, psychological forgiveness also involves the willingness to extend grace and goodness to those who have hurt us.

This doesn't mean victims give abusers free rein to hurt them again, for that would make a mockery of forgiveness. Rather, it means—based on the mercy and grace of God I have experienced—I'm willing to extend kindness even to my enemies (Matthew 5:43–47), with a view toward their own repentance and healing. For abuse victims, one of the most appropriate expressions of this type of forgiveness is simply the extending of grace through the inner desire and prayer for their perpetrators' healing.

Relational Forgiveness

Relational forgiveness is the restoration of relationship. It is synonymous with reconciliation. From a biblical perspective, this forgiveness is always desirable, though it's not always possible. God's desire for the human race is for healing and reconciliation, both individually with himself (2 Corinthians 5:18–21) and interpersonally with other humans (Ephesians 2:11–14; Colossians 3:10–13). Stanley Grenz, a leading theological researcher on the nature of the church as a community, summarizes the twofold reconciling work of God in human history:

> The vision of the Scriptures is clear: the final goal of the work of the triune God in salvation history is the establishment of the eschatological community—a redeemed people dwelling in a renewed earth, enjoying reconciliation with their God, fellowship with each other, and harmony with all creation. Consequently, the goal of community lies at the heart of God's actions in history.[21]

Though reconciliation is always the desired goal, many abusers cannot be given relational forgiveness, for they refuse to do the painful work of repentance. We must not soften the conditional force of Jesus' words in Luke 17:3: "If your brother sins, rebuke him; and *if* [emphasis added] he repents, forgive him." Jesus goes on to say that if this sinning brother repents repeatedly, he or she is to be forgiven repeatedly. Paul gives a similar teaching in 2 Corinthians 2:5–11, where he commands the Corinthians to now forgive the man they had excommunicated for his brazen sexual sin (1 Corinthians 5:1–13), as the excommunication seemed to have served the desired purpose of creating the shame and loneliness that stimulated repentance.

Thus, Christians are to offer relational forgiveness when genuine repentance has occurred. Some argue that forgiveness is not given at any level until the abuser repents,[22] but this approach fails to recognize that the biblical repentance demand applies to relational, not psychological, forgiveness. In other words, there are ways abuse survivors can offer forgiveness to their perpetrators that don't involve reconciliation or the establishment of a relationship.

The Greek word used in Luke 17:3 for "repents" is μετανοέω, which is a combination of two Greek words meaning "change" and "mind." This verb was used in the first century to indicate a definitive change of mind, a substantive shift in perspective. Inextricably connected with this change of mind is a change of life direction and behavior (Acts 26:20; 2 Corinthians 12:21; Revelation 2:5, 21–22; 9:20–21), which particularly from Luke's perspective means a "turning away from a sinful way of life . . . in light of the forgiveness of sins and salvation, which have come in Jesus."[23] Hence, in Luke 3:8, John the Baptist admonishes his audience to "bear fruits in keeping with repentance." Thus, the New Testament usage of repentance indicates that abusers who are to be reconciled must evidence a radical change of mind—particularly regarding their full responsibility for the abuse and for its sinful and destructive nature. Furthermore, this changed understanding must be evidenced in movement toward substantive (as opposed to superficial) changed behavior.

Let me summarize how psychological and relational forgiveness interact. In God's time and with his help, the abuse victim can learn to let go of hatred and extend appropriate grace to the perpetrator (psychological forgiveness). In this sense, the victim can only *remove the barriers* to relationship; ultimately, the responsibility for relational forgiveness lies with the abuser, who must *repent*.[24] This is the implication of Romans 12:18: "If possible, *so far as it depends on you* [emphasis added], be at peace with all men."

When is relational forgiveness appropriate? Religious people are often profoundly naive regarding the dynamics of abuse, and some can become indignant if reconciliation is not granted as soon as a perpetrator confesses and asks for forgiveness. Remember, though, an apology is not a sure indicator of repentance, and with both physical and sexual abusers, it often serves, in the "reconstitution phase," to help them convince themselves they're good people who don't have a serious problem.[25] Clearly, counselors and church leaders must be astute with regard to the characteristics of abusers and the dynamics of abuse, so they don't confuse a manipulative confession or apology with genuine repentance.

Two experts who treat offenders highlight the potential problems with abusers' apologies:

> Offenders are expert at manipulating people in order to justify their abuse to themselves and to others, as well as to maintain control and protect secret wishes and plans. Offenders often apologize in order to minimize the abuse, be forgiven, and assuage any guilt. Likewise, they may want to gain sympathy from other family members or to appear remorseful in the eyes of a court, and thereby get a lesser sentence. They may want to maintain power and set up a scenario that facilitates reabuse.[26]

Once their abuse has been made public, abusers will often ask their victims to forgive them. This can be problematic. In cases of sexual abuse, particularly of minors, it's generally inappropriate for the abuser unilaterally to ask his or her victim for forgiveness. If the offender wants judicial forgiveness, he or she must take that up with God.

In asking for forgiveness, offenders are typically seeking relational forgiveness (reconciliation), but the abuser's mere request for this is often reabusive. For instance, one expert notes that for incest victims, the request by their fathers to be forgiven is often "covert incest," for in asking for forgiveness, the fathers are treating the daughters as someone special, as the only ones who can help them with their problem, as their saviors.[27] This puts the child in a horribly difficult, unfair, and destructive position. I still affirm the propriety and desirability of relational forgiveness under the right circumstances, but given the dynamics of abuse, it is generally inappropriate for the offender to make an unsolicited request for forgiveness of his or her victim.

To determine the propriety of relational forgiveness, indicators of genuine repentance must be identified.[28] Repentance isn't easy to quantify, but an abuser who is truly repentant should in some fashion

- take full responsibility for the abuse (make a confession);
- acknowledge the widespread and extensive damage done to the victim and demonstrate remorse for the harm done;
- enact new boundaries that demonstrate respect for the victim and help ensure that the abuse will not reoccur; and
- take active steps to change the sinful patterns of behavior that led to the abuse.

Laurie Hall endured years of abuse from a husband who was a sex addict during their entire marriage. Eventually his addiction became so severe she was forced to separate from him. In the process, she sought the Lord and found herself needing to clarify what repentance looks like for an abuser:

> Just as forgiveness isn't cheap, repentance isn't cheap. Repentance isn't just being sorry we got caught. Repentance is learning from our mistakes. Repentance is walking a mile in the shoes of the one we've wounded. Repentance demands that we lie for a time in the bed we have made. In real repentance, we feel the pain we have caused others and ourselves.[29]

STEPS IN THE PRACTICE OF FORGIVENESS

It is one thing to argue for the biblical propriety of forgiving abusers and quite another matter to practice it. The following is a brief practical sketch to guide victims in forgiving their abusers. The steps are in logical order, but after the first two are taken, the sequencing of the remaining ones may vary.

1. Clarify the Offense(s) and the Resultant Negative Emotions

This essential preliminary step precedes actual forgiveness. One cannot truly forgive such a destructive offense as abuse until the specific offense(s) and emotional impact have been assessed and clarified. This is necessary, first of all, by virtue of the nature of forgiveness. Lewis Smedes correctly observes that human forgiveness is appropriate only for real offenses.[30] Thus, the victim must clarify the nature of the offense(s) he or she is considering forgiving. In other words, forgiveness can only happen in the light of a careful moral judgment.

It's very tempting for abuse victims to minimize or deny sin against them. Bitterness can also cause abuse victims to take offense at behavior that, in reality, was not harmful or abusive. In either case, one must prayerfully clarify the nature of the offense before forgiveness can be offered. Furthermore, if the emotional results of the abuse are not clarified, the victim risks offering a trivial forgiveness that is superficial, inappropriate, and unhealthy—unhealthy both for the abuse victim and the perpetrator, for it inevitably involves excusing or minimizing sin.

Certainly God's judicial forgiveness works this way, for he knows precisely what he is forgiving when he forgives us, including the heinousness of our behavior and its destructive results (see Psalm 32:1–5; 51:4; Isaiah 1:18; 40:27–28; Revelation 20:12). This is, in fact, what makes his forgiving grace so beautiful. One cannot, therefore, begin the real process of forgiving an abuser without painstakingly clarifying the nature and emotional results of the abuse.

This first step is also necessary in light of the nature and impact of abuse. Abuse victims often protect themselves through denial, distortion (such as self-contempt), and dissociation. They commonly blame themselves, not the perpetrators, for the abuse and often minimize the full extent of the abuse and its effects on them. Clarifying the offense and negative results stimulates the victim to break the pattern of denial and misplaced blame and is a necessary preliminary step to forgiveness.

One can now see how dangerous it is for counselors or church leaders to urge prompt (and hence premature) forgiveness of abusers. This is incredibly insensitive and destructive to the victims. It can not only hinder their healing (and often strengthen unforgiveness);[31] it can also contribute to additional abuse in the Christian community by promoting individual and corporate minimization and denial of evil. One theologian who works with abuse victims powerfully summarizes the allure and danger of immediate, premature forgiveness:

> Premature forgiveness may seem to smooth things over temporarily, and it appeals to most of us who were brought up to believe that being nice was a primary Christian virtue. But it has the effect of driving anger and pain underground where they then fester like a poisonous stream, under our houses and our churches and our communities. And it has the effect of relieving the abuser of any true responsibility to examine his behavior and to change. Because premature forgiveness bypasses consequences and rehabilitation for the offender, it is, in fact, tacit permission—perhaps even an invitation—to continue the violence.[32]

2. Determine Appropriate Boundaries to Check Evil and Stimulate Repentance

Since abuse is inherently about the perpetrator's abuse of power to violate personal boundaries, the victim must determine appropriate boundaries for self-protection. This element of boundary setting is preliminary to actual forgiveness, for one cannot truly forgive unless one can freely forgive—which likely can't

happen, particularly for a minor, until the cycle of victimization and powerlessness has been broken. When churches or families press abuse victims to forgive
promptly their abusers before protective boundaries are in place, they in essence
mock the victim. Church leaders, counselors, and families must instead take
seriously the biblical mandate to protect the vulnerable (Proverbs 24:11–12;
Isaiah 1:16–17; 58:6; James 1:27). Then, and only then, should forgiveness be
considered.

A second element of boundary setting will in many cases be the first aspect
of actual forgiving. Here the boundaries are set not only to protect the victim but
also to check the offender's evil and, in so doing, to stimulate repentance. Dan
Allender and Tremper Longman note that many evil people such as abusers are
manipulative and cunning and are accustomed to winning for their sordid purposes; therefore, erecting boundaries to prevent abuse also serves to thwart, or
check, their evil, giving them the "gift of defeat" that can be used by God to stimulate their repentance.[33]

If, after the boundaries are put in place, abusers are unrepentant and persist
in their abusive behavior, then they should be given the "gift of excommunication." As with corporate church discipline, the abuse victim does this to open the
door to loneliness and shame for the abuser, so that he or she may be led to
repent and find God's healing (1 Corinthians 5:5; 2 Thessalonians 3:14–15).

3. Deliberately Let Go of the Right to Hurt an Abuser for the Hurt He or She Has Inflicted

I've already given considerable attention to this aspect of forgiveness. I only want
to add here that this is an act of faith in which the victim prayerfully turns over
the need for justice and redress to God, who is the just Judge.

4. Reevaluate the Abuser and Discover His or Her Humanity

Forgiveness is in large measure a mental "reframing process" in which one rein-
terprets experiences and conclusions by means of biblical truth.[34] As one begins
the work of forgiveness, the abusive event(s), the abuser, God, and many other
entities and factors are reframed and given a fuller, more biblically accurate
understanding.

Victims have an understandable tendency to reduce those who wounded
them to the sum total of their hurtful act(s). While that one act *is* the most significant for the victim and must in no way, shape, or form be minimized, it's
helpful for victims to begin to look at offenders as fellow human beings and to
see other aspects of their lives as a whole. It may help victims both understand

the factors that led to the abuse (thus reducing the tendency to somehow blame themselves for the abuse) and gain a measure of compassion for offenders.

Michael McCullough, Steven Sandage, and Everett Worthington have developed a helpful empathy-humility model of forgiveness that relates this fourth forgiveness step to the transformation of a victim's memory.[35] Victims need to acknowledge the harmful actions committed against them, but they also must reflect on the neediness of their offenders—and on their own moral fallibility as well. In Colossians 3:12–13, we see that putting on a heart of compassion immediately precedes forgiving, implying that the former leads to the latter. It is well-known that a high percentage of abusers were themselves abused or neglected. Every abuser was once a vulnerable, needy child. Every abuser is a human being made in God's image. Every abuser has been manipulated by Satan into seeking to meet legitimate needs and cope with real pain in inappropriate, sinful ways.

Reflecting on an abuser's humanness, including his or her own trauma experiences, does not soften blame or lessen the reprehensibility of the behavior. But it may give the victim, who is trying to learn to forgive, a renewed ability to see the offender as a whole person—a mixture of hurts, fears, and evil responses. This in turn can help a victim loosen the grip of hatred in his or her own heart, so as to be able to extend psychological forgiveness.

5. Extend Appropriate Grace

Lewis Smedes describes the last stage of forgiveness as "revising our feelings" toward the one who sinned against us.[36] In this step, the victim moves from inner hatred toward the abuser to an inner desire that good things will come his or her way. This may well describe the first portion of the last phase, but full Christian forgiveness culminates in active commitment for one's abuser to experience God's healing and blessing.

Christians are called to extend grace even to evil, destructive people, desiring that this grace will transform them by God's power. Extending grace takes countless forms and can't be formularized, for the needs of each abuser and the personality and abilities of each abuse victim are different. Since the boundary steps determined in step 2 will seriously limit and in some cases preclude personal interaction with unrepentant abusers, this final step will for many abuse survivors primarily involve prayer for their abusers to be stripped of distorted beliefs, to repent, and to find God's forgiveness and healing. This is, in fact, a far more significant action than most realize. In many cases, it may be all the grace a survivor can extend, particularly when the victim has no contact with the abuser.

As noted earlier, Dan Allender and Tremper Longman also emphasize "bold love" as an act of grace toward evildoers.[37] This involves a willingness to do what it takes to bring about the abuser's health and salvation, including articulation of one's sorrow over the abuser's sin, confrontation (Proverbs 27:5–6), exhortation (2 Thessalonians 3:14–15), and excommunication (1 Corinthians 5:1–13). In other circumstances God has led abuse survivors to extend grace by visiting abusers in prison, by writing letters to abusers that explain the gospel, and by providing financial assistance for abusers to obtain professional counseling.

TO FORGIVE, OR NOT TO FORGIVE?

In conclusion, are we to forgive abusers? Yes, and no. It is God's desire to forgive evildoers. It is also his desire to create a community of forgiven sinners who are reconciled to each other. But we aren't always able to implement fully the three aspects of biblical forgiveness.

Only God can provide judicial forgiveness for the horrible sin of abuse. We can merely avoid hindering the process by pressing abusers to own their behavior and by never encouraging premature relational forgiveness. Relational forgiveness should only be offered when the abuser has shown a clear willingness to take responsibility for his or her abuse, is taking clear steps toward changed behavior, and is willing to enact firm and appropriate behavioral boundaries — and when the victim is not in significant danger of being revictimized. We should, however, offer psychological forgiveness to abusers — even to unrepentant abusers.

In time, we can learn to let go of our attempts to exact personal revenge on abusers and can, where possible, extend not hatred but grace and kindness toward the abusers. We do this with a view toward their healing, recognizing that their unrepentant evil of abuse will be judged righteously and decisively by God. A forgiveness that follows these principles breathes hope into malevolent human evil. It offers the hope of healing for abuse survivors and a call to repentance for abuse perpetrators.

epilogue:
a word from mary

*M*ary, the missionary daughter whose story was told at the beginning of the book, offered to write this epilogue to update readers on God's healing work.

Healing from abuse has been a long process for me. When I look back on my journey, it's hard to believe I'm the same person I was a few years ago. Last year I finished graduate school and now serve as a social worker for homeless and impoverished families. I recently celebrated five years of being married to an amazing Christian man, and all of my anger and bitterness toward God has been replaced by a sweet, sincere relationship with him. I now view God as my redeemer and rescuer. Hearing songs such as "Amazing Grace" never fails to bring tears to my eyes. I have turned my energy toward helping needy women and children, many of whom are abuse victims. I feel I can help them on a level that someone who has not been abused can't, because I can literally step into their shoes. I will never cease to be amazed at the way God uses evil for good if we let him.

But my healing didn't happen overnight. The years after my disclosure were the hardest years of my life. I want to remind readers that healing from abuse takes time, patience, and support from others. It is often "two steps forward and one step backward." I think it's important for victims of abuse to remember this and not to beat themselves up if the process is taking much longer than they expected. My healing came very slowly. It started with my parents, who loved me tenaciously. They loved me when I was acting unlovable, and they stuck by my side when I was angry. If possible, abuse victims should find someone who will love them like this. It could be a parent, a sibling, a friend, a pastor, or a counselor. Before victims can accept and love themselves, they must experience unconditional love from someone else. After I accepted that my parents would love me no matter what, I began to trust other people. I started by telling a close friend about the abuse. I gradually began to trust people in seemingly little ways, such as going on dates with guys or letting more of my true self show through to friends. I encourage abuse victims to open up to people, when they feel ready, so they can experience trust again. In my journey, I found the more I trusted other people, the more I could trust God.

As an abuse victim, healing my relationship with God has been the hardest thing I've ever done. It took the most time and was the most painful, but eventually it happened. For a long time I was very angry at God. Although I continued going to church, I didn't feel a lot of love for God, and that was OK. We are not responsible for our feelings; we're just responsible to keep obeying and pursuing God. During my healing I learned that it's OK to feel angry at God! He even wants us to *tell* him about this anger. I found it helpful to write letters to God about how confused and angry I was toward him, and to ask him to show himself to me.

My last step of healing from abuse was forgiving my abuser and those who had enabled him. I believe forgiving one's abuser can only be accomplished after the victim's relationship with God has been healed. Forgiving one's abuser is a supernatural event, and it can only be accomplished with God's help.

I'd like to reiterate to anyone reading this book who has been abused that deep healing takes time. Please don't rush the process. Pray for God to show you the good he wants to bring out of your abuse. Claim his promise in Jeremiah 29:11 (NIV): "'For I know the plans I have for you,' declares the LORD, 'plans to prosper you and not to harm you, plans to give you hope and a future.'" Look at the story of Joseph and read Genesis 50:20. What people meant for evil, God used for good. Claim these biblical promises, and pray that God will reveal their truth to you.

I'd like to conclude with some tips for pastors and others who want to help victims of abuse. First, *be very careful to support and believe the victim*. Abuse victims, as well as their abusers, deny and minimize abuse, so the story of abuse a victim reported to you was most likely only representing a fraction of the actual abuse he or she experienced. It's extremely difficult and painful for victims to disclose abuse to anyone, let alone an authority figure. So the last thing they need is for someone they trust—someone who's trying to help them—to question or deny the abuse. They desperately need your support.

Second, *remember that healing from abuse takes time*. It often takes years. This doesn't mean that abuse is too damaging for healing to occur quickly or that God is too weak to heal abuse damage instantly—but it's not the way God typically works. Accepting the fact that healing from abuse is generally a long, arduous process doesn't impugn God's power; it's simply a recognition of the way God has made us. Abuse is a powerful tool in Satan's hands because it creates deep soul damage.

Third, *allow the victim to be angry*—angry at God, angry at the abuser, even angry at you. Just love them and validate that it's OK they're angry—they have a lot to be angry about! Validating feelings is very important for any victim of abuse. Abuse has stripped them of worth, of feelings, and of life. Thus, they need all the validation they can get.

The final and perhaps most important tip is to *love, love, love*. If the victim is being mean and harsh, love him or her. If they are being self-destructive, love them. If they are being hurtful, love them. Victims often must *experience* love before they can *embrace* love and begin to trust others. Your role in this healing is vital. You have great potential for help, as well as great potential for harm—never forget that. Most of all, remember that if we are open and available, we can be vessels through whom God can work to bring tremendous healing. I am only where I am today because of God working in people like you! I truly believe that if I can experience healing, anyone can!

appendix 1:
child protection policy—
first church

Note: While First Church has worked and will work diligently to apply this policy, due to the nature of ministry it makes no written or implied guarantee that every aspect of the policy will be followed in every situation. Any concerns about the implementation of the policy should be directed to the senior pastor or the chairperson of the child protection committee.

I. **Summary Statement**

First Church is committed to the nurture and protection of all human beings, particularly those who are physically or emotionally vulnerable, such as children. Thus FC will not tolerate the physical or sexual abuse of minors in our ministries. FC will act decisively and assertively to protect children and youth and to help victims, as well as perpetrators, find personal and spiritual healing.

II. **Definitions of Child Abuse**

FC defines child or youth abuse as acts of mistreatment or neglect against minors (those under age eighteen). The child/youth abuse covered in this policy falls into three major areas, which FC defines as follows:

A. **Physical Abuse**

Physical abuse is any nonaccidental injury to a minor by an adult or older caregiver. This can include blows, shakings, or assaults that cause injury to the child. Disciplinary spankings by a parent that do not cause physical injury to the child are not considered physical abuse.

B. **Neglect**

Neglect is the chronic failure of a parent or adult guardian to provide a minor with adequate food, clothing, medical care, protection, and supervision.

C. **Sexual Abuse**

Sexual abuse is the exploitation of a minor for the sexual gratification of another person. Sexual abuse includes intercourse, sodomy,
oral sexual contact, fondling, prostitution, the production of pornography, exhibitionism, and the deliberate exposure of a minor to
pornography or sexual activity.

III. **Procedural Responses to Alleged Child Abuse**

For legal and moral reasons, it is imperative the following reporting procedures are carefully followed. These procedures apply to all paid or volunteer workers ("FC workers") who minister to minors at FC.

*Note: The child protection committee mentioned below will be chaired by a staff
member or other qualified individual who is chosen by the senior pastor in consultation with the church board. The child protection committee chairperson, in consultation with the senior pastor, will choose the child protection committee members.
The church board will approve all child protection committee members.*

When an FC worker suspects that a child/youth in an FC ministry has
been abused, the following steps should be taken:

Step 1: Maintain appropriate confidentiality. This includes not speaking
with fellow workers or the suspected victim's parents about the suspected
abuse.

Step 2: Contact the chairperson of the child protection committee and
indicate your observations and concerns regarding the suspected abuse.
If the chairperson of the child protection committee is not available, contact the senior pastor or his designee and share your concerns. The senior pastor and the chairperson of the child protection committee will
promptly inform each other of any abuse allegations regarding minors in
ministry at FC.

Step 3: If it is determined that there are reasonable grounds to believe a
minor has been abused, under the direction of the senior pastor and/or
the chairperson of the child protection committee, a member of the child
protection committee or pastoral staff by law shall immediately report
the suspected abuse by telephone to Child Protective Services and to the
local police department. Then within seventy-two hours, a written report
is to be submitted to CPS or to the police department that contains (1)
the names and addresses of the minor and his or her parents or
guardians, (2) the minor's age and nature and extent of injuries, and (3)
any other information that may be helpful in establishing the cause or

extent of abuse. The time, contents, and recipients of the abuse reports given to CPS or the police department should always be documented and kept in the secured child protection file at FC.

Step 4: If it is uncertain whether there are reasonable grounds to believe a minor has been abused, an inquiry team will be formed by the chairperson of the child protection committee. The senior pastor will be immediately informed of the allegation and of the formation of the inquiry team. The inquiry team will be composed of a small group of individuals selected from the child protection committee. Other qualified individuals, including the child/youth worker who made the abuse allegation/suspicion, may be chosen to join the inquiry team at the discretion of the senior pastor and chairperson of the child protection committee. No one will be chosen to serve on the inquiry team if they are the alleged perpetrator of the abuse, or if someone in their immediate family is the alleged victim or perpetrator of the abuse.

The sole function of the inquiry team is to determine whether there are reasonable grounds to believe a minor has been abused. If and when they determine there are reasonable grounds to believe a minor has been abused, they are immediately to follow step 3 above and notify the proper authorities. They are not to conduct a forensic (formal investigative) type of interview with the alleged victim, as this could impede a subsequent investigation by law enforcement officials. All they are to ask of the alleged victim are four questions: (1) What happened to you? (2) Where did it happen? (3) When did it happen? (4) Who did it? A written summary will be made of each phase of the investigation. At the completion of the investigation, all investigation documentation will be treated as strictly confidential and preserved in a secured file.

The worker who originally raised the abuse allegation will be advised of the outcome of the investigation, meaning they will be told either that the committee filed an abuse report with CPS and law enforcement or that the inquiry team determined there weren't reasonable grounds to believe a child had been abused and thus no report was filed. If the person who originally shared the abuse concern with the committee still believes a child has been abused and hence disagrees with the committee's conclusions, this person can and should file a report with CPS and with the local law enforcement agency.

Step 5: When it is determined there are reasonable grounds to believe a minor has been abused while at an FC function or church-sponsored ministry, or the alleged perpetrator attends First Church, the chairperson of the church board will be immediately contacted by a pastoral staff member and informed of the abuse allegation. The parents of the suspected victim are not to be contacted by the church leaders and told of the abuse allegation until law enforcement officials are able to do their investigation and give the church clearance to contact the parents.

Step 6: When it is determined there are reasonable grounds to believe a minor has been abused, and the alleged perpetrator is a member of the church staff or is a volunteer youth or children's worker at FC who allegedly abused a child or youth under his or her care while in ministry at or on behalf of FC, the church attorney should be immediately contacted, as well as the FC insurance carrier. In some cases, particularly if a church worker or staff member is accused of abuse, the church attorney may need to be contacted as soon as the allegation is made, before it is determined there are reasonable grounds to believe a minor has been abused.

Step 7: When it is determined there are reasonable grounds to believe a minor has been abused, and the alleged perpetrator is a member of the church staff or is a volunteer youth or children's worker at FC, the accused will be immediately removed from his or her ministry to children or youth. The church board, in consultation with the pastoral staff, will determine if and when the accused can resume ministry to children or youth at FC. It must be remembered, however, that an accusation is just that until adjudicated or admitted in a court of law. We must be mindful of the rights of the accused, as well as the damage a false accusation can bring.

Step 8: If the alleged abuse perpetrator (step 7 above) is a volunteer church worker or a church staff member who allegedly abused a child or youth under his or her care while in ministry at or on behalf of FC, the church will offer counseling to the alleged victim and to the alleged perpetrator and may also offer legal counsel. The type and duration of counseling offered will be at the discretion of the church leadership.

Step 9: The senior pastor and chairperson of the child protection committee, in consultation with the church leadership and legal or psychological counsel, will determine additional steps FC will take to minister to the alleged victim and alleged perpetrator.

IV. Selection of Workers

A. *All* children's and youth workers will receive the FC child protection policy summary and will attest in writing that they have read the policy, have never abused a minor, and will abide by the policy guidelines. All staff (i.e., paid workers) and volunteers who work with minors at FC will also fill out a written application. All janitors, adults who work with adolescents, children's ministry teachers and leaders, adults who take minors on overnight outings will also be fingerprinted and will participate in an oral interview. This will serve to evaluate, as much as is reasonably possible, the suitability of the individual for ministry to children or youth.

B. All individuals listed in A above will provide references as requested in the written application. The child protection committee and their designees will check references as they deem appropriate.

C. The church staff will initiate background checks of the individuals listed in A above as they deem appropriate.

D. Occasional children's workers may be asked to submit to the full screening outlined above, as the pastoral staff deems appropriate.

E. All children's and youth workers' applications, notes from the oral interviews, reference interviews, and background check data shall be kept in the secured child protection safe.

F. Child protection committee members, in general consultation with the pastoral staff, will evaluate the potential workers' applications, oral interviews, references, and background checks to determine suitability of the applicants for work with minors at FC. If for some reason it is determined an individual is unsuitable for ministry to children or youth (e.g., if they have ever committed child abuse, have ever committed sex crimes, or have a recent history of alcohol or drug abuse), every effort will be made to find another area of ministry they can engage in at FC. Every effort will be made to do this in a spirit of grace, while maintaining appropriate confidentiality.

V. Education and Monitoring of Workers Regarding Abuse

A. In consultation with the pastoral staff, the child protection committee will seek to develop an abuse education plan for the whole church family, including parents, children, and adolescents, as well as those who work with minors.

B. One of the most important steps we must take to implement a church child protection policy is to train all leaders thoroughly, so they can successfully educate and supervise the workers under them. Thus, FC will conduct or recommend child protection training and policy clarification meetings on a regular basis. It is expected that all workers and staff will attend these training sessions.

C. Children's and youth leaders will regularly monitor their workers through scheduled and unscheduled observations of their classrooms and ministries. This will be done expressly to help teachers and workers improve their skills and to become their best for Christ, as well as to identify potential problems.

VI. Workers' Procedures to Reduce Abuse and False Allegations of Abuse

In order to protect children and youth at FC and to reduce the likelihood of false abuse allegations, workers should do the following.

A. All teachers and assistants should strive to work as a team. Seek to avoid situations in which the worker and child/youth are alone without another worker present, particularly in the restroom, in disciplinary situations, and when counseling.

B. In the event a worker is left alone with children, be sure the door is ajar and windows are not obstructed. Always strive to avoid even the appearance of impropriety.

C. When workers assist in the restroom, they should alert other workers that they are taking a child to the restroom. The adult worker should secure the restroom by checking each stall. Then the worker should step to the doorway of the restroom, unless there are other adults inside the room. When assisting with a child's clothing, the worker should assist the child at the doorway of the restroom.

D. Children at play should be carefully supervised so that no sexual misconduct occurs between them while they are playing. The same principle applies to adolescents.

E. Junior and senior high workers should be particularly careful about spending time alone with youth of the opposite gender. When this is unavoidable, the worker should notify the youth's parents and another youth worker prior to the event.

F. Always report immediately any abuse concerns, suspicions, or nagging questions to the pastoral staff member who oversees your ministry (refer to section III).

appendix 2:
application for
children's/youth work—
first church

CONFIDENTIAL

The purpose of this application is to help the church provide a safe and secure environment for those children and youth under our care, as well as to place workers in ministries they are best suited for by virtue of their gifting, experience, and life history.

Applications will be reviewed only by the pastoral staff and children's administrator in consultation with the child protection committee. Upon review, all applications will be kept in a secured file.

The leadership of First Church will review all applications with confidentiality, sensitivity, and compassion.

Date: _____

Name: _____

Telephone (Home): _____ (Work): _____

Present Address: _____

_____

Date of birth: _____

This is merely a sample screening form and should not be construed as legal counsel. Abuse laws and liabilities vary. Churches should consult local professionals to create the most appropriate documents for their church or ministry.

Children's Names/Ages: _____

_____

If Married, Spouse's Name: _____

Occupation: _____

Place of Employment: _____

Past Employment: _____ From/to: _____

FC Membership Status (circle one):

          Member   Regular Attender   Seasonal Attender   N/A

Church Attendance (list last three churches attended):

Church Name/Address	Contact Person	From/To	Reason for Leaving

1. _____

_____

2. _____

_____

3. _____

_____

Present/Past Ministry or Volunteer Work
(church/parachurch/civic for past five years):

Organization	Location	Position	From/To	#Hours/Week

_____

_____

_____

_____

_____

Please indicate the type of youth or children's work you prefer:

_____

Please indicate the date you would be available to begin:

_____

Name the minimum length of commitment you can make:

_____

Have you ever been convicted of or pleaded guilty or no contest to a crime (other than non-DUI traffic offense)?____Yes   ____No

If yes, please explain; attach separate page, if necessary.

_____

_____

_____

Have you ever physically or sexually abused a minor? ____Yes   ____No
If yes, explain.

_____

_____

_____

(We define physical abuse as nonaccidental injury of a child, and sexual abuse as the sexual exploitation of a minor for the gratification of another person.) Were you a victim of abuse or molestation while a minor?____Yes   ____No

(Answering yes, or leaving the question unanswered, will not automatically disqualify an applicant for children's or youth work. Because abuse can leave long-lasting scars and in some cases seriously impair one's ability to work with children, we feel this is an important question.)

Have you ever committed a sex crime?   ____Yes   ____No
If yes, explain.

_____

_____

_____

Do you have a current driver's license?   ____Yes   ____No

If yes, list license #: _____

Have you ever had a problem with drugs or alcohol? ____Yes   ____No
If yes, explain.

_____

_____

_____

List any experience, education, or volunteer training that has prepared you for children's/youth ministry.

_____

_____

_____

What are your spiritual gifts, and how would you like to use them in children's/youth ministry?

_____

_____

_____

Personal References (not former employers/employees or relatives):
Name   Address   Telephone

1. _____

_____

2. _____

_____

3. _____

_____

Briefly describe how you became a Christian. Describe your relationship with Christ today.

_____

_____

_____

APPLICANT'S STATEMENT

The information contained in this application is correct to the best of my knowledge. I authorize any references or churches listed in this application to give you any information (including opinions) they may have regarding my character and fitness for children's or youth work. In consideration of the receipt and evaluation of this application by First Church, I hereby release any individual, church, youth organization, charity, employer, reference, or any other person or organization, including record custodians, both collectively and individually, from any and all liability for damages of whatever kind or nature that may at any time result to me, my heirs, or family on account of compliance, or any attempts to comply, with this authorization. I waive any right I may have to inspect any information provided about me by any person or organization identified by me in this application.

Should my application be accepted, I agree to be bound by the bylaws and policies of First Church and to refrain from unscriptural conduct in the performance of my services on behalf of the church.

I further state that I HAVE CAREFULLY READ THE FOREGOING RELEASE AND KNOW THE CONTENTS THEREOF, AND I SIGN THIS RELEASE AS MY OWN FREE ACT. This is a legally binding agreement, which I have read and understand.

Applicant's Signature: _____

Date: _____

Witness: _____

Date: _____

REQUEST FOR CRIMINAL RECORDS CHECK AND AUTHORIZATION

I hereby request the _____ Police Department to release any information that pertains to any record of convictions contained in its files or in any criminal file maintained on me, whether local, state, or national. I hereby release said police department from any and all liability resulting from such disclosure.

_____   _____   _____
Signature   Print Name   Date

Print maiden name if applicable:_____

Print all aliases: _____

Date of birth:_____Place of birth:_____

Social Security Number:_____

appendix 3:
child protection oral
screening—first church

Date: _____

Applicant: _____ Interviewer: _____

Note: All notes from this interview will be kept in a secured vault accessible only to the staff. The purpose of this interview is to get insights to help us place workers in ministries that are best for them and for children and youth at FC. To allow us to best minister to you and to the children and youth at FC, it is imperative that you are fully honest in answering the following questions.

1. **Please tell me a little bit about your experience in working with children.**
   (Watch for adults whose lives seem to revolve around spending time with children.)

2. **Why do you want to work with children?**
   (Again, watch for the adult who is too child focused or who wants to work with children because they are "pure," "innocent," "trusting," nonjudgmental," and so forth. Adults should want to work with children because they have something to offer the child, not because children can meet their adult need for control, love, or affection.)

This is merely a sample screening form and should not be construed as legal counsel. Abuse laws and liabilities vary. Churches should consult local professionals to create the most appropriate documents for their church or ministry.

3. **Tell me a little bit about your adult friendships here at FC and elsewhere.**
   (Beware of the adult who has poor peer relationships, especially if that person relates only to children or youth. Also, be thinking of ways we can help this person network with other adults at FC.)

4. **Do you understand the child protection policy? Do you agree to abide by it? Do you have any questions about the policy?**
   (Take time to answer their questions and clarify the policy.)

5. **Give an example of what you would consider inappropriate behavior between an adult and a child.**
   (This provides insight into what they consider to be acceptable and unacceptable and also gives a chance for you to clarify our policy and what we consider acceptable/unacceptable behavior.)

6. **Do you want to clarify any of your answers on the written application?**

7. In cases where the applicant had indicated he or she had been abused: **Please explain the general nature of the abuse you suffered. How has it affected you? How have you worked through the effects of the abuse? (What steps have you taken to experience healing?)**

8. In cases where the applicant had indicated they had been convicted of or pleaded guilty or no contest to a crime, and more data is needed than what they put in the written application: **Could you give the circumstances and details of the offenses you mention in the application?**

9. In cases where the applicant had indicated they had abused a minor: **Could you say more about the nature and circumstances of the abuse?**
   (Explain that our policy precludes us from allowing those with a history of abusing children to work in children's or youth ministry. Assure them that we want to help them grow, heal, and find suitable areas of service when they are ready.)

10. **Have you ever been accused of the abuse of a minor?** If they have: **Could you give the circumstances and details of the allegation?** (An accusation of abuse doesn't necessarily preclude a person from ministry at FC, but not being honest during this interview probably will. Get enough information to investigate the allegations if at all possible, and explain that we will need to do so. If they don't want us to do any investigation, explain that we will probably not be able to use them to work with minors.)

11. **Have you ever been accused of sexual harassment of an adult?** If they have: **Could you give the circumstances and details of the allegation?**

12. **In light of the things we've just talked about, are there any ways we as a church can help you grow in terms of your personal well-being or your skills for children's or youth ministry?**

appendix 4: warning signs of potential abusers

✳

Symptom: Are extremely possessive, jealous

Description: Insecure people may interpret this behavior as love (and an abuser will defend it this way), but healthy people do not endlessly scrutinize who their girlfriends, boyfriends, or spouses spend time with, call multiple times a day to check up on what they are doing and with whom, and so forth.

Symptom: Display smothering, controlling behavior

Description: Abusive people often seek to control virtually every aspect of another's life. They don't allow their loved ones to have their own views, their own lives, their own schedules, or their own possessions. Abusive husbands may not even allow their wives to buy the groceries on their own. Some don't even allow their wives to drive. Often every single purchase is scrutinized and controlled.

Symptom: Have unpredictable, extreme mood changes

Description: Some have described this as a "Dr. Jekyll and Mr. Hyde" pattern that is very confusing and often makes victims doubt their own judgment. The abuser can be very sweet one minute but explode in anger the next. Abusers' bad moods are unpredictable, causing family members to "walk on eggshells" so that they don't set them off.

Symptom: Are unable or unwilling to acknowledge any personal fault or responsibility

Description: This is a nearly universal characteristic of abusers. They simply will not take full responsibility for their behavior; it's always someone else's fault. Abusers have an uncanny way of finding unhealthy partners who struggle with low self-esteem and can be easily bullied and shamed into believing they (the nonabusers) are always the problem.

Symptom: Are hypercritical
Description: One of the ways abusers avoid taking responsibility for their
                unhealthy and sinful behavior is to be hypercritical of others,
                which is largely the result of their own deep-seated shame. Fur-
                thermore, abusers tend to be hypersensitive, so that any little
                thing upsets them. Family members of abusers can never "get it
                right" and constantly find themselves being scolded and shamed
                for their mistakes.

Symptom: Abuse alcohol
Description: Roughly 50 percent of domestic physical abusers have a serious
                drinking problem. They may blame their abusive behavior on the
                alcohol, but it's nothing but blame shifting. Alcohol and/or drug
                abuse is often their sinful way of numbing past trauma.

Symptom: Have unresolved family of origin trauma
Description: The most predictable trait of physical abusers (particularly men)
                is that they experienced physical abuse in their own childhood
                homes. They learned early in life that violence is an acceptable
                way to solve frustrations. Childhood trauma, especially physical
                or sexual abuse and neglect, create deep-seated soul damage that
                can lead to abusive behavior in adulthood unless the wounds are
                dealt with. One warning sign for potential abuse is seen in an
                adult who, in spite of having grown up in a dysfunctional or abu-
                sive family, denies or minimizes the abuse and its impact.

Symptom: Isolate the victims from family and friends
Description: Abusers cut off their victims from all other social resources. They
                accuse others of causing trouble. They may try to pull the victim
                away from family members by saying the victim is too dependent
                on his or her family or that the family is not supportive. They'll
                accuse the victim of having an affair if he or she has any opposite-
                gender friendships or even casual relationships. Sometimes
                abusers will even make victims quit their jobs to cut them off
                from other relationships (and to make them more dependent on
                the abusers).

Symptom: Insult and ridicules victims' family and friends
Description: Abusers justify isolating their partners from family and friends
                and promote their own superiority by insulting and ridiculing
                these individuals.

Symptom: Prevent victims from leaving
Description: Because an abuser likes to control all behavior and has no sense
                of appropriate boundaries, he will often refuse to allow a wife or
                girlfriend to leave, especially during an argument. He may do this
                by physically stopping her, by verbally harassing her, or by ver-
                bally manipulating her.

Symptom: Employ a rigid model of gender roles
Description: Abusers typically have a rigid, extremely conservative under-
                standing of male/female roles. They often place great emphasis
                on male headship and on the need for women and children to
                be submissive. They typically ignore the fact that the Bible never
                teaches that the man is to be "the boss" who demands obedience
                from his wife; rather, the Bible calls men to be loving servant-
                leaders. Females are often viewed and treated as inferior to men.
                Thus, female opinions and feelings can be readily discounted.
                Abusers often believe they must make their wives and children
                submit completely to them, even if they have to use physical
                force to do so. Ironically, while abusers demand unqualified sub-
                mission from others, they tenaciously resist submitting to civic
                or ecclesiastical authorities (CPS workers, the police, court-
                appointed counselors, their pastors, and so forth).

Symptom: Threaten to harm themselves
Description: Abusers often successfully manipulate their partners into remain-
                ing in an abusive relationship by threatening to harm themselves
                if the partner breaks off the relationship.

Symptom: Threaten to hurt victims or their families
Description: This is another common way abusers manipulate their part-
                ners to stay in the relationship and to passively accept abusive
                behaviors.

Symptom: Insult and degrade victims in private
Description: Often abusers are charming to their partners (and others) in
                public but are demeaning and degrading in private.

Symptom: Ignore or ridicule victims' feelings and wishes
Description: Abusers' inappropriate domination, control, and sense of supe-
                riority is evidenced by the way they constantly ignore, reject, and
                even ridicule their partners' feelings and wishes.

Symptom: Have a volatile history of broken romantic relationships and friendships

Description: Abusers often have extensive histories of broken relationships, and in these cases, it was always the other person's fault. Often abusers were physically and/or verbally abusive in these previous relationships.

Symptom: Always posture themselves as victims

Description: Everyone is out to get them; everyone mistreats them; their boss is unfair; they are never given a fair shake; and so forth.

Symptom: Cause victims to fear ever confronting or even disagreeing with them

Description: Abusers systematically and chronically erode their partners' self-confidence, sense of safety, and emotional well-being through manipulation, violent outbursts, and verbal intimidation. This makes partners of abusers fearful of ever disagreeing with or confronting them, even over trivial issues.

Symptom: Blame the victims for their feelings

Description: Abusers blame others for "making them mad," for "making them feel bad about themselves," and so forth.

Symptom: Have intense, quick development of romantic relationships

Description: Abusers are often very intense in the early stages of dating relationships. They smother and overwhelm the other person with attention and shows of affection. They often press for quick commitment and even marriage before the other person has a chance to really get to know them. Victims of abusers often report they had many nagging doubts when dating them, but they felt so pressured that they ignored their feelings and proceeded to get married and found themselves being abused.

Symptom: Place impossible demands on family members

Description: Abusers are very insecure and have quite distorted views of what others can and should do for them. Family members, girlfriends, or boyfriends are made 100 percent responsible for their happiness. In a very strange and sick way, abusers need to physically, emotionally, and verbally control family members because they have transferred responsibility for their emotional well-being to their spouses or children. Abusive mothers also tend to do this with their children.

appendix 5: bible passages that address abuse

JESUS' VIEW OF CHILDREN AND THOSE WHO HARM CHILDREN

Jeremiah 32:31–32, 35—"Indeed this city has been to Me a provocation of My anger and My wrath from the day that they built it, even to this day, so that it should be removed from before My face, because of all the evil of the sons of Israel and the sons of Judah.... They built the high places of Baal that are in the valley of Ben-hinnom to cause their sons and their daughters to pass through the fire to Molech, which I had not commanded them nor had it entered My mind that they should do this abomination."

Matthew 18:5–6—"And whoever receives one such child in My name receives Me; but whoever causes one of these little ones who believe in Me to stumble, it would be better for him to have a heavy millstone hung around his neck, and to be drowned in the depth of the sea."

Matthew 19:13–14—"Then some children were brought to Him so that He might lay His hands on them and pray; and the disciples rebuked them. But Jesus said, 'Let the children alone, and do not hinder them from coming to Me; for the kingdom of heaven belongs to such as these.'"

CONDEMNATION OF PHYSICAL ABUSE

Psalm 11:5—"The LORD tests the righteous and the wicked, and the one who loves violence His soul hates."

Proverbs 1:15–19—"My son, do not walk in the way with them. Keep your feet from their path, for their feet run to evil and they hasten to shed blood. Indeed, it is useless to spread the baited net in the sight of any bird; but they [abusers] lie in wait for their own blood; they ambush their own lives. So are the ways of everyone who gains by violence; it takes away the life of its possessors."

Proverbs 6:16–19—"These are six things which the LORD hates, yes, seven which are an abomination to Him: Haughty eyes, a lying tongue, and hands that shed innocent blood, a heart that devises wicked plans, feet that run rapidly to evil, a false witness who utter lies, and one who spreads strife among brothers."

Ezekiel 9:9 – 10 — "The iniquity of the house of Israel and Judah is very, very great, and the land is filled with blood and the city is full of perversion; for they say, 'The LORD has forsaken the land, and the LORD does not see!' But as for Me [God], My eye will have no pity [on abusers] nor will I spare, but I will bring their conduct upon their heads."

Ezekiel 18:10 – 13 — "Then he may have a violent son who sheds blood and who does any of these things to a brother ... defiles his neighbor's wife, oppresses the poor and needy, commits robbery. . . . He will not live! He has committed all these abominations, he will surely be put to death."

Romans 3:15 – 18 — "Their feet are swift to shed blood, destruction and misery are in their paths, and the path of peace they have not known. There is no fear of God before their eyes."

CONDEMNATION OF SEXUAL ABUSE

Deuteronomy 22:25 – 26 — "But if in the field the man finds the girl who is engaged, and the man forces her and lies with her, then only the man who lies with her shall die. But you shall do nothing to the girl; there is no sin in the girl worthy of death."

Judges 19:25 — "But the men would not listen to him. So the man seized his concubine and brought her out to them; and they raped her and abused her all night until morning, then let her go at the approach of dawn."

Lamentations 5:11 — "They ravished the women in Zion, the virgins in the cities of Judah."

Ezekiel 22:11, 21 — "One has committed abomination with his neighbor's wife and another has lewdly defiled his daughter-in-law. And another in you has humbled his sister, his father's daughter. . . . I will gather you and blow on you with the fire of My wrath, and you will be melted in the midst of it."

EFFECTS OF SEXUAL ABUSE

2 Samuel 13:19 – 20 — "Tamar put ashes on her head and tore her long-sleeved garment which was on her; and she put her hand on her head and went away, crying aloud as she went. . . . So Tamar remained and was desolate in her brother Absalom's house."

CONDEMNATION OF NEGLECT

1 Timothy 5:8 — "But if anyone does not provide for his own, and especially for those of his household, he has denied the faith and is worse than an unbeliever."

CONDEMNATION AND EFFECT OF VERBAL ABUSE

Proverbs 12:18 — "There is one who speaks rashly like the thrusts of a sword, but the tongue of the wise brings healing."

Proverbs 15:4 — "A soothing tongue is a tree of life, but perversion in it crushes the spirit."

Proverbs 18:21 — "Death and life are in the power of the tongue."

Romans 3:13–14 — "Their throat is an open grave, with their tongues they keep deceiving, the poison of asps is under their lips; whose mouth is full of cursing and bitterness."

James 3:5–6, 8–9 — "So also the tongue is a small part of the body, and yet it boasts of great things. See how great a forest is set aflame by such a small fire! And the tongue is a fire, the very world of iniquity; the tongue is set among our members as that which defiles the entire body, and sets on fire the course of our life, and is set on fire by hell. . . . But no one can tame the tongue; it is a restless evil and full of deadly poison. With it we bless our Lord and Father, and with it we curse men, who have been made in the likeness of God."

CONDEMNATION OF SPIRITUAL ABUSE

Ezekiel 22:25–26, 28 — "There is a conspiracy of her prophets in her midst like a roaring lion tearing the prey. They have devoured lives; they have taken treasure and precious things; they have made many widows in the midst of her. Her priests have done violence to My law. . . . Her prophets have smeared whitewash for them, seeing false visions and divining lies for them, saying, 'Thus says the Lord GOD,' when the LORD has not spoken."

Matthew 23:1–5, 11–13 — "Then Jesus spoke to the crowds and to His disciples, saying: 'The scribes and the Pharisees have seated themselves in the chair of Moses; therefore all that they tell you, do and observe, but do not do according to their deeds; for they say things and do not do them. They tie up heavy burdens and lay them on men's shoulders; but they themselves are unwilling to move them with so much as a finger. But they do all their deeds to be noticed by men. . . . But the greatest among you shall be your servant. Whoever exalts himself shall be humbled; and whoever humbles himself shall be exalted. But woe to you, scribes and Pharisees, hypocrites, because you shut off the kingdom of heaven from people.'"

Mark 7:5–8—"The Pharisees and the scribes asked Him, 'Why do Your disciples not walk according to the tradition of the elders, but eat their bread with impure hands?' And He said to them, 'Rightly did Isaiah prophesy of you hypocrites, as it is written: "This people honors Me with their lips, but their heart is far away from Me. But in vain do they worship Me, teaching as doctrines the precepts of men." Neglecting the commandment of God, you hold to the tradition of men.'"

RESPONSIBILITY OF LEADERS TO AID AND PROTECT THE VULNERABLE

Proverbs 24:11–12—"Deliver those who are being taken away to death, and those who are staggering to slaughter, Oh hold them back. If you say, 'See, we did not know this,' does He not consider it who weighs the hearts? And does He not know it who keeps your soul?"

Isaiah 1:17—"Learn to do good; seek justice, reprove the ruthless, defend the orphan, plead for the widow."

Jeremiah 22:3—"Thus says the LORD: 'Do justice and righteousness; and deliver the one who has been robbed from the power of his oppressor. Also do not mistreat or do violence to the stranger, the orphan, or the widow; and do not shed innocent blood in this place.'"

Jeremiah 22:15–17—"'Did not your father eat and drink and do justice and righteousness? Then it was well with him. He pled the cause of the afflicted and needy; then it was well. Is not that what it means to know Me?' declares the LORD. 'But your eyes and your heart are intent only upon your own dishonest gain, and on shedding innocent blood and on practicing oppression and extortion.'"

RESPONSIBILITY OF LEADERS TO CONFRONT ABUSE AND OTHER TYPES OF EVIL

1 Samuel 3:13—"For I have told him that I am about to judge his house forever for the iniquity which he knew, because his sons brought a curse on themselves and he did not rebuke them." [Eli was judged for failing to confront and stop his sons from physical and sexual abuse—see 1 Samuel 2:16, 22.]

Isaiah 1:17—"Learn to do good; seek justice, reprove the ruthless, defend the orphan, plead for the widow."

1 Timothy 5:20—"Those who continue in sin, rebuke in the presence of all, so that the rest also will be fearful of sinning."

Titus 3:10–11—"Reject a factious man after a first and second warning, knowing that such a man is perverted and is sinning, being self-condemned."

GOD'S RIGHTEOUS JUDGMENT ON ABUSERS

2 Kings 17:17–18—"Then they made their sons and their daughters pass through the fire [burned them alive], and practiced divination and enchantments, and sold themselves to do evil in the sight of the LORD, provoking Him. So the LORD was very angry with Israel and removed them from His sight; none was left except the tribe of Judah."

Joel 3:19—"Egypt will become a waste, and Edom will become a desolate wilderness, because of the violence done to the sons of Judah, in whose land they have shed innocent blood."

Nahum 3:1, 3, 5, 7—"Woe to the bloody city [Nineveh, the capital of the abusive, ruthless Assyrians], completely full of lies and pillage; her prey never departs. . . . Swords flashing, spears gleaming, many slain, a mass of corpses, and countless dead bodies [of her murder victims]. . . . 'Behold, I am against you,' declares the LORD of hosts. . . . And it will come about that all who see you will shrink from you and say, 'Nineveh is devastated! Who will grieve for her?'"

Philippians 1:27–28—"I will hear of you that you are . . . in no way alarmed by your opponents—which is a sign of destruction for them, but of salvation for you, and that too, from God."

Revelation 21:8—"But for . . . murderers and immoral persons and sorcerers and idolaters and all liars, their part will be in the lake that burns with fire and brimstone, which is the second death."

CONDEMNATION OF ABUSIVE LEADERS

Ezekiel 22:6–7, 13, 15—"Behold, the rulers of Israel, each according to his power, have been in you for the purpose of shedding blood. . . . The alien they have oppressed in your midst; the fatherless and the widow they have wronged in you. . . . Behold, then, I smite My hand at your dishonest gain which you have acquired and at the bloodshed which is among you. . . . I will scatter you among the nations and I will disperse you through the lands, and I will consume your uncleanness from you."

Micah 3:1–4, 9–10, 12—"'Hear now, heads of Jacob and rulers of the house of Israel. Is it not for you to know justice? You who hate good and love evil, who tear off their skin from them and their flesh from their bones, who eat the flesh of my people, strip off their skin from them, break their bones, and chop them up as for the pot and as meat in a kettle.' Then they [the abusive leaders] will cry out to the LORD, but He will not answer them. Instead, He will hide His face from them at that time because they have practiced evil deeds. . . . Now hear this, heads of the house of Jacob and rulers of the house of Israel, who abhor justice and twist everything that is straight, who build Zion with bloodshed and Jerusalem with violent injustice. . . . Therefore, on account of you Zion will be plowed as a field, Jerusalem will become a heap of ruins."

TRUE NATURE OF GODLY LEADERSHIP

Deuteronomy 24:5—"When a man takes a new wife, he shall not go out with the army nor be charged with any duty; he shall be free at home one year and shall give happiness to his wife whom he has taken."

Luke 22:25–26—"And He said to them, 'The kings of the Gentiles lord it over them; and those who have authority over them are called "Benefactors." But it is not this way with you, but the one who is the greatest among you must become like the youngest, and the leader like the servant.'"

Ephesians 5:25, 28—"Husbands, love your wives, just as Christ also loved the church and gave Himself up for her. . . . So husbands ought also to love their own wives as [they love] their own bodies."

Colossians 3:19, 21—"Husbands, love your wives and do not be embittered against them. . . . Fathers, do not exasperate your children, so that they will not lose heart."

1 Peter 3:7—"You husbands in the same way, live with your wives in an understanding way, as with someone weaker, since she is a woman; and show her honor as a fellow heir of the grace of life, so that your prayers will not be hindered."

1 Peter 5:2–3—"Shepherd the flock of God among you, . . . nor yet as lording it over those allotted to your charge, but proving to be examples to the flock."

GOD'S REDEMPTION OF ABUSE

Genesis 50:20—"As for you, you meant evil against me, but God meant it for good in order to bring about this present result, to preserve many people alive."

Isaiah 53:5—"But He was pierced through for our transgressions, He was crushed for our iniquities; the chastening for our well-being fell upon Him, and by His scourging we are healed."

1 Corinthians 1:18—"For the word of the cross is foolishness to those who are perishing, but to us who are being saved it is the power of God."

2 Corinthians 4:8–10—"We are afflicted in every way, but not crushed; perplexed, but not despairing; persecuted, but not forsaken; struck down, but not destroyed; always carrying about in the body the dying of Jesus, so that the life of Jesus also may be manifested in our body."

notes

chapter 1: a wake-up call regarding the extent and power of abuse

1. The only offensive weapon listed in Scripture for spiritual warfare is the word of God, the sword of the Spirit (Ephesians 6:17). The language Paul uses in this passage is significant, for there are two words for "sword" used in the New Testament. The ῥομφαια, or broadsword, was used to slash from a distance, but it isn't the term used in this verse. Paul uses the other term for sword in Ephesians 6:17 (μακαιρα), which indicates the short dagger used in close hand-to-hand combat to stab an open spot in the enemy's armor. This suggests that in spiritual warfare our goal is not to simply thrust large amounts of Scripture at a problem but rather to gain a precise understanding of the issue (and Satan's lies), so that we can use the appropriate Scripture with precision to deal with the problem.

2. Reported in World Health Organization, "Violence against Women: A Priority Health Issue" (July 1997); can be viewed on the Web at www.who.int/gender/violence/v4.pdf.

3. Reported in the Majority Staff of the Senate Judiciary Committee, "Violence against Women: A Week in the Life of America" (October 1992); can be viewed on the Web at www.mith2.umd.edu/WomensStudies/GenderIssues/Violence+Women/WeekIn America/full-text.

4. Reported in Antonio C. Novello et al., "From the Surgeon General, US Public Health Service," *Journal of the American Medical Association* 267 (1992): 3132.

5. Reported in Callie Marie Rennison and Sarah Welchans, "Bureau of Justice Statistics Special Report: Intimate Partner Violence" (May 2000); can be viewed on the Web at www.ojp.usdoj.gov/bjs/pub/pdf/ipv.pdf.

6. Ibid.

7. Reported in American Psychological Association, "Violence and the Family: Report of the American Psychological Association Presidential Task Force on Violence and the Family" (1996), 10. A group of researchers found a 31 percent lifetime prevalence for domestic violence among adult women using a screening questionnaire recommended by the American Medical Association (R. M. Siegel et al., "Screening for Domestic Violence in the Community Pediatric Setting," *Pediatrics* 104 [1999]: 874–77).

8. Lee Bowker, "Religious Victims and Their Religious Leaders," in *Abuse and Religion: When Praying Isn't Enough*, ed. Anne L. Horton and Judith A. Williamson (Lexington, Mass.: Lexington Books, 1988), 230–31.

9. One of the most comprehensive discussions of the research supporting the prevalence of sexual abuse and sexual assault is Diana E. H. Russell and Rebecca M. Bolen, *The*

Epidemic of Rape and Child Sexual Abuse in the United States (Thousand Oaks, Calif.: Sage, 2000).

10. M. P. Koss, C. A. Gidycz, and W. Wisniewski, "The Scope of Rape: Incidence and Prevalence of Sexual Aggression and Victimization in a National Sample of Higher Education Students," *Journal of Consulting and Clinical Psychology* 55 (1987): 162–70. Most research puts the sexual abuse rates for female American college students between 15 percent and 25 percent (Martin D. Schwartz and Walter S. DeKeseredy, *Sexual Assault on the College Campus: The Role of Male Peer Support* [Thousand Oaks, Calif.: Sage, 1997], 13).

11. Robin Warshaw, *I Never Call It Rape* (New York: Harper and Row, 1988), 11. More recent studies suggest that dating violence has gotten even worse. Jay G. Silverman et al. found that about 20 percent of female high school students report being physically or sexually abused by a dating partner ("Dating Violence against Adolescent Girls and Associated Substance Abuse, Unhealthy Weight Control, Sexual Risk Behavior, Pregnancy, and Suicidality," *Journal of the American Medical Association* 286 (2001): 572–79.

12. Reported in David Finkelhor, "Current Information on the Scope and Nature of Child Sexual Abuse," *Future of Children* 4 (1994): 31–53; can be viewed on the Web at www.futureofchildren.org/usr_doc/vol4no2ART2.pdf. Diana Russell and Rebecca Bolen give considerable evidence that sexual abuse rates for females are over 35 percent (*The Epidemic of Rape and Child Abuse*, 205–12).

13. Reported in A. J. Sedlak and D. D. Broadhurst, *Executive Summary of the Third National Incidence Study of Child Abuse and Neglect* (Washington, D.C.: U. S. Department of Health and Human Services, 1996); can be viewed on the Web at www.healthieryou.com/cabuse.html. Two sets of definitional standards were applied in the study: the Harm Standard and the Endangerment Standard. The Harm Standard is fairly stringent in that it generally requires that an act (or failure to act) must result in demonstrable harm to the child if it is to be classified as abuse. Given the careful and repeatedly replicated research that reveals that child abuse is rampant, it is irresponsible for Christian writers who have no graduate training or professional experience in the discipline to declare that child abuse is not epidemic in America (for example, see Brenda Scott, *Out of Control: Who's Watching Our Child Protection Agencies?* [Lafayette, La.: Huntington House, 1994], 35, 430.

14. Sedlak and Broadhurst note that it is inconceivable that the actual abuse rates were actually four times higher than reported in the 1986 study but somehow escaped the notice of the professional community. Hence, they argue that the findings of the 1993 incidence study "herald a true rise in the scope and severity of child abuse in the United States" (*Executive Summary*).

15. Reported in Charles L. Whitfield, M.D., *Memory and Abuse: Remembering and Healing the Effects of Trauma* (Deerfield Beach, Fla.: HCI, 1995), 51.

16. Pamela Cooper-White notes that virtually everyone has a reason, conscious or unconscious, to minimize abuse ("An Emperor without Clothes: The Church's Views about Treatment of Domestic Violence," *Pastoral Psychology* 45 [1996]: 4). Even trained professionals often minimize abuse. For instance, in one study, physicians correctly identified domestic violence in only 0.3 percent of instances (B. D. Kerker et al.,

"Identification of Violence in the Home: Pediatric and Parental Reports," *Archives of Pediatric Adolescent Medicine* 154 [2000]: 457–62).

17. While sinful depravity and the capacity for abuse are equally shared by both genders, throughout human history men have generally held more power and hence have been responsible for a disproportionate share of sexual abuse and domestic violence. While I can't subscribe to all of the solutions to abuse proposed by feminists, I deeply appreciate their exposure of the problem. The following works have been particularly influential in documenting the widespread abuse of male power against women and children: Carol J. Adams and Marie M. Fortune, eds., *Violence Against Women and Children: A Christian Theological Sourcebook* (New York: Continuum, 1995); Susan Brownmiller, *Against Our Will: Men, Women, and Rape* (New York: Simon and Schuster, 1975); R. Emerson Dobash and Russell Dobash, *Violence Against Wives: A Case Against the Patriarchy* (New York: Macmillan, 1979); Diana E. H. Russell, *Rape in Marriage*, rev. ed. (Indianapolis: Indiana Univ. Press, 1990); Lenore E. Walker, *The Battered Woman* (New York: Harper and Row, 1979).

18. For a basic overview of the nature and activity of angels, see C. Fred Dickason, *Angels Elect and Evil*, rev. ed. (Chicago: Moody, 1995). For a scholarly treatment of the biblical doctrine of angels, see Stephen F. Noll, *Angels of Light, Powers of Darkness* (Downers Grove, Ill.: InterVarsity Press, 1998). For a comprehensive biblical treatment of Satan and demons, see Sydney H. T. Page, *Powers of Evil: A Biblical Study of Satan and Demons* (Grand Rapids: Baker, 1995).

19. For an excellent overview of historical and contemporary theological models of evil, see Hans Schwarz, *Evil: A Historical and Theological Perspective* (Minneapolis: Fortress, 1995).

20. Dickason, *Angels Elect and Evil*, 130, regarding the articular use of the adjective πονηρος to refer to Satan. On other uses of this phrase to refer to Satan, particularly in Matthew, see Page, *Powers of Evil*, 112–14.

21. The use of the verb σφάζω highlights the brutal nature of Cain's act, for it means to kill by violence, to slaughter (LXX Jeremiah 52:10; Revelation 6:4, 9). Satan's being "a murderer from the beginning" may refer to his influence on Cain but more likely refers to his influence in the temptation of Adam, which would then make Satan the murderer of the entire human race (Romans 5:12–21; Wisdom of Solomon 2:23–24).

22. The use of the Greek verb συνευδοκεω in Acts 8:1 makes it clear that Paul did not passively consent to Stephen's murder, for this term indicates active consent and hearty approval (Acts 22:20; Romans 1:32; 1 Corinthians 7:12). Furthermore, Acts 8:3 shows that Paul was actively ravaging the church (ελυμαινετο — the imperfect tense indicates ongoing action).

chapter 2: abuse as a perversion of the image of God

1. Steven Levenkron, a psychologist who specializes in treating self-mutilators, estimates that there are two million Americans who self-mutilate, and the vast majority do so because of unresolved childhood trauma, especially sexual abuse (*Cutting: Understanding and Overcoming Self-Mutilation* [New York: Norton, 1999]).

2. Kathleen Potter, Judy Martin, and Sarah Romans conducted a study of prostitutes in New Zealand and found that 80 percent of them had experienced physical abuse and 36 percent experienced genital sexual abuse before the age of sixteen ("Early Developmental Experiences of Female Sex Workers: A Comparative Study," *Australian and New Zealand Journal of Psychiatry* 33 [1999]: 935−40). A larger study of 237 prostitutes and 407 comparison women at an STD clinic found that 32 percent of the prostitutes had experienced severe childhood sexual abuse (nonconsensual prepubertal intercourse). This rate was two and a half times higher than that experienced by the control group from an STD clinic—and a control group from an STD clinic will most likely reflect considerably higher childhood abuse rates than the general populace (John J. Potterat et al., "Pathways to Prostitution: The Chronology of Sexual and Drug Abuse Milestones," *Journal of Sex Research* 98 [1998]: 333−41). These abuse rates are three to four times the national average.

3. Studies conducted by Patrick Carnes reveal that 72 percent of the sex addicts surveyed reported physical abuse in their history, and 81 percent reported a history of sexual abuse (*Don't Call It Love: Recovery from Sexual Addiction* [New York: Bantam, 1991], 146). Interestingly, the partners of sex addicts have histories of physical and sexual abuse mirroring that of the addicts.

4. Reported in M. S. Wylie, "The Shadow of a Doubt," *Family Therapy Networker* 17 (1993): 70−73. David Finkelhor et al. conclude that abuse is "a serious mental health problem, consistently associated with very disturbing problems in a significant portion of its victims" (*A Sourcebook on Child Sexual Abuse* [Beverly Hills, Calif.: Sage, 1986], 163).

5. See L. L. Merrill, L. K. Hervig, and J. S. Milner, "Childhood Parenting Experiences, Intimate Partner Conflict Resolution, and Adult Risk for Child Physical Abuse," *Child Abuse and Neglect* 20 (1996): 1049−65. A shockingly high percentage of parents who experienced abuse as children will become abusers. J. Kaufman and E. Ziglar report that approximately 30 percent of abused children become physically abusing parents ("Do Abused Children Become Abusive Parents?" *American Journal of Orthopsychiatry* 57 [1987]: 186−92).

6. Paul K. Jewett, *Who We Are: Our Dignity as Humans* (Grand Rapids: Eerdmans, 1996), 54.

7. I'm indebted to Anthony A. Hoekema for this perspective of the image of God. He argues that the image of God in humans is multifaceted and involves a structural aspect (innate qualities such as rationality) as well as relational and functional aspects (*Created in God's Image* [Grand Rapids: Eerdmans, 1986], 66−101); see also Wayne Grudem, *Systematic Theology* (Grand Rapids: Zondervan, 1994), 443−44.

8. Anthony Hoekema notes, "Men and women cannot attain to true humanity in isolation; they need the fellowship and stimulation of others. We are social beings" (*Created in God's Image*, 77); see also Ranald Macaulay and Jerram Barrs, *Being Human: The Nature of Spiritual Experience* (Downers Grove, Ill.: InterVarsity Press, 1978), 171.

9. The literature on attachment is voluminous. Robert Karen gives an excellent overview of the research (*Becoming Attached: First Relationships and How They Shape Our Capacity to Love* [New York: Oxford Univ. Press, 1998]). As a theologian, I'm amazed at the way secular attachment research harmonizes with the biblical teaching on the relational

aspect of the image of God, especially the profound significance of intimate relationships.

10. *Marasmus* (wasting away) is the medical term for this condition, which was identified after World War II when large numbers of infant orphans, cared for in Allied orphanages, began dying for no apparent medical reason. Once these infants who were being changed, fed, and given warm cribs but receiving little or no physical contact by the busy nurses began to be held by caregivers, the exploding infant mortality rates dramatically reversed.

11. The Hebrew word for "image" *(ṣelem)* indicates concrete similarity, such as that found in a coin or a statue (Daniel 3:1). The word for "likeness" *(demût)* indicates abstract similarity (Daniel 10:16). The terms are probably mutually defining.

12. See Erich Sauer, *The King of the Earth* (Exeter, England: Paternoster, 1959), 72–91.

13. The prediction that Eve's desire would be for her husband is difficult to interpret. Susan Foh forcefully argues that, based on the use of the same word in Genesis 4:7, this refers to the woman's desire to master or usurp her husband's authority (*Women and the Word of God: A Response to Biblical Feminism* [Grand Rapids: Baker, 1979], 67–69). While this view has exegetical merit, I believe it places too much emphasis on the meaning of "desire" in Genesis 4:7, while ignoring the fact that the only other time the term is used in the Old Testament, it refers to emotional, romantic desire (Song of Solomon 7:10). Donald Joy convincingly argues that the context of Genesis 1–3, as well as human experience, suggests that the woman's desire here is one of inappropriate idolatrous attachment to her husband (*Bonding: Relationships in the Image of God* [Waco, Tex.: Word, 1991], 21–24).

14. The majority of commentators recognize that "he will rule over you" is no divine prescription but a tragic prediction of sin's effects on the human race. The Hebrew term for "rule" found in Genesis 3:16 is the same term found in Genesis 4:7 of Cain's need to harshly dominate or master that which would harm him, namely, sin. This lexical observation, along with the fact that Genesis 3:16 gives several unfortunate negative consequences of the fall, lead me to conclude that "he will rule over you" reflects not God's desire but a realistic prediction of the results of sinful depravity on males who will routinely seek to abuse their power. Thus, Victor Hamilton argues that this phrase means "the sinful husband will try to be a tyrant over his wife" (*The Book of Genesis Chapters 1–17* [Grand Rapids: Eerdmans, 1990], 202).

15. Interestingly, the same Greek word used in Luke 22:25 to denote harsh lordship or domination (κυριεύω) is the same word used in Genesis 3:16 in the Septuagint to indicate that the man will rule over the woman.

16. For a nonfeminist analysis of the abuse of male headship and biblical correctives, see Steven R. Tracy, "1 Corinthians 11:3: A Corrective to Distortions and Abuses of Male Headship," *Journal for Biblical Manhood and Womanhood* 8 (2003): 17–22.

17. Mark Chaffin, Elizabeth Letourneau, and Jane Silovsky cite research that indicates women are responsible for 17 percent of child sexual abuse and 20 percent of adolescent sexual abuse ("Adults, Adolescents, and Children Who Sexually Abuse Children: A Developmental Perspective," in *The APSAC Handbook on Child Maltreatment*, 2d ed., ed. John E. B. Myers et al. [Thousand Oaks, Calif.: Sage, 2002], 219). David

Finkelhor argues that 95 percent of child sexual abuse of girls is perpetrated by men, and 80 percent of child sexual abuse of boys is perpetrated by men (*Child Sexual Abuse: New Theory and Research* [New York: Free Press, 1984], 184).

18. Callie Marie Rennison and Sarah Welchans, "Bureau of Justice Statistics Special Report: Intimate Partner Violence" (May 2000); can be viewed on the Web at www.ojp.usdoj.gov/bjs/pub/pdf/ipv.pdf.

19. Reported in A. J. Sedlak and D. D. Broadhurst, *Executive Summary of the Third National Incidence Study of Child Abuse and Neglect* (Washington, D.C.: U. S. Department of Health and Human Services, 1996); can be viewed on the Web at www.healthieryou.com/cabuse.html. However, while 65 percent of all maltreated children are maltreated by a female, 54 percent of maltreated children are also maltreated by a male; and while 75 percent of all children maltreated by a parent are maltreated by their mother, 46 percent of children maltreated by a birth parent are maltreated by their father. These figures add up to much more than 100 percent because many children are maltreated by both parents.

20. When we look just at sexual abuse, the picture is somewhat different. Nearly half of sexually abused children were abused by a parent or parent-substitute, but just over one-fourth were sexually abused by a birth parent.

21. While I'm focusing on five types of abuse, these are the major categories and by no means exhaust the spectrum of abuse. Paul Hegstrom, a man who physically abused his wife for years while serving as a Protestant pastor, charts sixteen different varieties of wife abuse, including stalking, economic abuse, intimidation, property violence, emotional abuse, and the use of children (*Angry Men and the Women Who Love Them* [Kansas City, Mo.: Beacon Hill, 1999], 30–42).

22. Dan Allender's definition of sexual abuse is helpful: "Sexual abuse is any contact or interaction (visual, verbal, or psychological) between a child/adolescent and an adult when the child/adolescent is being used for the sexual stimulation of the perpetrator or any other person" (*The Wounded Heart*, rev. ed. [Colorado Springs: NavPress, 1995], 48).

23. I'm utilizing Diana Russell's six categories of sexual abuse (*The Secret Trauma: Incest in the Lives of Girls and Women* [New York: Basic Books, 1986], 144).

24. Reported in Russell, *The Secret Trauma*, 142–44. By way of contrast, 54 percent of severe sexual abuse resulted in extreme trauma.

25. For a technical exegesis that supports my conclusions, see Bruce Fisk, "Πορνευειν as Body Violation: The Unique Nature of Sexual Sin in 1 Corinthians 6:18," *New Testament Studies* 42 (1996): 540–58.

26. See Carol J. Adams, *Woman-Battering* (Philadelphia: Fortress, 1994), 12.

27. Children who witness family violence suffer extremely serious consequences. Child psychiatrist and brain researcher Bruce Perry has done groundbreaking work on the permanent effects on children who witness domestic violence, documenting the permanent changes in brain physiology of children who witness abuse (*Maltreated Children: Experience, Brain Development, and the Next Generation* [New York: Norton, 1996]).

28. Art therapy pictures are included in several of the following chapters. The vast majority of these come from my wife's counseling practice. They give the reader a graphic window into the world of abuse survivors and into the dynamics of abuse.

29. For more on spiritual abuse, see David Johnson and Jeff VanVonderen, *The Subtle Power of Spiritual Abuse* (Minneapolis: Bethany House, 1991), 20; Ken Blue, *Healing Spiritual Abuse: How to Break Free from Bad Church Experiences* (Downers Grove, Ill.: InterVarsity Press, 1992), 12.

30. Ken Blue organizes much of his book around Matthew 23 and the spiritual abuse of the Pharisees. He concludes by identifying seven symptoms of abusive religion seen in Matthew 23 (*Healing Spiritual Abuse*, 134–35).

31. See Johnson and VanVonderen, *The Subtle Power of Spiritual Abuse*, 63–71.

32. Caregivers' responses to children's abuse disclosures often have profound long-term effects. Inappropriate responses to an abuse disclosure (shaming, blaming, denial, passivity, etc.) can be just as damaging as the abuse itself (see Leonard T. Gries et al., "Positive Reaction to Disclosure and Recovery from Child Sexual Abuse," *Journal of Child Sexual Abuse* 9 [2000]: 29–51); Thomas A. Roesler, "Reactions to Disclosure of Childhood Sexual Abuse: The Effect on Adult Symptoms," *Journal of Nervous and Mental Diseases* 182 (1994): 618–24.

33. Tragically, parents often do not respond properly to disclosures of abuse. In a study of 755 adult women who had disclosed incest to a nonoffending parent in childhood (before age eighteen), 52 percent of the time the incest continued for more than one year after the disclosure. In a high percentage of instances, mothers disbelieved or blamed their daughters for the incest (see Thomas A. Roesler and Tiffany Weissmann Wind, "Telling the Secret: Adult Women Describe Their Disclosure of Incest," *Journal of Interpersonal Violence* 9 [1994]: 327–38).

34. "Shimmer," words and music by Shawn Mullins. Copyright © 1998 EMI BLACKWOOD MUSIC, INC. and ROADIEODIE MUSIC, INC. All rights controlled and administered by EMI BLACKWOOD MUSIC, INC. All rights reserved. International rights secured. Used by permission.

chapter 3: profiles of abusers

1. Hannah Arendt, *Eichmann in Jerusalem: A Report on the Banality of Evil*, rev. ed. (New York: Penguin, 1965), 228–232.

2. Reported in Anna C. Salter, *Transforming Trauma: A Guide to Understanding and Treating Adult Survivors of Child Sexual Abuse* (Thousand Oaks, Calif.: Sage, 1995), 27–28.

3. See Arendt, Eichmann in Jerusalem, 21–25. The extreme extent to which Eichmann denied responsibility is seen in his last statement to the court. He declared that his only crime was that he was virtuous, i.e., that he was an obedient, law-abiding German citizen, and his virtuous obedience had been abused by Nazi leaders, 247.

4. Eric Leberg gives helpful insights into the various ways child molesters maintain secrecy and deny responsibility (*Understanding Child Molesters: Taking Charge* [Thousand Oaks, Calif.: Sage, 1997], 57–80).

5. Reported in N. L. Pollock and J. M. Hashmall, "The Excuses of Child Molesters," *Behavioral Sciences and the Law* 9 (1991): 53–59. H. E. Barbaree and W. L. Marshall argue regarding child molesters that "denial of the offense and minimization of the offender's responsibility and the harm he has done is so common . . . as to be regarded

as a defining characteristic of this population" ("Treatment of the Sexual Offender," in *Treatment of Offenders with Mental Disorders*, ed. Robert M. Wettstein [New York: Guilford, 1998], 294).

6. Cited in James Ptacek, "How Men Who Batter Rationalize," in *Abuse and Religion: When Praying Isn't Enough*, ed. Anne L. Horton and Judith A. Williamson (Lexington, Mass.: Lexington Books, 1988), 249-50.

7. For an excellent discussion of the way child molesters blame victims and victims' mothers, see Leberg, *Understanding Child Molesters*, 81-87.

8. Ptacek, "How Men Who Batter Rationalize," 251, 254.

9. Ibid., 252-53.

10. See Dan Allender and Tremper Longman, *Bold Love* (Colorado Springs: NavPress, 1992), 236. Hannah Arendt describes the incredible way Nazis used "language rules" both to camouflage their brutal actions and to program their own executioners. For instance, the word for "murder" was replaced by "to grant a mercy death." The code words for "execution" were "final solution," "evacuation," and "special treatment." The soldiers were programmed for their task by being told, "We realize that what we are expecting of you is superhuman," when in reality their orders were "superhumanly inhuman" (Arendt, *Eichmann in Jerusalem*, 85-86, 105-8).

11. David enjoined Uriah to go home and "wash his feet." On this phrase being a euphemism for sexual relations, see Gale A. Yee, "Fraught with Background: Literary Ambiguity in 2 Samuel 11," *Interpretation* 42 (1988): 245.

12. Ronald Youngblood notes the similarity of David's three-phase, increasingly ruthless plan to deal with his "problem" to the abusive plan used earlier by an Egyptian pharaoh, who first oppressed the Israelites with forced labor. When that didn't work, the pharaoh commanded the Hebrew midwives to kill newborn Hebrew males. When that didn't work, he ordered all Egyptians to drown newborn Hebrew male children (Frank E. Gaebelein, ed., *The Expositor's Bible Commentary*, vol. 3 [Grand Rapids: Zondervan, 1993], 932-33). As abusers become more desperate, they often become more ruthless and deceptive.

13. Leberg, *Understanding Child Molesters*, 65-66.

14. Restitution for the stealing of sheep was expressly said to be fourfold (Exodus 22:1), as it was for stealing other goods and for extortion (Leviticus 6:1-5; Luke 19:8; cf. 2 Samuel 12:6).

15. Murder was a capital offense (Genesis 9:6; Numbers 35:33), and David was ultimately responsible, not just for Uriah's murder, but for the murder of other unnamed soldiers with him (2 Samuel 11:24). He was also guilty of adultery with (or rape of) a married woman, both of which were capital offenses (Deuteronomy 22:22, 25).

16. See Salter, *Transforming Trauma*, 104-16. Unlike other kinds of abusers, sadistic offenders do not deny the victims' pain and suffering; rather, they feed off of it. It's one of the primary reasons they intimidate—it creates even greater emotional pain and degradation for the victims.

17. For a general discussion of Assyrian cruelty to those they defeated, see Georges Contenau, *Everyday Life in Babylon and Assyria* (New York: W. W. Norton, 1966), 141-57.

18. Reported in David Finkelhor et al., "Sexual Abuse in a National Survey of Adult Men and Women: Prevalence, Characteristics, and Risk Factors," *Child Abuse and Neglect* 14 (1990): 19–28.

19. David Finkelhor offers an excellent theoretical model to analyze the complex dynamics of child sexual abuse. He argues that four preconditions must be met for someone to sexually violate a child (*Child Sexual Abuse: New Theory and Research* [New York: Free Press, 1984], 36–46, 53–61).

20. Reported in David M. Fergusson and Paul E. Mullen, *Childhood Sexual Abuse: An Evidence-Based Perspective* (Thousand Oaks, Calif.: Sage, 1999), 49; see Rochelle F. Hanson, Julie A. Lipovsky, and Benjamin E. Saunders, "Characteristics of Fathers in Incest Families," *Journal of Interpersonal Violence* 9 (1994): 155–69.

21. Reported in Hanson, Lipovsky, and Saunders, "Characteristics of Fathers in Incest Families," 164.

22. Reported in Julie McCormack, Stephen M. Hudson, and Tony Ward, "Sexual Offenders' Perceptions of Their Early Interpersonal Relationships: An Attachment Perspective," *Journal of Sex Research* 39 (2002): 85–94.

23. Reported in Daniel Salter et al., "Development of Sexually Abusive Behavior in Sexually Victimized Males: A Longitudinal Study," *The Lancet* 361 (2003): 471–76.

24. Reported in Fergusson and Mullen, *Childhood Sexual Abuse*, 45–47.

25. Ibid., 47.

26. Reported in J. C. Anderson et al., "The Prevalence of Childhood Sexual Abuse Experiences in a Community Sample of Women," *Journal of the American Academy of Child and Adolescent Psychiatry* 32 (1993): 911–19; see also Diana E. H. Russell, *The Secret Trauma: Incest in the Lives of Girls and Women* (New York: Basic Books, 1986), 388.

27. Reported in G. G. Abel et al., "Self-reported Sex Crimes of Nonincarcerated Paraphiliacs," *Journal of Interpersonal Violence* 2 (1987): 3–25.

28. Abel et al. calculate that child molesters have only a 5 percent chance of getting caught. M. R. Weinrott and M. Saylor document the large number of nonsexual crimes committed by child molesters ("Self-report of Crimes Committed by Sex Offenders," *Journal of Interpersonal Violence* 6 [1991]: 286–300); see also Salter, *Transforming Trauma*, 21–23.

29. R. T. Rada found that 50 percent of the molesters he surveyed had been drinking at the time they molested—30 percent had been drinking heavily ("Alcoholism and the Child Molester," *Annals of the New York Academy of Sciences* 273 [1979]: 492–96). Be aware, though, that while this may provide a partial explanation for molesters' overcoming inhibitions, it should never be accepted as an excuse or justification for sexual offenses against minors.

30. Reported in Salter, Transforming Trauma, 13–17.

31. Reported in John B. Murray, "Psychological Profile of Pedophiles and Child Molesters," *The Journal of Psychology* 134 (2000): 212.

32. Ibid., 214; see also A. N. Groth, W. F. Hobson, and T. S. Gary, "The Child Molester: Clinical Observations," *Social Work and Human Sexuality* 1 (1982): 129–44.

33. Eric Leberg gives helpful examples of the calculated grooming that sex offenders, especially pedophiles, utilize (*Understanding Child Molesters*, 15 – 45, 139 – 43).

34. Reported in Finkelhor et al., "Sexual Abuse in a National Survey of Adult Men and Women," 19 – 28.

35. See Anna C. Salter, *Predators, Pedophiles, Rapists, and Other Sex Offenders: Who They Are, How They Operate, and How We Can Protect Ourselves and Our Children* (New York: Basic Books, 2003), 76 – 79; see also Ruth Mathews, Jane Matthews, and Kate Speltz, "Female Sexual Offenders," in *The Sexually Abused Male: Prevalence, Impact, and Treatment, ed. Mic Hunter* (Lexington, Mass.: Lexington Books, 1990), 275 – 93.

36. Reported in Craig S. Cashwell and Michele E. Caruso, "Adolescent Sex Offenders: Identification and Intervention Strategies," *Journal of Mental Health Counseling* 19 (1997): 336 – 49.

37. Reported in Gary P. Bischof and Sandra M. Stith, "Family Environments of Adolescent Sex Offenders and Other Juvenile Delinquents," *Adolescence* 30 (1995): 157 – 71.

38. Reported in Mark Chaffin, Elizabeth Letourneau, and Jane F. Silovsky, "Adults, Adolescents, and Children Who Sexually Abuse Children: A Developmental Perspective," in *The APSAC Handbook on Child Maltreatment*, 2d ed., ed. John E. B. Myers et al. (Thousand Oaks, Calif.: Sage, 2002), 208 – 9; see also G. Lane Ryan, J. S. Davis, and C. Isaac, "Juvenile Sex Offenders: Development and Correction," *Child Abuse and Neglect* 11 (1987): 385 – 95.

39. Reported in Judith V. Becker, "What We Know about the Characteristics and Treatment of Adolescents Who Have Committed Sexual Offenses," *Child Maltreatment* 3 (1998): 317 – 29.

40. Some experts suggest it's improper to use the terms "molester" and "perpetrator" for children who initiate sexually inappropriate acts on other children because of children's limited cognitive development, the legal inappropriateness of these terms, and the fact that such labels can do more harm than good developmentally (see Chaffin, Letourneau, and Silovsky, "Adults, Adolescents, and Children Who Sexually Abuse Children," 208 – 9).

41. Ibid., 209.

42. Reported in Callie Marie Rennison and Sarah Welchans, "Bureau of Justice Statistics Special Report: Intimate Partner Violence" (May 2000); can be viewed on the Web at www.ojp.usdoj.gov/bjs/pub/pdf/ipv.pdf.

43. Reported in Centers for Disease Control Fact Sheet, "The Co-occurrence of Intimate Partner Violence against Mothers and the Abuse of Children" (2002).

44. Reported in Ola W. Barnett, Cindy L. Miller-Perrin, and Robin D. Perrin, eds., *Family Violence across the Lifespan: An Introduction* (Thousand Oaks, Calif.: Sage, 1997), 239.

45. See Lundy Bancroft and Jay G. Silverman, *The Batterer as Parent: Addressing the Impact of Domestic Violence on Family Dynamics* (Thousand Oaks, Calif.: Sage, 2002), 5 – 7.

46. See David J. Livingston, *Healing Violent Men: A Model for Christian Community* (Philadelphia: Fortress, 2002), 18 – 21; Diane Goldstein and Alan Rosenbaum, "An

Evaluation of the Self-Esteem of Maritally Violent Men," *Family Relations* 34 (1985): 425–28.

47. Reported in Bancroft and Silverman, *The Batterer as Parent*, 7–16; see also Mary Nomme Russell, *Confronting Abusive Beliefs: Group Treatment for Abusive Men* (Thousand Oaks, Calif.: Sage, 1995), 36–46. One influential typology proposes three types of physical male abusers in ascending order of violence: the family-only batterer, the borderline/dysforic batterer, and the generally violent/antisocial batterer (A. Holtzworth-Munroe and G. L. Stuart, "Typologies of Male Batterers: Three Subtypes and the Differences among Them," *Psychological Bulletin* 116 [1994]: 476–97). Lundy Bancroft describes ten different types of abusive men (*Why Does He Do That? Inside the Minds of Angry and Controlling Men* [New York: G. P. Putnam's Sons, 2002], 76–105).

chapter 4: portrait of an abusive family

1. David Noel Freedman notes that the birth of Solomon precedes this section, and the account of the rape of Tamar is foundational to explaining the "fulfillment of the quest for an heir in the rise of Solomon, the fourth and the youngest of the sons to seek or claim the throne" ("Dinah and Shechem, Tamar and Amnon," *Austin Seminary Bulletin* [1990]: 60). Similarly, Andrew E. Hill argues that Tamar is just a pawn in the power play for the throne ("A Jonadab Connection in the Absalom Conspiracy," *Journal of the Evangelical Theological Society* 30 [1987]: 389).

2. Many researchers note that in abusive families, particularly in incestuous families, role reversal is very common, with one or more of the older children taking care of both a physically and emotionally frail mother and younger siblings (see Catherine Cameron, *Resolving Childhood Trauma: A Long-Term Study of Abuse Survivors* [Thousand Oaks, Calif.: Sage, 2000], 32); see also Judith Lewis Herman, *Father-Daughter Incest*, rev. ed. (Cambridge, Mass.: Harvard Univ. Press, 2000), 78–81. This helps explain why victims of father-daughter incest are most often firstborn children (see David Finkelhor, *Sexually Victimized Children* [New York: Free Press, 1979], 129).

3. Anna C. Salter notes that those who are violent toward people they are connected to tend to distance themselves from them with their words, just as they do with their emotions (*Predators, Pedophiles, Rapists, and Other Sex Offenders* [New York: Basic Books, 2003], 220).

4. Research shows that support and guidance from family members can significantly reduce abuse by fathers. See Carol Coohey, "The Role of Friends, In-Laws, and Other Kin in Father-Perpetrated Child Physical Abuse," *Child Welfare* 79 (2000): 373–403.

5. I am not disputing the fact that God had forgiven David or that God was blessing David but asserting that, based on the events that follow, the composite family appearance did not mirror the composite family reality.

6. Herman, *Father-Daughter Incest*, 71.

7. Diana Russell found that in cases of incest, family members are least likely to support the victim (including accepting the evidence) if the perpetrator is a member of the

nuclear family (*The Secret Trauma: Incest in the Lives of Girls and Women* [New York: Basic Books, 1986], 373).

8. The verb *ḥazaq* means "to fasten upon, to seize, to bind." It is used just a few verses later in 2 Samuel 13:14 to describe Amnon's being "stronger" than Tamar.

9. I've heard some pastors suggest that Tamar bore some moral guilt for the rape, based on the fact that when Amnon grabbed and propositioned her, she did not cry out as Deuteronomy 22:24 requires a victim to do. This assertion is absurd. The text doesn't tell us she did not cry out. What it does tell us is that, with no provocation whatsoever, Amnon forcefully grabbed Tamar and sexually forced himself on her. Furthermore, three times Tamar told Amnon "don't" (2 Samuel 13:12). Apparently some pastors, as well as rapists ancient and modern, still do not believe that "don't" means "don't."

10. Lenore E. Walker analyzes this dynamic with respect to battered women who stay with their abusers. She explains it in terms of a psychosocial theory of learned helplessness (*The Battered Woman* [New York: Harper and Row, 1979], 42–54). While Walker has a jaded view of male and female roles that makes no allowance for a male servant leadership that lifts up females, I believe her model is still helpful.

11. It is significant that Amnon's sexual proposition of Tamar is identical to that given by Potiphar's wife to Joseph (Genesis 39:12) except that he adds "my sister," making it all the more confusing and manipulative. In this respect, family members have more power to hurt by their abuse than do outsiders, for one should expect tender care from those in one's own family. Diana Russell's study shows repeatedly that the least severe form of sexual abuse, such as erotic kissing by a family member, is more traumatic and damaging than violent rape perpetrated by a nonfamily member (*The Secret Trauma*, 362, 365, 372).

12. "Sister" has a nonliteral usage that can have an erotic connotation (Song of Solomon 4:9–10), but this metaphorical use probably draws on the tenderness implicit in a healthy brother-sister relationship. Amnon's use of "sister" is neither metaphorical (she was his blood sister) nor tender (he was her violent rapist).

13. Florence Rush insightfully illustrates the ambiguous, confusing messages that cloud reality for abuse victims by referencing the 1944 Ingrid Bergman film *Gaslight* (*The Best-Kept Secret: Sexual Abuse of Children* [Englewood Cliffs, N.J.: Prentice-Hall, 1980], 81–82).

14. The Hebrew word translated "violate" *(anah)* indicates sexual intercourse—often referring to forced sexual intercourse that violates the law of God (Genesis 34:2; Deuteronomy 22:29; Judges 19:24; Ezekiel 22:10–11). This leads to the second "don't"—"such a thing is not done in Israel" because it is a violation of God's law. The "disgraceful thing" mentioned in the final "and" ties this together. P. Kyle McCarter (*II Samuel* [New York: Doubleday, 1984], 322–23) notes that the term for "disgraceful thing" *(nebala)* is often translated "folly," but here it conveys the idea of a "sacrilege," for it refers to "a violation of the sacred taboos that define, hedge, and protect the structure of society.... *Nebala* is used especially of sexual misconduct, including rape (Judges 20:6, 10), promiscuity (Deuteronomy 22:21), adultery (Jeremiah 29:23), and homosexual assault (Judges 19:23)." These violations have far-reaching individual and societal consequences.

15. It's impossible to know whether Tamar was suggesting a course of action she truly believed King David would follow and one she would have cooperated with—or whether she was bluffing to avoid being raped. While marriage between a half brother and half sister was expressly condemned in the Torah (Leviticus 18:9, 11; 20:17), some commentators argue there's no way to know if the law was in practice at this time, especially in royal families that may have felt the normal rules didn't apply to them. They might have argued, for instance, that Sarah and Abraham were married siblings (Genesis 20:12). McCarter contends convincingly that the use of "brother" and "sister" six times in 2 Samuel 13:1−14 emphasizes that this is incest as well as rape (*II Samuel*, 328).

16. Reported in Cameron, *Resolving Childhood Trauma*, 35.

17. Herman, *Father-Daughter Incest*, 73.

18. Reported in Finkelhor, *Sexually Victimized Children*, 144, 211−12.

19. A number of researchers have noted that fathers and stepfathers who commit incest often take advantage of their wives' powerlessness (and much of their powerlessness is financial); see, for instance, Russell, *The Secret Trauma*, 363−67; Herman, *Father-Daughter Incest*, 72−73, 78−79.

20. Reported in Denise Pintello and Susan Zuravin, "Intrafamilial Child Sexual Abuse: Predictors of Postdisclosure Maternal Belief and Protective Action," *Child Maltreatment* 6 (2001): 349−50.

21. This finding helps explain why victims of extrafamilial abuse consistently receive more support from family members than do victims of intrafamilial abuse; see Ann N. Elliott and Connie N. Carnes, "Reactions of Nonoffending Parents to the Sexual Abuse of Their Child: A Review of the Literature," *Child Maltreatment* 6 (2001): 314−31.

22. The rabbis were so puzzled by this verse they imaginatively postulated that Amnon hated Tamar because, when he had sexual relations with her, he hurt himself by becoming tangled in her pubic hair (Babylonian Talmud, Tractate Sanhedrin, Folio 21a).

23. For this reason some have described life in an abusive family as constantly walking on eggshells to keep the peace and avoid setting off the abuser (see Lynn Heitritter and Jeanette Vought, *Helping Victims of Sexual Abuse* [Minneapolis: Bethany House, 1989], 72−73).

24. An especially articulate account of this dynamic is given by Diana Russell, "The Making of a Whore," *Violence Against Women* 1 (1995): 77−98.

25. Barbara's story, along with excellent commentary on it, is told by David Finkelhor (*Sexually Victimized Children*, 185−214).

26. Finkelhor, *Sexually Victimized Children*, 187, 191, 193, 201.

27. Exodus 22:16−17 and Deuteronomy 22:28−29 address the sexual seduction of a nonengaged virgin. If a man raped an *engaged* woman, he was to be stoned to death, but nothing punitive was to be done to the woman (Deuteronomy 22:25−26)—which seems to imply that if an engaged woman is raped, her fiancé will go through with the wedding.

28. See Dominic Rudman, "Reliving the Rape of Tamar: Absalom's Revenge in 2 Samuel," *Old Testament Essays* 11 (1998): 332−33. Joyce G. Baldwin argues that the bolting of the

door reinforces this message, for once Tamar was thrown out and the door bolted, "she knew deep down that the door to marriage was bolted against her for good" (*1 and 2 Samuel* [Downers Grove, Ill.: InterVarsity Press, 1988], 249).

29. Mary J. Evans suggests that the Hebrew phrase rendered "this woman" *(zot)* is very demeaning and could be translated "this thing" (*1 and 2 Samuel* [Peabody, Mass.: Hendrickson, 2000], 963–64). Supporting this rendering is the derogatory use of the equivalent masculine term "this one" *(zeh)* in 1 Samuel 10:27.

30. See Herman, *Father-Daughter Incest*, 36–49. In the case of Tamar, amazingly (and with no coherent textual justification), Pamela Tamarkin Reis blames Tamar for being raped, for she argues that Amnon and Tamar's sexual intimacy was consensual and was encouraged by Tamar's flirtatiousness ("Cupidity and Stupidity: Woman's Agency and the 'Rape' of Tamar," *Journal of the Ancient Near Eastern Society* 25 [1997]: 43–60).

31. Many researchers note the social isolation of abusive families, both as a cause and as a result of abuse (see Lucy Berlinger and Diana Elliot, "Sexual Abuse of Children," in *The APSAC Handbook on Child Maltreatment*, 2d ed., ed. John E. B. Myers et al. [Thousand Oaks, Calif.: Sage, 2002], 57; Diane DePanfilis, "Social Isolation of Neglectful Families: A Review of Social Support Assessment and Intervention Models," *Child Maltreatment* 1 [1996]: 37–52). Edward W. Gondolf notes the social isolation of physically abusive husbands and their wives (*Men Who Batter: An Integrated Approach for Stopping Wife Abuse* [Holmes Beach, Fla.: Learning Publications, 1985], 131–32).

32. Cited in Cameron, *Resolving Childhood Trauma*, 32.

33. This may explain, for instance, why nonperpetrating mothers of incest victims are often abuse victims themselves (see Herman, *Father-Daughter Incest*, 107–8). It may also explain why women who grow up witnessing domestic violence in their own homes are considerably more likely to end up in physically abusive relationships (see Richard J. Gelles, "No Place to Go: The Social Dynamics of Marital Violence," in *Battered Women: A Psychosociological Study of Domestic Violence*, ed. Maria Roy [New York: Van Nostrand Reinhold, 1977], 60).

34. Phyllis Trible notes that Absalom's words to Tamar are the only kindness she experiences in this entire episode (*Texts of Terror* [Philadelphia: Fortress, 1984], 51). Absalom also permanently took her into his home and cared for her (2 Samuel 13:20), and named his own daughter after her (2 Samuel 14:27).

35. See Carol E. Barringer, "The Survivor's Voice: Breaking the Incest Taboo," *NWSA Journal* 4 (1992): 4–22; see also Cameron, *Resolving Childhood Trauma*, 241.

36. Reported in Russell, *The Secret Trauma*, 85–87. Other experts assert that at least 90 percent of incest cases go unreported (see Herman, *Father-Daughter Incest*, 223). More recently, Benjamin Saunders et al. conducted local and national surveys of childhood abuse victims and found that in the local study (Charleston, South Carolina), only 5.7 percent of the 139 abuse incidents had been reported to the authorities, and only 12 percent of the 699 sexual abuse incidents in the national study had been reported ("Child Sexual Abuse as a Risk Factor for Mental Disorders Among Women: A Community Survey," *Journal of Interpersonal Violence* 7 [1993]: 189–204).

37. The problem with abusers is not just that they lack positive emotions but that they don't have the appropriate ones at the appropriate times. For example, in Lenore

Walker's widely accepted cycle theory of violence, there are three phases of domestic violence: (1) tension buildup, (2) acute battering incident, and (3) kindness and contrite loving behavior. While the third phase may appear to be an appropriate expression of healthy emotions, it is not, for these emotions are based on denial and manipulation (*The Battered Woman*, 65–70).

38. This additional clarifying sentence, which is left out of the Masoretic (Hebrew) text, is found in the Septuagint and in the Dead Sea texts (4QSam). P. Kyle McCarter convincingly argues that the Masoretic text reflects scribal error, for the scribe's eye must have skipped from the "wl" at the beginning of the last passage to "wl" at the beginning of verse 22 (*II Samuel*, 319–20).

39. For example, the seventy-two incest survivors in Catherine Cameron's study were abused by over two hundred different family members, and yet not one of these perpetrators was ever charged with a sex crime. Clearly, the families these incest survivors grew up in were highly committed to protecting perpetrators, not victims (*Resolving Childhood Trauma*, 268).

40. See The Investigative Staff of the Boston Globe, *Betrayal: The Crisis in the Catholic Church* (Boston: Little, Brown, & Company, 2002). For a similar account written by an investigative reporter who is Catholic, see Jason Berry, *Lead Us Not into Temptation: Catholic Priests and the Sexual Abuse of Children* (Chicago: University of Illinois Press, 1992).

41. The Investigative Staff of the Boston Globe, *Betrayal*, 174.

chapter 5: shame

1. John Bradshaw argues that shame is the "master emotion" because when it is internalized, all other emotions are bound by it (*Healing the Shame That Binds You* [Deerfield Beach, Fla.: Health Communications, 1988], 55). Shame is a profoundly influential emotion because, as Gershen Kaufman points out, it is intrinsic to one's development of personal identity (*The Psychology of Shame: Theory and Treatment of Shame-Based Syndromes* [New York: Springer, 1989], 17–20).

2. The catch-22 here is obvious: If bad things happen to me, it's my fault (which shows I'm a bad person). If good things happen to me, it's not because of me (so good things do *not* show that I'm a good person). Candice Feiring, Lynn Taska, and Michael Lewis describe this shame dynamic in terms of internality (the self is the cause) versus externality (something outside of me is the cause). Their research shows that an internal attributional style for negative events is one of the three most influential factors that lead to shame in abuse victims ("A Process Model for Understanding Adaptation to Sexual Abuse: The Role of Shame in Defining Stigmatization," *Child Abuse and Neglect* 20 [1996]: 769).

3. An excellent overview of secular models and definitions of shame is given by Paul Gilbert, "What Is Shame: Some Core Issues and Controversies," in *Shame: Interpersonal Behavior, Psychology, and Culture*, ed. Paul Gilbert and Bernice Andrews (New York: Oxford Univ. Press, 1998), 3–38. For a survey of contemporary theological models of

shame, see Stephen Pattison, *Shame: Theory, Therapy, and Theology* (New York: Cambridge Univ. Press, 2000), 189–228.

4. Sandra D. Wilson highlights the relational disconnection shame produces. She says shame is "the strong sense of being uniquely and hopelessly different and less than other human beings" (*Released from Shame*, rev. ed. [Downers Grove, Ill.: InterVarsity Press, 2002], 23).

5. Lewis B. Smedes, *Shame and Grace: Healing the Shame We Don't Deserve* (San Francisco: HarperSanFrancisco, 1993), 5.

6. My definitions are theologically grounded and shouldn't be confused with definitions given by psychologists who use different terminology. For example, Michael Lewis distinguishes between shame and guilt by arguing that shame, not guilt, is most damaging, for guilt is an alterable negative emotion related to one's behavior, whereas shame is a fixed negative emotion related to one's being (*Shame: The Exposed Self* [New York, Free Press, 1992]).

7. Anthony A. Hoekema, *Created in God's Image* (Grand Rapids: Eerdmans, 1986), 85.

8. Thus, I strongly disagree with Karen A. McClintock, who asserts in the context of sexual behavior that chronic shame is never helpful, for it eats away at one's sense of well-being (*Sexual Shame: An Urgent Call to Healing* [Minneapolis: Fortress, 2001], 21–22). It is a fool's paradise to have a sense of well-being when one's moral condition has created guilt and condemnation. Jeremiah condemned those who tried to heal Israel's moral sickness superficially by crying out, "Peace, peace" when there was no peace (Jeremiah 6:14). Jeremiah instead asked God to cause shame to fall on the people so that they would feel the weight of their sin and repent (Jeremiah 3:11–13, 25; 8:11–12).

9. Smedes, *Shame and Grace*, 37.

10. See Wilson, *Released from Shame*, 60–65. Two insightful books that can help parents learn to avoid shame-based parenting are Sandra D. Wilson, *Shame-Free Parenting* (Downers Grove, Ill.: InterVarsity Press, 1992), and Jeff VanVonderen, *Families Where Grace Is in Place* (Minneapolis: Bethany House, 1992).

11. Richard T. Frazier, "The Subtle Violations—Abuse and the Projection of Shame," *Pastoral Psychology* 48 (2000): 322.

12. Reported in Carlos Miller and Katie Nelson, "Phoenix Parents Charged after 'Tortured' Boy, 7, Found in Closet," *Arizona Republic* (10 June 2003); can be viewed on the Web at www.azcentral.com/specials/special46/articles/0610malnourished10.html.

13. Judith Lewis Herman, *Trauma and Recovery*, rev. ed. (New York: Basic Books, 1997), 103; see also Kaufman, *The Psychology of Shame*, 32–35, 66–67; Dan B. Allender, *The Wounded Heart: Hope for Adult Victims of Childhood Sexual Abuse*, rev. ed. (Colorado Springs: NavPress, 1995), 67.

14. Note, for instance, the contrast between the harsh, judgmental way the Pharisees responded to "sinners"—which only served to intensify their shame—and the way Jesus drew sinners to repent of their sins by treating them with outrageous love and grace (see Matthew 9:9–13; Luke 7:36–50; 19:1–10; John 8:1–11).

15. Lewis Smedes notes a strange paradox: "Some shamed people do shameful things to prove to themselves that they are not ashamed to be what they are ashamed of being.

They act out their shame with a fury in the hope that if they flaunt their shame they will convince themselves that they deserve it" (*Shame and Grace*, 94). Thus, shamed people, in essence, create self-fulfilling shame prophecies.

16. Philip Yancey, *What's So Amazing About Grace?* (Grand Rapids: Zondervan, 1997), 275.

17. Joanna and Alister McGrath note the importance of affirming those who are emotionally beaten down and have little self-esteem, as this is what Jesus modeled. They clarify, however: "Affirmation of people does not mean leaving them where they are; it means meeting them where they are—wherever that may be, and however distasteful that may be—and moving them on in love" (*The Dilemma of Self-Esteem: The Cross and Christian Confidence*, rev. ed. [Wheaton, Ill.: Crossway, 2002], 147). It should be noted that Alister McGrath is arguably the world's foremost living theological expert on the doctrine of justification, and his comments on self-esteem are rooted solidly in the soil of theology.

18. The Hebrew words *ḥerpâ* and *qālôn*, which most often mean "reproach," or "shame," have a literal usage of "pudenda," that is, the external genital organs, especially of females.

19. Reported in Candice Feiring, Lynn Taska, and Michael Lewis, "Adjustment Following Sexual Abuse Discovery: The Role of Shame and Attributional Style," *Developmental Psychology* 38 (2002): 87.

20. See Candice Feiring, Lynn Taska, and Michael Lewis, "The Role of Shame and Attributional Style in Children's and Adolescents' Adaptation to Sexual Abuse," *Child Maltreatment* 3 (1998): 130.

21. Reported in Bonnie L. Kessler and Kathleen J. Bieshke, "A Retrospective Analysis of Shame, Dissociation, and Adult Victimization in Survivors of Childhood Sexual Abuse," *Journal of Counseling Psychology* 46 (1999): 335–41; see also Bernice Andrews, "Bodily Shame as a Mediator between Abusive Experience and Depression," *Journal of Abnormal Psychology* 104 (1995): 277–85.

22. The complex symptomology of shame is largely the result of what John Bradshaw calls "feeling conversion," in which individuals convert shameful feelings into other feelings that are more acceptable (*Healing the Shame*, 77).

23. Most of these characteristics are covered in Marie Powers, *Shame: Thief of Intimacy* (Ventura, Calif.: Gospel Light, 1998), 19–21.

24. For instance, one of the most respected academic biblical encyclopedias, *The Anchor Bible Dictionary*, has no entry under "shame" or "honor." Of all the New Testament writers, Paul most fully develops the concept of shame, using sixteen different Greek terms for shame or aspects of shame in his letters and eight terms for honor; yet, a widely respected dictionary on Paul has no entry for "shame" or "honor" (*Dictionary of Paul and His Letters*, ed. Gerald F. Hawthorne, Ralph P. Martin, and Daniel G. Reid [Downers Grove, Ill.: InterVarsity Press, 1993]). The past decade has seen renewed interest in the concept of shame in the New Testament, but this research has primarily been of a sociological rather than psychological nature.

25. Thus, one of the three primary meanings for αἰσχύνη (shame) is "a shameful deed, which one commits" (Walter Bauer et al., *A Greek-English Lexicon of the New Testament and Other Early Christian Literature*, 2d ed. [Chicago: University of Chicago Press, 1979],

25). Throughout Scripture shame is associated with intrinsically indecent or disgraceful behavior committed by someone: Judges 19:24 ("act of folly"); Jeremiah 11:13 ("shameful thing"); Romans 1:27 ("indecent acts"—ἀσχημοσύνη); Ephesians 5:4 ("filthiness"—αἰσχρότης); Philippians 3:19 ("shame"—αἰσχύνη); Titus 1:11 ("sordid gain"—αἰσχρός); Jude 13 ("shame"—αἰσχύνη).

26. See Psalm 71:13; Isaiah 7:20; Jeremiah 46:24–25; Daniel 12:2. This concept is also seen in the Septuagint with the αἰσχύνω word group, which most often has God as the subject and refers to the shame he brings in judgment (Gerhard Kittel, ed., *Theological Dictionary of the New Testament*, vol. 1 [Grand Rapids: Eerdmans, 1964], 189). Since physical exposure is a great source of psychological shame, God promises to strip and expose unrepentant sinners in judgment, thus shaming them for their evil (Ezekiel 23:25–29; Hosea 2:3). Hence, the Hebrew word ʿerwâ literally refers to nakedness, but it is often associated with shame that both leads to and results from divine judgment (Isaiah 3:17; Ezekiel 16:22–23; Habakkuk 3:13; Zephaniah 2:14; cf. Zephaniah 3:5).

27. Dan Allender explains this shame confusion in terms of depravity and longings: "We ignore the issue of depravity and feel shame about our longing for what God intended us to enjoy" (*The Wounded Heart*, 68).

28. See Judith Lewis Herman, *Father-Daughter Incest*, rev. ed. (Cambridge, Mass.: Harvard Univ. Press, 2000), 232.

29. Reported in J. Wormith, "A Survey of Incarcerated Sexual Offenders," *Canadian Journal of Criminology* 25 (1983): 384.

30. Cited in Fox News, "Tyson: 'I Really Do Want to Rape Her'" (May 30, 2003); can be viewed on the Web at www.foxnews.com/story/0,2933,88206,00.html.

31. Antwone Fisher and Mim Eichler Rivas, *Finding Fish: A Memoir* (New York: HarperCollins, 2001), 44.

32. There are repeated references in 1 Peter to the verbal abuse being experienced by Christians (1 Peter 2:12; 3:16; 4:4, 14). But the verb used in 1 Peter 2:20 (κολαφίζω) clearly refers to physical abuse—literally, beatings.

33. In the biblical world, "honor and dishonor represents the primary means of social control in the ancient Mediterranean world" (Craig A. Evans and Stanley E. Porter, eds., *Dictionary of New Testament Background* [Downers Grove, Ill.: InterVarsity Press, 2000], s.v. "Honor and Shame").

34. The Hebrew word šimṣâ means "shame or scornful whispering; derision" (Exodus 32:25) and comes from šemeṣ ("to make a sound").

35. The Hebrew word kālam is used by various Old Testament writers to indicate shame or reproach and often indicates social shame (Numbers 12:14; Judges 18:7; Ruth 2:15; 1 Samuel 20:34; 2 Samuel 10:5; Isaiah 50:7).

36. R. Laird Harris, Gleason L. Archer Jr., and Bruce K. Waltke, eds., *Theological Wordbook of the Old Testament*, vol. 2 (Chicago: Moody, 1980), 799.

37. Anthony A. Hoekema notes, "When we commit a grave sin, we lose our consciousness of forgiveness; we lose our sense of peace with God. When we confess our sins to God, he awakens our sense of forgiveness and revives our assurance that we have been justified once for all" (*Saved by Grace* [Grand Rapids: Eerdmans, 1989], 181).

38. This is what justification means—Christ's righteousness imputed to sinners (Romans 3:24–26). See John W. Stott, *The Cross of Christ* (Downers Grove, Ill.: InterVarsity Press, 1986), 182–92; Hoekema, *Saved by Grace*, 172–78.

39. On how believers can learn to cultivate a deeper sense of God's love for and delight in them, see Brennan Manning, *Abba's Child*, rev. ed. (Colorado Springs: NavPress, 2002); Brennan Manning, *The Ragamuffin Gospel* (Portland, Ore.: Multnomah, 1990); Robert Wicks, *Touching the Holy: Ordinariness, Self-Esteem, and Friendship* (Notre Dame, Ind.: Ave Maria, 1992). Wicks astutely contends that the critical question of spiritual health is not whether we believe God loves us but whether God *likes* us.

40. Neil Anderson gives a helpful list of what constitutes the believer's identity in Christ (*Victory Over the Darkness: Realizing the Power of Your Identity in Christ*, rev. ed. [Ventura, Calif.: Regal, 2000], 38–39).

41. See Psalm 35:4–8, 24–26; 40:14; 69:19–28; 70:2; 71:13; 83:13–17.

42. Praying for God to judge unrepentant abusers may seem to be at odds with Jesus' command to love one's enemies (Luke 6:27–35), but Jesus' message and ministry repeatedly intertwine both divine love for sinners and divine judgment on the unrepentant; see Willard M. Swartley, "Luke's Transformation of Tradition: *Eirēnē* and Love of Enemy," in *The Love of Enemy and Nonretaliation in the New Testament*, ed. Willard M. Swartley (Louisville, Ky.: Westminster/John Knox, 1992), 165–71.

43. On the social ignominy and shame attached to crucifixion in the ancient Roman world, see Martin Hengel, *Crucifixion* (Philadelphia: Fortress, 1977).

44. The Greek phrase here (αἰσχύνης καταφρονήσας) is best translated "disregarding the shame." Similarly, in Isaiah 50:6–8 God's righteous servant, who is physically abused by evil men, is not disgraced (does not absorb the shame) because of his determination to accept God's vindication and reject the verdict of his abusers.

45. While I disagree with John Bradshaw that constructive criticism has little value (see Proverbs 12:1; 27:5–6), he does point to helpful ways to deal with unjustified criticism (*Healing the Shame*, 209–13).

46. Ronald F. Youngblood notes that the Today's English Version's "you bastard" and the New Jerusalem Bible's "you son of a rebellious slut" are vulgar but capture the Hebrew (1 and 2 Samuel, in *The Expositor's Bible Commentary*, vol. 3 [Grand Rapids: Zondervan, 1992], 724).

47. Secular literature also emphasizes the importance of community in overcoming the shame of abuse. See Bradshaw, *Healing the Shame*, 119–31; Herman, *Trauma and Recovery*, 214–36; Christine A. Courtois, *Healing the Incest Wound: Adult Survivors in Therapy* (New York: W. W. Norton, 1988), 244–74.

chapter 6: powerlessness and deadness

1. In outlining the history of trauma research, I've drawn heavily on Judith Lewis Herman, *Trauma and Recovery: The Aftermath of Violence from Domestic Abuse to Political Terror*, rev. ed. (New York: Basic Books, 1997), 10–28. J. David Kinzie and Rupert R. Goetz offer an excellent summary of the history of trauma research ("A Century of

Controversy Surrounding Posttraumatic Stress-Spectrum Syndromes: The Impact on DSM-III and DSM-IV," *Journal of Traumatic Stress* 9 [1996]: 159–79).

2. Sigmund Freud most fully developed this theory with the publication of *The Aetiology of Hysteria* in 1896 (included in *The Standard Edition of the Complete Psychological Works of Sigmund Freud*, ed. James Strachey [Stanford, Calif.: Meridian, 1997]).

3. Various writers have documented Freud's dramatic reversal in his theory of hysteria, including Judith Lewis Herman, *Father-Daughter Incest*, rev. ed. (Cambridge, Mass.: Harvard Univ. Press, 2000), 7–12; J. M. Masson, *The Assault on Truth: Freud's Suppression of the Seduction Theory* (New York: Farrar, Straus, and Giroux, 1984); Florence Rush, *The Best-Kept Secret: Sexual Abuse of Children* (New York: McGraw-Hill, 1980), 80–104.

4. Pierre Janet was the only major nineteenth-century researcher who continued to maintain that hysteria was the result of trauma. His views were unpopular but are now widely accepted and foundational for much of current trauma theory.

5. See Kinzie and Goetz, "A Century of Controversy," 171; see also Richard A. Kulka et al., *Trauma and the Vietnam War Generation: Report of Findings from the National Vietnam Veterans Readjustment Study* (New York: Brunner/Mazel, 1990), 268–70.

6. Several population studies of trauma and PTSD suggest that, based on various risk factors, approximately 25 percent of those exposed to an extreme stressor event will develop full-blown PTSD. See Bonnie L. Green, "Psychological Research in Traumatic Stress: An Update," *Journal of Traumatic Stress* 7 (1994): 345; Bessel A. van der Kolk, "The Psychological Consequences of Overwhelming Life Experience," in *Psychological Trauma*, ed. Bessel A. van der Kolk (Washington, D.C.: American Psychiatric Press, 1987), 10–12.

7. *The Diagnostic and Statistical Manual of Mental Disorders* places PTSD under anxiety disorders and notes that it is characterized by "the reexperiencing of an extremely traumatic event accompanied by symptoms of increased arousal and by avoidance of stimuli associated with the trauma" ([Washington, D.C.: American Psychiatric Association, 1994], 393).

8. See Bessel A. van der Kolk and Alexander C. McFarlane, "The Black Hole of Trauma," in *Traumatic Stress: The Effects of Overwhelming Experience on Mind, Body, and Society*, ed. Bessel A. van der Kolk, Alexander C. McFarlane, and Lars Weisaeth (New York: Guilford Press, 1996), 7–9. Babette Rothschild also notes the way trauma is reexperienced in those with PTSD. She places particular emphasis on the somatic (body) symptoms (*The Body Remembers: The Psychophysiology of Trauma and Trauma Treatment* [New York: W. W. Norton, 2000], 6–7).

9. See Matthew J. Friedman, Dennis S. Charney, and Ariel Y. Deutch, eds., *Neurobiological and Clinical Consequences of Stress: From Normal Adaptation to Post-Traumatic Stress Disorder* (Philadelphia: Lippincott-Raven, 1995), xx.

10. See Herman, *Trauma and Recovery*, 35–73. Herman actually gives four primary characteristics of trauma, but I'll deal with the fourth (disconnection) in the next chapter. For the characteristics of trauma observable in children, see Lenore C. Terr, "Childhood Traumas: An Outline and Overview," *American Journal of Psychiatry* 148 (1991): 12.

11. Babette Rothschild explains that hyperarousal results when the "alarm response" of the brain fails to turn off. Specifically, the limbic system, or survival center of the brain, keeps setting the hypothalamic-pituitary-adrenocortical systems in motion, repeatedly releasing hormones that prepare the body for defensive action (*The Body Remembers*, 45–48).

12. On the research noting the correlation between anxiety disorders and abuse, see Anna C. Salter, *Transforming Trauma: A Guide to Understanding and Treating Adult Survivors of Child Sexual Abuse* (Thousand Oaks, Calif.: Sage, 1995), 171–75.

13. John N. Briere, *Child Abuse Trauma: Theory and Treatment of the Lasting Effects* (Thousand Oaks, Calif.: Sage, 1992), 21. Briere notes that these nightmares are typically one of two types: (1) graphic and realistic dreams of the original abuse, or (2) symbolic representations of the original abuse trauma, involving themes of violence, violation, and danger. The first type appears soon after the abuse and often decreases in frequency over time, whereas the second type is both a short-term and long-term trauma effect.

14. See Ron Zaczek, *Farewell Darkness: A Veteran's Triumph over Combat Trauma* (Annapolis, Md.: Naval Institute Press, 1994), 160–63. Bessel A. van der Kolk and Alexander C. McFarlane note that, over time, "triggers for intrusive traumatic memories may become increasingly more subtle and generalized; what should be irrelevant stimuli may become reminders of the trauma" ("The Black Hole of Trauma," in *Traumatic Stress*, 10).

15. Diana Russell gives a lucid account of this dynamic in her detailed case study of a South African woman who as a young girl was chronically abused by her grandfather ("The Making of a Whore," *Violence Against Women* 1 [1995]: 77–98).

16. Ronnie Janoff-Bulman, "The Aftermath of Victimization: Rebuilding Shattered Assumptions," in *Trauma and Its Wake: The Study and Treatment of Post-Traumatic Stress Disorder*, ed. Charles R. Figley (New York: Brunner/Mazel, 1985), 16.

17. In the technical sense, dissociation is more of an impairment of memory and consciousness than emotion, though there is much overlap here (see *The Diagnostic and Statistical Manual*, 477).

18. Joyanna L. Silberg notes that the exact etiology of dissociation is unclear, but it is "likely a complex interaction of psychobiological, familial, and cultural processes" ("Fifteen Years of Dissociation in Maltreated Children: Where Do We Go from Here?" *Child Maltreatment* 5 [2000]: 127).

19. See Salter, *Transforming Trauma*, 239–40. A large study of adults being treated for alcohol dependency revealed that almost 60 percent of the participants reported lifetime abuse (Christopher Rice et al., "Self-Reports of Physical, Sexual and Emotional Abuse in an Alcoholism Treatment Sample," *Journal of Studies on Alcohol* 62 [2001]: 114–23). Richard A. Kulka et al. discovered that almost 40 percent of male Vietnam combat veterans have a lifetime prevalence of alcohol abuse or dependence (*Trauma and the Vietnam War Generation*, 274–75).

20. Salter, *Transforming Trauma*, 246.

21. Three of the best works on the impact of abuse on memory are Jennifer J. Freyd, *Betrayal Trauma: The Logic of Forgetting Childhood Abuse* (Cambridge, Mass.: Harvard Univ. Press, 1996); Charles L. Whitfield, *Memory and Abuse: Remembering and Healing the Effects*

of Trauma (Deerfield Beach, Fla.: Health Communications, 1995); Linda M. Williams and Victoria L. Banyard, eds., *Trauma and Memory* (Thousand Oaks, Calif.: Sage, 1999).

22. The False Memory Syndrome Foundation (FMSF), founded in 1991, has been particularly vocal in proclaiming that childhood abuse rarely, if ever, results in repressed memories. In reality, there is no "False Memory Syndrome." David Calof documents the defamatory, destructive tactics used by the FMSF against psychologists and researchers identified with abuse and trauma treatment ("Notes from a Practice Under Siege: Harassment, Defamation, and Intimidation in the Name of Science," *Ethics and Behavior* 8 [1998]: 161–87). Stephanie J. Dallam notes the way the FMSF and some of its leaders have justified abuse and enabled abusers ("Unsilent Witness: Ralph Underwager and the FMSF," *Treating Abuse Today* 7 [1997]: 31–39).

23. Lenore Terr notes several aspects of false memories: (1) they can be planted by suggestions from outside agents, such as parents or counselors; (2) they more commonly come when someone is receiving help from a counselor who works exclusively with abuse victims; and (3) they will not create the cluster of trauma symptoms that are caused by actual childhood abuse (*Unchained Memories: True Stories of Traumatic Memories, Lost and Found* [New York: Basic Books, 1994], 159–62). The last point is the most important in determining the historical veracity of abuse memories, for false trauma memories do not have the same kind of collective emotional and somatic effects that real ones do.

24. See Linda Meyer Williams, "Recall of Childhood Trauma: A Prospective Study of Women's Memories of Child Sexual Abuse," *Journal of Consulting and Clinical Psychology* 62 (1994): 1167–76. It's highly unlikely that these women had not actually forgotten the abuse but were simply too embarrassed to mention it to the interviewers, since 68 percent of the women who had no memory of the documented abuse told about other sexual assaults they had experienced.

25. Cathy Spatz Widom and Suzanne Morris conducted a study of 653 individuals with a childhood history of officially documented physical, sexual, and neglect abuse. Some twenty years after the abuse, they interviewed these individuals and found that only 64 percent of the women who had been sexually abused recalled being abused, and only 16 percent of the men recalled being sexually abused ("Accuracy of Adult Recollections of Childhood Victimization: Part 2. Childhood Sexual Abuse," *Psychological Assessment* 9 [1997]: 42). Of those with documented histories of childhood physical abuse, 40 percent reported not remembering being abused (Cathy Spatz Widom and Suzanne Morris, "Accuracy of Adult Recollections of Childhood Victimization: Part 1. Childhood Physical Abuse," *Psychological Assessment* 8 [1996]: 418).

26. See Rothschild, *The Body Remembers*, 12; see also Bessel A. van der Kolk, "The Body Keeps the Score," *Harvard Review of Psychiatry* 1 (1994): 253–65.

27. See Bessel A. van der Kolk and Rita Fisher, "Dissociation and the Fragmentary Nature of Traumatic Memories: Overview and Exploratory Study," *Journal of Traumatic Stress* 8 (1995): 511–12, 519–20.

28. Judith Herman and Emily Schatzow, "Recovery and Verification of Memories of Childhood Sexual Trauma," *Psychoanalytic Psychology* 4 (1987), 11; see also Freyd, *Betrayal Trauma*, 9–11.

29. Reported in John P. Wilson, W. Ken Smith, and Suzanne K. Johnson, "A Comparative Analysis of PTSD among Various Survivor Groups," in *Trauma and Its Wake*, 142–72.

30. Ibid., 149–53.

31. See W. Op den Velde et al., "Current Psychiatric Complaints of Dutch Resistance Veterans from World War II: A Feasibility Study," *Journal of Traumatic Stress* 3 (1990): 351–58; Nancy Speed et al., "Posttraumatic Stress Disorder as a Consequence of the POW Experience," *Journal of Nervous and Mental Disease* 177 (1989): 147–53.

32. Reported in Cathy Spatz Widom, "Posttraumatic Stress Disorder in Abused and Neglected Children Grown Up," *American Journal of Psychiatry* 156 (1999): 1223–29.

33. Judith Lewis Herman argues for the existence of a form of post-traumatic disorder in survivors of prolonged or repeated trauma she calls "Complex PTSD" ("Complex PTSD: A Syndrome in Survivors of Prolonged and Repeated Trauma," *Journal of Traumatic Stress* 5 [1992]: 377–91).

34. See van der Kolk and McFarlane "The Black Hole of Trauma," in *Traumatic Stress*, 6–7. D. Finkelhor and A. Browne argue that powerlessness is one of the four primary dynamics that create long-term trauma damage ("The Traumatic Impact of Child Sexual Abuse: A Conceptualization," *American Journal of Orthopsychiatry*, 55 [1985]: 530–41). The fact that trauma comes from the victim's perception of threat and powerlessness helps explain why Ron Zaczek, a Vietnam veteran who suffered with severe PTSD for years after the war, discovered in the course of therapy that the primary source of his chronic nightmares was not his 393 combat helicopter missions during which he frequently faced hostile enemy fire, but his nights "on the wire" as a perimeter guard in which he never once actually saw an enemy soldier or faced hostile fire but experienced intense vulnerability (see Zaczek, *Farewell Darkness*, 132–77).

35. See Dan B. Allender, *The Wounded Heart: Hope for Adult Victims of Childhood Sexual Abuse*, rev. ed. (Colorado Springs: NavPress, 1995), 114.

36. See Lenore C. Terr, "Children of Chowchilla: A Study of Psychic Trauma," *Psychoanalytic Study of the Child* 34 (1979): 552–623; Lenore C. Terr, "Chowchilla Revisited: The Effects of Psychic Trauma Four Years after a School-Bus Kidnapping," *The American Journal of Psychiatry* 140 (1983): 1543–50.

37. In fact, terrifying nightmares of dying increased over time. In the initial study, only five children reported these, whereas twelve reported them in the second study four to five years after the kidnapping (Terr, "Chowchilla Revisited," 1547–48).

38. See Henk M. van der Ploeg and Wim Chr. Kleijn, "Being Held Hostage in the Netherlands: A Study of Long-Term Aftereffects," *Journal of Traumatic Stress* 2 (1989): 153–69.

39. Depression is a common symptom of both physical and sexual abuse and is particularly associated with the latter. Anna Salter notes that depression "appears to be found more often in adult survivors of child sexual abuse than any other symptom (*Transforming Trauma*, 165).

40. The best treatment of this concept is John Piper, *Desiring God: Meditations of a Christian Hedonist*, rev. ed. (Sisters, Ore.: Multnomah, 1996). Piper's thesis is that the noblest, most godly motivation for all human behavior is pleasure. All of life should be driven by the prospect of experiencing joy and delight in God.

41. Dan Allender states this well: "Denial is an affront to God. It assumes that a false reality is better than the truth. It assumes that God is neither good nor strong enough" (*The Wounded Heart*, 202).

42. Alistair McFayden argues that abuse is so damaging because it threatens to distort the abuse survivor's experience of enrichment, life, and abundance that come from our Creator, who wants to bless his creation (*Bound to Sin: Abuse, Holocaust, and the Christian Doctrine of Sin* [Cambridge: Cambridge Univ. Press, 2000], 238).

chapter 7: isolation

1. See P. C. Alexander, "The Differential Effects of Abuse Characteristics and Attachment," *Journal of Interpersonal Violence* 8 (1993): 346–62.

2. See David DiLillo and Patricia J. Long, "Perceptions of Couple Functioning Among Female Survivors of Child Sexual Abuse," *Journal of Child Sexual Abuse* 7 (1999): 59–76; Liz Grauerholz, "An Ecological Approach to Understanding Sexual Revictimization: Linking Personal, Interpersonal, and Sociological Factors and Processes," *Child Maltreatment* 5 (2000): 5–17; Gina P. Owens and Kathleen M. Chard, "Cognitive Distortions Among Women Reporting Childhood Sexual Abuse," *Journal of Interpersonal Violence* 16 (2001): 178–91; David A. Wolfe et al., "Factors Associated with Abusive Relationships Among Maltreated and Nonmaltreated Youth," *Development and Psychopathology* 10 (1998): 61–85.

3. Reported in David Finkelhor et al., "Sexual Abuse and Its Relationship to Later Sexual Satisfaction, Marital Status, Religion, and Attitudes," *Journal of Interpersonal Violence* 4 (1989): 384, 392; Diana E. H. Russell, *The Secret Trauma: Incest in the Lives of Girls and Women* (New York: Basic Books, 1986), 118–19.

4. See Candice Feiring, Saul Rosenthal, and Lynn Taska, "Stigmatization and the Development of Friendship and Romantic Relationships in Adolescent Victims of Sexual Abuse," *Child Maltreatment* 5 (2000): 317–19; S. Salzinger et al., "The Effects of Physical Abuse on Children's Social Relationships," *Child Development* 64 (1993): 177–84; Jeffrey G. Parker and Carla Herrera, "Interpersonal Processes in Friendship: A Comparison of Abused and Nonabused Children's Experiences," *Developmental Psychology* 32 (1996): 1025–38.

5. See Judith Lewis Herman, *Trauma and Recovery: The Aftermath of Violence—from Domestic Abuse to Political Terror*, rev. ed. (New York: Basic Books, 1997), 51–73.

6. The Hebrew word used here for "helper" (*ʿezer*) does not connote inferiority. This term is used twenty-nine times in the Hebrew Scriptures, and in every other usage except for one, it is used of God himself. The phrase "helper suitable for him" indicates the woman corresponded to Adam and complemented him as an intimate equal.

7. See Victor P. Hamilton, *The Book of Genesis: Chapters 1–17* (Grand Rapids: Eerdmans, 1990), 181. Hamilton notes three major uses of "nakedness" in the Old Testament, but all three are connected with some form of humiliation.

8. The fact that Adam and Eve used fig leaves showed how desperate they were to overcome their shame, since fig leaves are rough in texture and would have been quite irritating, particularly in the genital region. Victor Hamilton suggests that Adam and

Eve used fig leaves because they were the largest leaves in the garden (*The Book of Genesis*, 191).

9. Herman, *Trauma and Recovery*, 52.

10. See Pamela M. Cole and Frank W. Putnam, "Effect of Incest on Self and Social Functioning: A Developmental Psychopathology Perspective," *Journal of Consulting and Clinical Psychology* 60 (1992): 174–84; Christine A. Courtois, *Healing the Incest Wound: Adult Survivors in Therapy* (New York: W. W. Norton, 1988), 111, 215–16; D. Finkelhor and A. Browne, "The Traumatic Impact of Child Sexual Abuse: A Conceptualization," *American Journal of Orthopsychiatry*, 55 (1985): 531–32; Jennifer J. Freyd, *Betrayal Trauma: The Logic of Forgetting Childhood Trauma* (Cambridge, Mass.: Harvard Univ. Press, 1996), 3–11.

11. David Finkelhor, *Sexually Victimized Children* (New York: Free Press, 1979), 214.

12. Reported in Judith Lewis Herman, *Father-Daughter Incest*, rev. ed. (Cambridge, Mass.: Harvard Univ. Press, 2000), 30–31, 81–89, 184.

13. C. S. Lewis, *The Four Loves* (New York: Harcourt Brace Jovanovich, 1960), 169.

14. Reported in Finkelhor et al., "Sexual Abuse and Its Relationship to Later Sexual Satisfaction, Marital Status, Religion, and Attitudes," 382.

15. Russell, *The Secret Trauma*, 119–21. The adult religious defection rate for women with no incest history was 32 percent. The most dramatic differences were found among Catholics, with twice as many Catholics who experienced incest defecting from the church as Catholics who did not experience incest.

16. Elie Wiesel, *Night* (New York: Bantam Books, 1960), 61–62.

17. Linda Cutting, *Memory Slips: A Memoir of Music and Healing* (New York: HarperCollins, 1997), 165.

18. Ibid., 156.

19. Cited in Courtois, *Healing the Incest Wound*, 111; see also Clark E. Barshinger, Lojan E. LaRowe, and Andres Tapia, *Haunted Marriages: Overcoming the Ghosts of Your Spouse's Childhood Abuse* (Downers Grove, Ill.: InterVarsity Press, 1995), 206–7.

20. Reported in P. E. Mullen et al., "The Effect of Child Sexual Abuse on Social, Interpersonal and Sexual Function in Adult Life," *British Journal of Psychiatry* 165 (1994): 39.

21. For more on this, see Steven R. Tracy, "The Marriage Mystery," *Christianity Today* (January 7, 2002), 63.

22. See Finkelhor et al., "Sexual Abuse and Its Relationship to Later Sexual Satisfaction, Marital Status, Religion, and Attitudes," 379–99; Katarina Oberg, Kerstin S. Fugl-Meyer, and Axel R. Fugl-Meyer, "On Sexual Well-Being in Sexually Abused Swedish Women: Epidemiological Aspects," *Sexual and Relationship Theory* 17 (2002): 329–41; David B. Sarwer and Joseph A. Durlak, "Childhood Sexual Abuse as a Predictor of Adult Female Sexual Dysfunction: A Study of Couples Seeking Therapy," *Child Abuse and Neglect* 20 (1996): 963–72. Sarwer and Durlak report that up to 95 percent of female survivors of penetration sexual abuse experience adult sexual dysfunction.

23. See Johann F. Kinzl et al., "Sexual Dysfunction in Males: Significance of Adverse Childhood Experiences," *Child Abuse and Neglect* 20 (1996): 759–66; Cindy M. Meston and Julia R. Heiman, "The Relation between Early Abuse and Adult Sexuality," *Journal*

of Sex Research 36 (1999): 385–96; David B. Sarwer, Isaiah Crawford, and Joseph A. Durlak, "The Relationship between Childhood Sexual Abuse and Adult Male Sexual Dysfunction," *Child Abuse and Neglect* 21 (1997): 649–55.

24. See Meston and Heiman, "The Relation between Early Abuse and Adult Sexuality," 385.

25. Reported in Oberg et al., "On Sexual Well-Being," 339.

26. See Suzanne Prescott and Carolyn Letko, "Battered Women: Social Psychological Perspective," in *Battered Women: A Psychosociological Study of Domestic Violence*, ed. Maria Roy (New York: Van Nostrand Reinhold, 1977), 72–96; Bessel A. van der Kolk, "The Compulsion to Repeat the Trauma: Re-enactment, Revictimization, and Masochism," *Treatment of Victims of Sexual Abuse* 12 (1989): 393–95.

27. See Don Dutton and Susan Lee Painter, "Traumatic Bonding: The Development of Emotional Attachments in Battered Women and Other Relationships of Intermittent Abuse," *Victimology: An International Journal* 6 (1981): 139–55; Alytia A. Levendosky and Sandra A. Graham-Bermann, "Trauma and Parenting in Battered Women: An Addition to an Ecological Model of Parenting," *Journal of Aggression, Maltreatment & Trauma* 3 (2000): 25–35.

28. Reported in Herman, *Father-Daughter Incest*, 114–16.

29. See David Finkelhor, "Early and Long-Term Effects of Child Sexual Abuse: An Update," *Professional Psychology: Research and Practice* 21 (1990): 326.

30. Depression is the most commonly cited symptom reported by adults molested as children (see John N. Briere, *Child Abuse Trauma: Theory and Treatment of the Lasting Effects* [Thousand Oaks, Calif.: Sage: 1992], 29–32), and it is considerably more common in children who have been sexually abused (see Lucy Berliner and Diana M. Elliot, "Sexual Abuse of Children," in *The APSAC Handbook on Child Maltreatment*, 2d ed., ed. John E. B. Myers et al. [Thousand Oaks, Calif.: Sage, 2002], 59–60).

31. See Salzinger et al., "The Effects of Physical Abuse on Children's Social Relationships," 169–87; S. M. Alessandri, "Play and Social Behavior in Maltreated Preschoolers," *Development and Psychopathology* 3 (1991): 191–205; M. E. Haskett and J. A. Kistner, "Social Interaction and Peer Perception of Young Physically Abused Children," *Child Development* 62 (1991): 979–90; David J. Kolko, "Child Physical Abuse," in *The APSAC Handbook on Child Maltreatment*, 32.

32. Reported in Parker and Herrera, "Interpersonal Processes in Friendship," 1034–35.

33. Reported in Martha Farrell Erickson and Byron Egeland, "Child Neglect," in *The APSAC Handbook on Child Maltreatment*, 7–8.

34. Reported in J. Adams et al., "Sexually Inappropriate Behaviors in Seriously Mentally Ill Children and Adolescents," *Child Abuse and Neglect* 19 (1995): 555–68; see also Berliner and Elliot, "Sexual Abuse of Children," in *The APSAC Handbook on Child Maltreatment*, 60.

35. See Catalina M. Arata, "From Child Victim to Adult Victim: A Model for Predicting Sexual Revictimization," *Child Maltreatment* 5 (2000): 30–31; A. Browne and D. Finkelhor, "Impact of Child Sexual Abuse: A review of the research," *Psychological Bulletin* 99 (1986): 70–71; Courtois, *Healing the Incest Wound*, 107–8; Meston and Heiman, "The Relation between Early Abuse and Adult Sexuality," 385–96.

36. Reported in Wolfe et al., "Factors Associated with Abusive Relationships," 61.

37. Reported in Feiring, Rosenthal, and Taska, "Stigmatization and the Development of Friendship and Romantic Relationships in Adolescent Victims of Sexual Abuse," 317–19.

38. See Acts 2:41–47; Romans 12:4–5; 12:13–15:2; 1 Corinthians 12:12–27; Galatians 6:1–2; Ephesians 4:7–16; Philippians 2:1–4.

39. Leonard T. Gries and David S. Goh studied twenty-one children who had been placed in foster care because of parental abuse. The reaction of the foster parents to the children's disclosure of abuse was identified as the most salient feature connected with the children's subsequent emotional functioning ("Positive Reaction to Disclosure and Recovery from Child Sexual Abuse," *Journal of Child Sexual Abuse* 9 [2000]: 29–51). Caregivers' reactions to disclosures have long-term consequences as well. Thomas A. Roesler, in a study of sixty-six adults who had been sexually abused as children and disclosed the abuse during childhood, found that the reaction of the family members to the disclosure had a mediating effect (positively and negatively) on adult emotional well-being, specifically on scores assessing general trauma, post-traumatic stress disorder, and dissociation ("Reaction to Disclosure of Childhood Sexual Abuse: The Effects of Adult Symptoms," *Journal of Nervous and Mental Diseases* 182 [1994]: 618–24).

40. Reported in Gail E. Wyatt, Michael D. Newcomb, and Monika H. Riederle, *Sexual Abuse and Consensual Sex: Women's Developmental Patterns and Outcomes* (Thousand Oaks, Calif.: Sage, 1993), 187.

41. Reported in A. W. Burgess and L. L. Holmstrom, "Adaptive Strategies and Recovery from Rape," *American Journal of Psychiatry* 136 (1979): 1278–82.

42. Cited in Barshinger, LaRowe, and Tapia, *Haunted Marriages*, 206–7.

chapter 8: facing the brokenness

1. See Ed Bulkley, *Only God Can Heal the Wounded Heart* (Eugene, Ore.: Harvest House, 1995), 59, 83–108, 117.

2. This isn't the only time Paul is candid about his past. In two different speeches recorded by Luke, Paul chronicles his preconversion past (Acts 22:3–6; 26:4–14), including his shameful persecution and abuse of Christians some twenty years earlier. In Acts 22:4 Paul even admits that he persecuted Christians to death (ἐδίωξα ἄχρι θανάτου) and imprisoned both men and women.

3. See Thomas R. Schreiner, *Paul: Apostle of God's Glory in Christ* (Downers Grove, Ill.: InterVarsity Press, 2001), 46, 122–23.

4. Dan B. Allender, *The Wounded Heart: Hope for Adult Victims of Childhood Sexual Abuse*, rev. ed. (Colorado Springs: NavPress, 1995), 202.

5. The beatitude in Matthew 5:4 uses a present tense participle (οἱ πενθοῦντες), indicating ongoing mourning.

6. Anna Salter, *Transforming Trauma: A Guide to Understanding and Treating Adult Survivors of Child Sexual Abuse* (Thousand Oaks, Calif.: Sage, 1995), 262.

7. See James A. Chu, *Rebuilding Shattered Lives: The Responsible Treatment of Complex Post-Traumatic and Dissociative Disorders* (New York: Wiley, 1998), 82.

8. See Judith Lewis Herman, *Trauma and Recovery: The Aftermath of Violence—from Domestic Abuse to Political Terror*, 2d ed. (New York: Basic Books, 1997), 105; Charles Whitfield, *Memory and Abuse: Remembering and Healing the Effects of Trauma* (Deerfield Beach, Fla.: Health Communications, 1995), 32.

9. Babette Rothschild, *The Body Remembers: The Psychophysiology of Trauma and Trauma Treatment* (New York: W. W. Norton, 2000), 6.

10. See Claire Burke, *Counseling Survivors of Childhood Sexual Abuse*, 2d ed. (Thousand Oaks, Calif.: Sage, 2000), 42–43; Catherine Cameron, *Resolving Childhood Trauma: A Long-Term Study of Abuse Survivors* (Thousand Oaks, Calif.: Sage, 2000), 211–35; Katherine Steele and Joanna Colrain, "Abreactive Work with Sexual Abuse Survivors: Concepts and Techniques," in *The Sexually Abused Male: Application of Treatment Strategies*, vol. 2, ed. Mic Hunter (Lexington, Mass.: Lexington Books, 1990), 1–55.

11. See J. T. L. Messman and P. J. Long, "Child Sexual Abuse and Its Relationship to Revictimization in Adult Women: A Review," *Clinical Psychology Review* 16 (1996): 397–420; Diana Russell, *Rape in Marriage* (New York: Macmillan, 1982); John J. Potterat et al., "Pathways to Prostitution: The Chronology of Sexual and Drug Abuse Milestones," *Journal of Sex Research* 35 (1998): 333–41.

12. Reported in Emily Bittner, "Hotel Guest Heard the Fatal Fight," *Arizona Republic* (September 12, 2003).

13. See Mary Elizabeth Collins, "Parents' Perceptions of the Risk of Child Sexual Abuse and Their Protective Behaviors: Findings from a Qualitative Study," *Child Maltreatment* 1 (1996): 53–64.

14. See Judith Lewis Herman, *Father-Daughter Incest*, 2d ed. (Cambridge, Mass.: Harvard University Press, 2000), 72–73, 88–91; Diana E. H. Russell, *The Secret Trauma: Incest in the Lives of Girls and Women* (New York: Basic Books, 1986), 362–68; Ann M. Gresham, "The Role of the Nonoffending Parent When the Incest Victim Is Male," in *The Sexually Abused Male*, 171–72.

15. Salter, *Transforming Trauma*, 232–33.

16. Ibid., 221–28.

17. There are two DSM-IV categories of amnesia: (1) amnestic disorders, which results from physical or biological causes, and (2) dissociative disorders, which results from psychological trauma (*Diagnostic and Statistical Manual of Mental Disorders*, 4th ed. [Washington, D.C.: American Psychiatric Association, 1994], 156–63, 447–81). The focus here is on the amnesia that results from psychological trauma.

18. See J. M. Arrigo and K. Pezdek, "Lessons from the Study of Psychogenic Amnesia," *Current Directions in Psychological Science* 6 (1997): 148–52; K. S. Pope and L. S. Brown, *Recovered Memories of Abuse* (Washington, D.C.: American Psychological Association, 1996); Onno van der Hart and Danny Brom, "When the Victim Forgets: Trauma-Induced Amnesia and Its Assessment in Holocaust Survivors," in *International Handbook of Human Response to Trauma*, ed. Arieh Y. Shalev, Rachel Yehuda, and Alexander C. McFarlane (New York: Plenum, 2000), 233–48.

19. See Cameron, *Resolving Childhood Trauma*, 96–97; Whitfield, *Memory and Abuse*, 117–26.

20. This is similar to what Peter Dale calls "disowned abuse memories" (*Adults Abused as Children: Experiences of Counseling and Psychology* [Thousand Oaks, Calif.: Sage, 1999], 175).

21. See C. B. Draucker, *Counseling Survivors of Childhood Sexual Abuse*, 2d ed. (London: Sage, 2000), 26–27.

22. Mic Hunter and Paul N. Gerber view the therapy process for abuse survivors as a five-stage grief process that largely revolves around overcoming denial and facing the truth of the abuse ("Use of the Terms 'Victim' and 'Survivor' in the Grief Stages Commonly Seen during Recovery from Sexual Abuse," in *The Sexually Abused Male*, 84).

23. See Dan B. Allender and Tremper Longman, *The Cry of the Soul: How Our Emotions Reveal Our Deepest Questions about God* (Colorado Springs: NavPress, 1994), 13–27.

24. See Herman, *Trauma and Recovery*, 155–74; Bessel A. van der Kolk and Alexander C. McFarlane, "The Black Hole of Trauma," in *Traumatic Stress: The Effects of Overwhelming Experience on Mind, Body, and Society*, ed. Bessel A. van der Kolk, Alexander C. McFarlane, and Lars Weisaeth (New York: Guilford, 1996), 17–19. Some therapeutic models identify self-care as the first step in healing from abusive trauma (Chu, *Rebuilding Shattered Lives*, 78–80). While self-care is a broader category than establishing safety, establishing safety is a central aspect of self-care.

25. See Lundy Bancroft, *Why Does He Do That? Inside the Minds of Angry and Controlling Men* (New York: G. P. Putnam's Sons, 2002), xxii–xxiii; John N. Briere, *Child Abuse Trauma: Theory and Treatment of the Lasting Effects* (Thousand Oaks, Calif.: Sage, 1992), 23–27, 69–73.

26. John Oswalt notes that *bāṭaḥ* is similar to the theological term "faith" but this Hebrew word stresses the emotional aspect of trust and of feeling secure (R. Laird Harris, Gleason L. Archer Jr., and Bruce K. Waltke, eds., *Theological Workbook of the Old Testament*, vol. 1 [Chicago: Moody Press, 1980], 101).

27. Ibid., 102. See such Bible passages as Deuteronomy 28:52; Psalm 31:6; 49:6; 118:8; 146:3; Jeremiah 7:4; Ezekiel 33:3.

28. Cameron, *Resolving Childhood Trauma*, 211.

29. Peter Dale has an excellent discussion for therapists on the challenges and the process of helping clients talk about their abuse (*Adults Abused as Children*, 103–25).

30. Antwone Fisher, whose foster parents abused him for fifteen years and then abandoned him to the streets, eventually dealt with the hidden rage and soul damage that was destroying him. His poem "Recollections" is written to his abusive foster parents and is an excellent example of facing and telling the truth about one's abusive family (*Who Will Cry for the Little Boy?* [New York: HarperCollins, 2003], 61).

31. See Mary Ann Donaldson and Russell Gardner, "Diagnosis and Treatment of Traumatic Stress among Women after Childhood Incest," in *Trauma and Its Wake: The Study and Treatment of Post-Traumatic Stress Disorder*, ed. Charles R. Figley (New York: Brunner/Mazel, 1985), 368–73; Herman, *Trauma and Recovery*, 177–78.

32. See John Briere, "Treating Adult Survivors," in *The APSAC Handbook on Child Maltreatment*, 2d ed., ed. John E. B. Myers et al. (Thousand Oaks, Calif.: Sage, 2002), 179–80.

33. A woman identified as Lydia offers several lies that were created by her abuse. She categorizes these into lies about Christ, the Holy Spirit, Satan, the church, men, women, the family, herself, and authority ("Testimony of an Abuse Survivor," in *Healing the Hurting: Giving Hope and Help to Abused Women*, ed. Catherine Clark Kroeger and James R.

Beck [Grand Rapids: Baker, 1998], 71–74). See also Derek Jehu, Carole Klassen, and Marjorie Gazan, "Cognitive Restructuring of Distorted Beliefs Associated with Childhood Sexual Abuse," *Journal of Social Work and Human Sexuality* 4 (1986): 49–69.

34. Sandra Wilson offers a helpful visual that contrasts various shame-based lies with the corresponding truth (*Released from Shame*, rev. ed. [Downers Grove, Ill.: InterVarsity Press, 2002], 115). The truth that challenges shame-based lies must ultimately come from Scripture, our only sure source of truth in this life (2 Timothy 3:16–17). Once the lies and the biblical truth have been identified, the abuse survivor must learn to discipline the mind to embrace the truth and reject the lies (2 Corinthians 10:5— "taking every thought captive to the obedience of Christ").

35. Dan B. Allender, *The Wounded Heart: Hope for Adult Victims of Childhood Sexual Abuse*, rev. ed. (Colorado Springs: NavPress, 1995), 207.

36. Steele and Colrain, "Abreactive Work with Sexual Abuse Survivors," 4–5.

37. Constance Hoenk Shapiro and Susan Turner note, for instance, that mourning anticipated losses is a critical part of the early stages of healing for battered women ("Helping Battered Women through the Mourning Process," in *Abuse and Religion: When Praying Isn't Enough*, ed. Anne L. Horton and Judith A. Williamson [Lexington, Mass.: Lexington Books, 1988], 123–25).

38. See H. L. Ellison, "Lamentations," in *The Expositor's Bible Commentary*, ed. Frank E. Gaebelein (Grand Rapids: Zondervan, 1986), 6:697; Delbert R. Hillers, *Lamentations* (Garden City, N.Y.: Doubleday, 1972), xl. Later on, Tisha b'Av also became a day of remembrance and mourning for the defeat of Bar Kochba's fortress, Betar, by the Roman army in AD 135.

39. These events are recorded in 2 Kings 25 and Jeremiah 39 and 52. These atrocities are also mentioned in Lamentations 2:20–22; 4:9–10; 5:11–14.

40. It's clear from Scripture that the Babylonian conquest was a direct result of Judah's sin (Jeremiah 26:1–6; Lamentations 1:18; 2:1–10) and was permitted in order to stimulate the people's repentance (Lamentations 3:39–42). The fact remains, however, that Jeremiah, like most modern abuse survivors, was not responsible for the abuse he suffered but rather was suffering because of his ancestors' sins (Lamentations 5:7).

41. In introducing the theme and purpose of Lamentations, Walter C. Kaiser notes, "Suffering cannot adequately be dealt with by pretending that it does not exist. It will not do to try to minimize it or to 'talk' it out of existence. It does exist and it does hurt…. The most comforting news Scripture has for the sufferer is that where pain, grief, and hurt are, there is God" (*A Biblical Approach to Suffering* [Chicago: Moody Press, 1982], 14).

42. See Lamentations 1:3, 4, 7, 16; 2:15; 3:4, 17; 5:8–16.

43. H. L. Ellison's comments on Lamentations 3:21 are instructive: "The 'hope' that the writer expressed here is not created by denying or minimizing suffering and misery. Rather, these are transformed when the mind is turned to God" ("Lamentations," 720).

chapter 9: rebuilding intimacy with God

1. Fyodor Dostoyevsky, *The Brothers Karamazov* (1880; reprint [New York: Bantam Books], 1970), 295–96.

2. Konstantin Mochulsky, cited in Dostoyevsky, *The Brothers Karamazov*, xii.

3. This is similar to the list developed by Joanne Ross Feldmeth and Midge Wallace Finley (*We Weep for Ourselves and Our Children: A Christian Guide for Survivors of Childhood Sexual Abuse* [New York: HarperCollins, 1990], 88–89).

4. See 1 Kings 9:4; 11:4; 2 Kings 14:3; 16:2; Job 1:1, 8; Habakkuk 3:17–19.

5. Mochulsky, cited in Dostoyevsky, *The Brothers Karamazov*, xiii.

6. For a detailed treatment of this issue, see Jeffrey Kauffman, ed., *Loss of the Assumptive World: A Theory of Traumatic Loss* (New York: Brunner-Routledge, 2002).

7. It is significant that here God changes Jacob's name from Jacob, which means "supplanter," or "trickster" (Genesis 25:26), to Israel, which means "one who struggles with God." Thus, in this historical incident the spiritual value and propriety of wrestling with God are strongly affirmed.

8. Philip Yancey, *Disappointment with God: Three Questions No One Asks Aloud* (Grand Rapids: Zondervan, 1988), 235.

9. See Feldmeth and Finley, *We Weep for Ourselves and Our Children*, 103–10.

10. Linda Cutting, *Memory Slips: A Memoir of Music and Healing* (New York: HarperCollins, 1997), 156.

11. Ibid.

12. See Francis Martin, *The Feminist Question: Feminist Theology in the Light of Christian Tradition* (Grand Rapids: Eerdmans, 1994), 265–92. Mary Daly's assault on the fatherhood of God has been influential among feminists. She reasons, "If God is male, then the male is God" (*Beyond God the Father* [Boston: Beacon Press, 1973], 19). Rejecting the fatherhood of God hasn't helped women in general or abuse victims in particular; it has created a host of new problems. When Daly moved "beyond God the Father," she and others who followed her embraced goddess worship and lesbianism, which they erroneously found to be more affirming for women (see Carol P. Christ, "Feminist Theology as Post-Traditional Theology," in *The Cambridge Companion to Feminist Theology*, ed. Susan Frank Parsons [Cambridge: Cambridge Univ. Press, 2002], 79–96).

13. John Cooper, *Our Father in Heaven: Christian Faith and Inclusive Language for God* (Grand Rapids: Baker, 1998), 261.

14. Herman Bavinck argues that "Father" (πατήρ) is the New Testament equivalent of Yahweh (*The Doctrine of God* [Grand Rapids: Baker, 1951], 263). For a broad evangelical discussion of the divine name and gender, see Alvin F. Kimel Jr., ed., *This Is My Name Forever: The Trinity and Gender Language for God* (Downers Grove, Ill.: InterVarsity Press, 2001).

15. I affirm (along with John Cooper) that Scripture overwhelmingly but not exclusively describes God in masculine language (Cooper, *Our Father in Heaven*, 65–114); see also Donald G. Bloesch, *Is the Bible Sexist?* (Westchester, Ill.: Crossway, 1982), 66, 68, 76–77. Thus, if we are going to do justice to the biblical record and to abuse victims who have an aversion to masculine imagery, we need to recognize the feminine/maternal descriptions of God in the Bible. This doesn't mean, however, that we should refer to God as our heavenly Mother, for God is expressly called "our Father" in Scripture (and he is never called "Mother"). This is a divine title and a term of direct address. Feminine or maternal descriptions of God in the Bible occur exclusively as figures of speech, never as titles (see Cooper, *Our Father in Heaven*, 108).

16. Craig Keener gives an excellent, detailed explanation of why tax collectors and sinners were hated by the Pharisees. According to Keener, "sinners" likely refers to those who were blatant violators of the law (*A Commentary on the Gospel of Matthew* [Grand Rapids: Eerdmans, 1999], 292-96).

17. See Luke 8:1-3; 10:38-42; 24:1-11; John 4:7-27. On the status and treatment of women in first-century Palestine, see Tal Ilan, *Integrating Women into Second Temple Judaism* (Tübingen: J. C. B. Mohr, 1999); Tal Ilan, *Jewish Women in Greco-Roman Palestine* (Peabody, Mass.: Hendrickson, 1996); Joachim Jeremias, *Jerusalem in the Time of Jesus* (Philadelphia: Fortress, 1969), 359-76.

18. A helpful academic work on the person and character of God is Donald G. Bloesch, *God the Almighty: Power, Wisdom, Holiness, Love* (Downers Grove, Ill.: InterVarsity Press, 1995). Two classics on the attributes of God are J. I. Packer, *Knowing God* (Downers Grove, Ill.: InterVarsity Press, 1973), and A. W. Tozer, *The Knowledge of the Holy* (New York: Harper & Row, 1961).

19. Gary Haugen, *Good News about Injustice: A Witness of Courage in a Hurting World* (Downers Grove, Ill.: InterVarsity Press, 1999), 68.

20. Martin Luther, cited in Bloesch, *God the Almighty*, 151-52.

21. Paul endured multiple stonings, beatings, imprisonments, and ultimately execution by the Roman authorities (2 Corinthians 11:23-33; 2 Timothy 4:6). On Paul's prison experience based on the historical setting, see Brian Rapske, *The Book of Acts and Paul in Roman Custody* (Grand Rapids: Eerdmans, 1994).

22. See Dorothee Soelle, *Suffering* (Philadelphia: Fortress, 1975), 148. I agree with J. Christian Becker that Soelle has helpful insights on suffering, but (among other departures from evangelical theology) she fails to distinguish between tragic suffering and redemptive suffering (*Suffering and Hope: The Biblical Vision and the Human Predicament* [Grand Rapids: Eerdmans, 1987], 110-12).

23. Dietrich Bonhoeffer, *Letters and Papers from Prison: The Enlarged Edition* (London: SCM, 1953), 361; see also Charles Ohlrich, *The Suffering God: Hope and Comfort for Those Who Hurt* (Downers Grove, Ill.: InterVarsity Press, 1982).

24. See Corrie ten Boom, *The Hiding Place* (Minneapolis: World Wide Publications, 1971), 196-97.

25. This concept is conveyed in the verb θριαμβεύω ("to lead in triumphal procession").

26. See 1 Corinthians 2:6-10; 2 Corinthians 4:5-12; C. Marvin Pate, *The End of the Age Has Come: The Theology of Paul* (Grand Rapids: Zondervan, 1995), 43-70. On the cross and the conquest of evil, see John R. Stott, *The Cross of Christ* (Downers Grove, Ill.: InterVarsity Press, 1986), 231-51.

27. Νίκη, νικάω. On the theme of the believer's victory in the book of Revelation, see Stott, *The Cross of Christ*, 246-51.

28. Henri Blocher, *Evil and the Cross* (Downers Grove, Ill.: InterVarsity Press, 1994), 132.

chapter 10: forgiveness

1. See K. E. Gerdes et al., "Adult Survivors of Childhood Sexual Abuse: The Case of Mormon Women," *Affilia* 11 (1996): 39-60; C. Taylor and L. Aronson-Fontes, "Seventh

Day Adventists and Sexual Child Abuse," in *Sexual Abuse in Nine North American Cultures*, ed. L. Aronson Fontes (Thousand Oaks, Calif.: Sage, 1995), 176–99.

2. See Pamela Cooper-White, *The Cry of Tamar: Violence Against Women and the Church's Response* (Philadelphia: Fortress, 1995), 253–57; C. Holderread-Heggen, *Sexual Abuse in Christian Churches* (Scottsdale, Pa.: Herald, 1993), 121–34.

3. See David Augsburger, *Caring Enough to Forgive: True Forgiveness* (Ventura, Calif.: Regal, 1981), 18–21; Augsburger, *Caring Enough to Not Forgive: False Forgiveness* (Ventura, Calif.: Regal, 1981), 67–68.

4. John Kselman, "Forgiveness," in *The Anchor Bible Dictionary*, vol. 2, ed. David Noel Freedman (New York: Doubleday, 1992), 831.

5. Ellen Bass and Laura Davis, *The Courage to Heal: A Guide for Women Survivors of Child Sexual Abuse* (New York: Harper & Row, 1988), 348.

6. John Patton makes this argument, asserting that the gospel writers misinterpreted Jesus' teachings on forgiveness and mistakenly made forgiveness a condition for entering the kingdom (*Is Human Forgiveness Possible? A Pastoral Care Perspective* [Nashville: Abingdon, 1985], 157).

7. See Walter Bauer et al., *A Greek-English Lexicon of the New Testament and Other Early Christian Literature*, 2d ed. [Chicago: University of Chicago Press, 1979], 125.

8. See L. Gregory Jones, *Embodying Forgiveness: A Theological Analysis* (Grand Rapids: Eerdmans, 1995), 78–91.

9. See P. U. Maynard-Reid, "Forgiveness," in *Dictionary of the Later New Testament and Its Development*, ed. R. P. Martin and P. H. Davis (Downers Grove, Ill.: InterVarsity Press, 1997), 379–82; in contrast to Jones, *Embodying Forgiveness*, 158–59.

10. See Holderread-Heggen, *Sexual Abuse in Homes and Churches*, 127.

11. See B. Moller, "When Your Children Pay the Price, " *Leadership* 14 (1993): 87–95; M. Morris, *Sins of the Father* (Boise, Ida.: Pacific Press, 1993), 104–6, 133–50, 155, 173–87.

12. See M. M. Fortune, *Sexual Violence: The Unmentionable Sin* (Cleveland, Ohio: Pilgrim, 1983), 61–87; Holderread-Heggen, *Sexual Abuse in Homes and Churches*, 98–115; A. J. Morey, "Blaming Women for the Sexually Abusive Male Pastor," *The Christian Century* 5 (October 1988): 866–69; Laurie Hall, *An Affair of the Mind: One Woman's Courageous Battle to Salvage Her Family from the Devastation of Pornography* (Colorado Springs: Focus on the Family, 1998), 18–19, 54–56, 190–91.

13. See J. G. Haber, *Forgiveness* (Savage, Md.: Rowman and Littlefield, 1991), 35, 37; J. C. Murphy and J. Hampton, *Forgiveness and Mercy* (Cambridge: Cambridge Univ. Press, 1988), 14–34.

14. R. D. Enright and R. L. Zell, "Problems Encountered When We Forgive One Another," *Journal of Psychology and Christianity* 8 (1989): 54–55.

15. The Greek word for "wrath" at the end of Ephesians 4:26 is παροργισμος, which is an intensive form of anger. In this context it indicates a settled bitterness.

16. See Marilyn McCord-Adams, "Forgiveness: A Christian Model," *Faith and Philosophy* 8 (1991): 296.

17. Ibid., 297; see Dan B. Allender and Tremper Longman, *Bold Love* (Colorado Springs: NavPress, 1992), 183–204; Maxine Hancock and Karen Burton-Mains, *Child Sexual Abuse: A Hope for Healing* (Wheaton, Ill.: Shaw, 1987), 65.

18. See Allender and Longman, *Bold Love*, 197–200; G. M. Zerbe, *Non-Retaliation in Early Jewish and New Testament Texts* (Sheffield: Sheffield Academic Press, 1993), 261, 292; in contrast to C. F. D. Moule, "The Christian Understanding of Forgiveness," *Theology* 71 (1968): 437–39.

19. See John Piper, *Love Your Enemy: Jesus' Love Command in the Synoptic Gospels and in Early Christian Paraenesis* (Cambridge: Cambridge Univ. Press, 1979), 115–19; Zerbe, *Non-Retaliation*, 241–49.

20. See Philip Yancey, "An Unnatural Act," *Christianity Today* 35 (April 1991), 36–39.

21. Stanley J. Grenz, *Revisioning Evangelical Theology: A Fresh Agenda for the 21ˢᵗ Century* (Downers Grove, Ill.: InterVarsity Press, 1993), 158.

22. See M. M. Fortune, "Forgiveness: The Last Step," in *Violence Against Women and Children*, ed. C. J. Adams and M. M. Fortune (New York: Continuum, 1995), 201–6; J. Wilson, "Why Forgiveness Requires Repentance," *Philosophy* 63 (1988): 534–35.

23. Horst Balz and Gerhard Schneider, eds., *Exegetical Dictionary of the New Testament*, vol. 2 (Grand Rapids: Eerdmans, 1991), s.v. μετανοέω, μετάνοια.

24. See P. Ellingworth, "Forgiveness of Sins," in *Dictionary of Jesus and the Gospels*, ed. J. B. Green, S. McKnight, and I. H. Marshall (Downers Grove, Ill.: InterVarsity Press, 1994), 241–43.

25. See Ralph H. Earle and Marcus R. Earle, *Sex Addiction: Case Studies and Management* (New York: Brunner/Mazel, 1995), 63–64. Lenore E. Walker similarly notes the powerful role of apology and contrition in helping physical abusers convince themselves and their partners that they don't have a problem (*The Battered Woman* [New York: HarperCollins, 1979], 65–70).

26. H. Eldridge and J. Still, "Apology and Forgiveness in the Context of the Cycles of Adult Male Sex Offenders Who Abuse Children," in *Transforming Trauma: A Guide to Understanding and Treating Adult Survivors of Child Sexual Abuse*, ed. A. C. Salter (Thousand Oaks, Calif.: Sage, 1995), 153–54.

27. See Sharon Lamb, *The Trouble with Blame: Victims, Perpetrators, and Responsibility* (Cambridge, Mass.: Harvard Univ. Press, 1996).

28. See Lewis Smedes, "Forgiving People Who Do Not Care," *Reformed Journal* 33 (1983): 13–18.

29. Hall, *An Affair of the Mind*, 220.

30. Lewis B. Smedes, *Forgive and Forget: Healing the Hurts We Don't Deserve* (San Francisco: HarperSanFrancisco, 1984), 5–9.

31. See P. C. Vitz, "Kernbergian Psychodynamics and Religious Aspects of the Forgiveness Process," *Journal of Psychology and Theology* 25 (1997): 72–80.

32. Cooper-White, *The Cry of Tamar*, 256.

33. Allender and Longman, *Bold Love*, 243–49.

34. See B. B. Cunningham, "The Will to Forgive: A Pastoral Theological View of Forgiving," *Journal of Pastoral Care* 34 (1985): 143.

35. See Michael E. McCullough, Steven J. Sandage, and Everett L. Worthington, *To Forgive Is Human* (Downers Grove, Ill.: InterVarsity Press, 1997), 110–26.

36. See Smedes, *Forgive and Forget*, 10–11.

37. See Allender and Longman, *Bold Love*, 243–54.

scripture index

subject index

We want to hear from you. Please send your comments about this
book to us in care of zreview@zondervan.com. Thank you.

ZONDERVAN.com/
AUTHORTRACKER
follow your favorite authors